IS IT AN OMEN?
By

STELLA STICKLAND

IS IT AN OMEN?

STELLA STICKLAND

Blackie & Co
Publishers Ltd

A BLACKIE & CO
PUBLISHERS LIMITED PAPERBACK

© Copyright 2003

Stella Stickland

First published in 2003

A CIP catalogue record for this title is
available from the British Library

ISBN 1-84470-039-9

Blackie & Co Publishers Ltd
107-111 Fleet Street
LONDON EC4A 2AB

Printed and Bound in Great Britain

This book is dedicated to my husband

Mike – with all my love

Is It An Omen?

Chapter 1 - Formation

When I was a child I thought I was the same as every other child, I thought everybody saw ghosts and auras and could feel the pain of a person if they touched them. I soon realised that they couldn't, and I was to be regarded by my family as a very strange child. I learnt loneliness from an early age.

I was born in Broadwater, Worthing, during the first hour of the first day of January, 1946. The third daughter for my parents, Joan and Clarence Golds. I later learned that my mother hadn't wanted another child and had tried the usual things to try to budge me, but I was obviously a very determined person even then. I can appreciate that it must have been very difficult for my mother finding out that she was pregnant again, with my sister Eileen only four months old, and the war just ending. Money was tight for everybody.

I was delivered by my maternal grandmother in the back bedroom of a very pretty flint cottage in Kingsland Road. My parents, once they'd reconciled the fact that I was going to be born, were hoping for a son, as they already had two daughters, Elizabeth, known as Betty, and Eileen. My name was to be Jack if I was a boy and Edith if I was a girl, but when I arrived, my mother decided I should be called Stella instead, what a relief, I don't think Edith would have suited me at all.

1

My father's middle name was Septimus, so named because he was the seventh son of a seventh son. He was the youngest of eleven children. Dad's parents had been market gardeners in a village called Washington, on the outskirts of Worthing, but Dad decided to be a builder instead, and was to teach me much about the building industry, which proved to be invaluable later in my life, when my destiny was revealed. Dad was an avid reader, absorbing about five books a week from the library, and could hold a conversation on nearly any topic under the sun. When he was in full flow we didn't dare interrupt him, as he held us captivated, literally! He was a very smart man, who paid a lot of attention to how he looked, and Mum used to tell us a funny story about how, before they were married, Dad used to get his leg pulled because he used to wear silk shirts and silk socks to work, on a building site! And I gather from Mum, that he played the ukulele rather well. My mother was one of five children (one died), so I wasn't short of aunts, uncles and cousins! Mum was a nursery woman, whose ability to propagate just about anything was an amazing gift. This combination was to prove invaluable to me during my early to middle life.

Being a very sensitive child, I found life difficult, and it didn't help me being constantly reminded by my grandmother of the great disappointment of my parents when I arrived, because I wasn't a son. This hurt me very much, but she seemed to delight in telling me over and over again. I was also left-handed, which in those days was not as accepted as it is today, and I was constantly reminded of my affliction. Cackhanded was an expression, which seemed to be used all the time at home, when referring to me, whatever I did I was told I looked awkward and unnatural. If I needed to be shown how to do anything, from threading a needle, to learning how to cast on stitches for knitting, it was always met with a derisory remark. Whenever I laid the table for tea, someone would always say 'Oh, you can tell who's laid the table!', because I had the cutlery round the wrong way. This had a very bad effect on me. I never liked anybody watching me do anything, and I became more and more self-conscious. My family couldn't have envisaged the long-term effects that their remarks would have on me.

2

Eileen was only fourteen months older than me, and I used to follow her around, hoping to play with her, but she regarded me as a thorough nuisance and would send me off to find my own friends. If we had been twins I think it would have been easier for her, but because the gap was so small we were rivals. I do not really remember much about Betty during the early years, because of the age gap, as she was five years older than I was. She was a bit daunting, very studious and serious. I do however remember her calling me 'Little Pygmy', because I looked just like one, with my fat stomach. We used to laugh about it, and that amused me. My school friends would not come into the house if Betty was around because they were afraid of her. They would hang around the back door, and if they caught sight of her they would run.

Broadwater was a lovely place to spend ones childhood. We had the best of both worlds - the downs and the sea. I was part of a group of six children from the neighbourhood who all went to the same school and Sunday school. We were the famous five plus one. We spent all of our leisure time together, either swimming in the sea or roaming the downs. I could see the downs from my parents' bedroom window, and I loved going up onto them. Sometimes we explored the ruins of what had been Charmandean Girls Boarding School before the Germans bombed it. It really gave me the creeps, but I had to follow the others into it because the alternative was to be left outside on my own, which was creepier still. Opposite the school on the other side of the lane, was a chalk pit, at the top of which grew the loveliest lilacs. I loved climbing to the top and picking them. Because of my Mother's love of flowers she knew where everything grew. In the spring we would go off to the woods and pick primroses, and then Eileen and I would distribute them to various old ladies in the neighbourhood. This brought them a lot of pleasure, as they were unable to get out much themselves. In the house next to ours, there were two elderly sisters, the Misses Jenson. Their house was detached whereas ours was semi-detached, and they had an immaculate garden with lawns. We were a little in awe of them well scared stiff actually. We thought they were witches, and if our ball went into their garden we always had to ask permission to retrieve it, hoping that we wouldn't be turned into toads or the like. One of the sisters was made a Dame for her services to the Red Cross during the war. We didn't learn this until much later, so she was probably a lovely old soul. Children can be horrible.

When the weather was warm enough we used to go to the beach and maybe spend all day there, with our egg sandwiches and Tizer. My mother used to work full time at a nursery, and I grew up thinking it was the norm for women to work and raise a family. But I remember times as well when I wished she was with us on the beach, so that she could have enjoyed some leisure as well. Both my parents worked very hard. The gang would go blackberrying in the summer up towards Chanctonbury Ring. My mother used to laugh, because we would all come back separately, having fallen out with each other, and with no blackberries, because we had eaten them all on the way home. This also happened on Saturdays, when some of us went to Saturday morning pictures. Again we would set off together, then arrive home separately. The boys usually fought over who was going to sit next to who, firstly on the bus and then at the pictures. Boys, what a pain they were!

We lived across the road from the dairy, and Eileen and I spent a lot of time over there, visiting the horses that pulled the milk carts. Three of the horses were named "Betty", "Eileen" and "Stella". I never knew if it was a coincidence or not. They seemed to have a horse named after every child in the neighbourhood so perhaps it wasn't a coincidence. Perhaps when there was a child born in the area they used the name for the next horse. Well you never know do you? One day a year the dairy held an open day, and we used to be able to ride the horses.

I showed a keen interest in building from about the age of ten. I used to stand by my father's car at weekends if I thought there were any signs that he was going to the building site, hoping he might take me with him when he went to check that everything was alright. I was often lucky. I used to think that he explained everything to me because he really wanted a son, but years later, when my destiny was revealed, I realised that he had known that I needed to learn as much as I could about all aspects of the building industry. He used to go to great lengths to explain everything from footings and drains, to windows and lead work on roofs to me from a very early age. I can remember on one occasion being very disappointed because my mother wouldn't buy me boys' wellingtons, which were so much nicer than the girls' wellingtons. I liked the big ridges in the soles, they were just like Dad wore on the building site. She was adamant that little girls didn't wear boys' boots. Poor Mum, she had no idea! Today the girls wear the most masculine heavy shoes, but in my day, girls were girls.

I used to be able to discuss anything with my father, absolutely anything. I remember getting agitated and very upset in the sixties, when toplessness came into fashion, to the point of bursting into tears one day. I thought it so embarrassing and horribly cheap. How could nice girls want to parade around like that? Especially with boys the way they were, with one-track minds. I found out from a very early age what boys were like, what with the boy next door and his cousin always trying to lure some unsuspecting female into their sheds. I got street wise from a very early age, through sheer necessity. I broke Tommy's arm, (he lived next door), I pushed him off the fence because he was being obnoxious, then I ran as fast as I could, and hid in the airing cupboard, because his mum was on the war path, looking for me. So for girls to want to parade themselves topless, I thought they were definitely looking for trouble. After my outburst and tears, Dad told me straight that I would have to cope with lots of things in my life, that I would not like, and that I should try harder not to let things get to me if possible, or I wouldn't cope with life. They were wise words indeed, but I had a lot of trouble with not letting things affect me for years. It was also about this time that the birth pill was readily available, and what was intended to make married women's lives better and easier by not having so many unwanted pregnancies, was to cause a sexual revolution later on, with it even being prescribed for girls as young as eleven. Who could have predicted then that we would end up with teenage pregnancies the highest in Europe, and that marriage would be regarded as an unnecessary state for many. None of what was about to happen over the next four decades was going to get true equality for the majority of women, quite the reverse, and the majority of the children from those single mothers were to live well below the poverty line. I think I knew, even at that tender age of fifteen, what was going to happen in my beloved country, and that was why it all upset me so much. I was extremely psychic from a very early age.

My father had two homes – the Wigmore Arms Public House and ours. He was a dab hand at shove-halfpenny and cribbage, as well as darts, cards and dominoes. We soon learned never to bet with him, as he always won, and usually with a wicked grin on his face. I was often sent to fetch him at dinnertime. I used to hang right over the counter of the bottle and jug, which enabled me to see right into the public bar, and attract his attention. It usually annoyed him, as he was invariably in full flow, either lecturing them on some aspect of the building trade or else about some obscure tribe of Indians from the Rain Forests or such like. Such information came from his National Geographic Magazine. If ever there was a born Anthropologist it was Dad. He was actually a very knowledgeable man, brought up in Hove, which was very smart at the turn of the Century. He was an educated man who wrote in script, who'd been a choirboy, and who later on played cricket, and was asked to play for Sussex. Dad was also quite a political person. As a young man he belonged to the Labour party, and then he very reluctantly, because it was the thing to do, had to join a Trade Union. Later on, when he was doing fairly well, he changed over to the Conservative Party, and was treasurer of the local Conservative Working Men's Club.

During the war he was in the home guard, a reserved occupation, because he was needed to put houses back together. He was stationed in Coventry, so as fast as he was putting them back together, Hitler was knocking them down again. He was close to Coventry Cathedral the night it was bombed, and watched it burn to the ground. He had always been a pacifist so this job suited him, trying to put some sort of a roof over people's heads again. I remember being told as a child that his gun had stayed in our airing cupboard throughout the war, with the ammunition. There was no way that Dad was going to kill anyone!

Apart from my interest in the building industry, I was nevertheless a very feminine little girl. I'd always liked playing with my dolls, and walking around the streets after school with my smart doll's

6

pram pretending I was a Mum. At the age of ten I switched to real babies and to looking after a neighbour's baby girl called Lorna. I loved babies and could hardly wait to grow up and have my own.

I helped my Mother as much as I could in the house. As I said she worked full time at the nursery, leaving the house at eight thirty in the morning and returning at five p.m. I was always aware of how hard she worked, and so I did as much as I could to help her. Mum suffered with the most dreadful migraines and would at times have to take to her bed. She would then not appear for about three days, during which time she had nothing to eat and very little to drink. She was physically very sick with her headaches and the only thing she could do was to lay in bed, in the dark and hopefully sleep. On other occasions I would see her hanging over the sink with dreadful nosebleeds, the pressure in her head must have been awful and probably accounted for her quick temper at times. If my Mother was cross, you disappeared as quickly as possible, she was a big woman, very strong, and one of her smacks would leave hand imprints on you that lasted for days. She was always telling me that the Russians would come and take me away if I was naughty, they knew just what to do with naughty girls, and for a highly sensitive child to be told that was nothing short of terrifying. Later on in life when I asked her what sort of child I had been, she replied that I had been a good girl, and that I had never given her any trouble. The main reason I was ever told off was because I was very outspoken, I had an opinion on most things from a very young age, and children were supposed to be seen and not heard. I was always wanting to be heard! So I spent a lot of time in my bedroom! As a punishment. But the Russian thing did nothing for my confidence and made me even more nervous. I was afraid of almost everything. I was afraid of the dark and of being sent to bed first because of all the people I saw in my parent's bedroom ghosts walking out of the wardrobe. No one would believe me when I told them what I saw. I was afraid of spiders because I used to be shut in the coal shed, the neighbourhood kids would chant 'Stella, smell her, shut her in the coal cellar'. I was so afraid, I hated the dark and I could feel the cobwebs touch my bare arms. And I was afraid of school.

My father believed in sexual equality, and that included all women working. He was a man born before his time, and in retrospect I am so grateful to have been brought up in a household like that. I learnt life was hard from an early age and it gave me the back bone I was to need much later in my life when I was a divorced mum, working particularly hard with my business to give my sons the opportunities they needed in order for them to do well. My sons used to tell people that I belonged on the Russian Front. Charming! Didn't all women shovel up yards of sand and carry bricks? Obviously not!

My mother used to work at the nursery with a woman who lived across the street. We called her Auntie Edie. I liked her very much, and I knew she was a good friend to my mother. After I'd completed my daily chores, lighting the fire if it was winter, laying the table for tea, I then took the dog out for a walk. Spot was a sweet little black and white mongrel, I used to train her to sit at kerbs and carry the news paper home, I would often meet my mother and Auntie Edie from work and walk home with both of them. My mother often referred to me as her little maid, for obvious reasons. Auntie Edie always called me Star. I liked that. The cottage was very basic, like so many others at the time. Although we hade an outside toilet, we did have a room containing just a bath. But as there was no central heating we preferred the tin bath in front of the fire.

School was the bugbear of my life. I don't ever remember liking it, especially infant and junior school. It wasn't that I found the work difficult, I actually enjoyed learning. I just found going to school a terrifying experience for me. I realised much later in my life, that I did not like being with lots of people. It was a kind of agoraphobia even at that young age, (fear of the marketplace). Teachers today are thankfully much more understanding of sensitive children. Years later I had a son who was very sensitive like me, and through my own experiences I knew how to make his childhood more bearable. This aspect I will cover later in the book.

I started school at Whitemead Primary School, which was within walking distance of our house. I never liked that school, it had a horrible smell of school dinners and lavatories, and the teachers seemed like monsters. My only memories of that school are standing outside the classroom in the corridor because I had been sent out of a lesson for talking, or standing in the corner with the dunces' hat on, again for talking when I should not have been. The trouble was that I was so nervous that I thought talking to someone would help me. It actually had the opposite effect, and got me into a lot of trouble. I never liked the teachers, they seemed to be just grown up bullies. I have just three happy memories of that school. The first memory was of May Day, when we were allowed to dance around the Maypole, I loved the colours of the ribbons. The second was a painting of mine going to Worthing art gallery. I was only five or six, and can still remember going along to see it hanging on the wall at the gallery, and I remember a photograph of me with my classmates holding up pictures we had drawn, and mine was, of course, a house, which was to prove very significant. The third happy memory was when I left the school.

I then crossed the road to the junior school, which was a little better, but not a lot. I was always in the top stream, and enjoyed arithmetic, as it was called, especially problems (you know - if it takes four men eight hours to dig a hole, and all that), and I loved reading and being read to. I used to sit next to a boy whose mother was in and out of the local psychiatric hospital, and as a result he was maybe not as clean as he might have been. Nobody wanted to sit next to him except me, and he and I used to race through the arithmetic cards, really enjoying ourselves. I often wondered what happened to him. He passed the eleven plus whereas I failed, much to my surprise and horror.

I got used to being overlooked. When the Head, one day, asked who was the fastest runner in my class, a girl called Marion shot her hand up in the air, and said "I am". I could not believe it. She could no way out-run me, but they took her word for it.

I have always seen auras around trees and plants, and as a child I thought they glowed beautifully. To me it was normal, and I thought everybody saw them. It's quite a shock when you realise other people don't see what you do. I also used to ask my mother to touch me if I had a pain, for example, if my leg hurt I would ask her to put her hand on it because I thought she could feel my pain, but she never could. She would smile and say 'But how can I feel it?' But I could feel other people's pain, and that used to intrigue me. I knew just where to touch them, to feel the pain. When I became a healer I knew exactly where to touch them, I could even read their minds.

Apart from the never-ending people coming out of the wardrobe in my parent's bedroom, something used to wander around our bedroom at night (I shared a room with Eileen). So I used to sleep right down the bottom of my bed, and from there I could feel its presence, night after night. It's a wonder I didn't suffocate. I had a frequent recurring dream as a child about being chased up and down staircases, and along landings to the next staircase. Nothing else - just running up and down stairs all night. I was always relieved once the night was over, I can tell you. Years later I understood what the dream meant but at that time no one was into dreams like they are today. The dream was telling me about the relentless tests I was going to have to experience, pushing me to the very limits of endurance at times. I used to hear voices as well and I would answer them. Mum would ask me, who I was talking to and when I told her, a look of exasperation would come over her. Years later, my mother said that the family in general had always found me to be a little strange, but she said it nicely. It is uncomfortable though to be thought of as strange or odd. I knew there wasn't anything strange about me it was just that they didn't understand me. Hence my loneliness.

My love of God and "upstairs" as I now call it, I have always had, right from my childhood. I always loved singing "There is a green hill far away". My sister Eileen was tone deaf, and I used to give her singing lessons in bed at night, much to my mother's annoyance. I gave up though - Eileen could not sing! I used to question my elders constantly, and as you can imagine in those days, children were not treated in the same way as they are today. You were supposed to be seen but not heard. This used to get me into lots of trouble, as you can imagine, and I was often sent to bed as a punishment. This actually wasn't a punishment as I

loved my bed and I liked being alone and reading.   I was always
surprised at grown ups - the way they never seemed to question
anything.   If I asked why something had to be done there was
never a constructive answer.   It was always 'Because that's what
everybody does'.   Why wasn't 'Bureaucracy' and the 'Powers
that be' questioned more? Would we all grow up into mindless
sheep? Shudder at the thought.

We, like most children, used to go to Sunday school every week.
I loved bible stories and one year I put myself forward for the
scripture examination, which was held every year.   I came top of
the juniors.   My favourite teacher knew Gladys Aylward the
missionary, and I loved listening to stories about her.   I belonged
to the local library, and the books I liked to read the best were all
biographies.   Gladys Aylward, Florence Nightingale, Grace
Darling to name but a few.   The minister at our local Church was
all fire and brimstone.   I knew his God was not my God.   His
God was scary, whereas my God was all loving and protective.
This was the local Baptist Church, and the Vicar was against any
enjoyment on Sunday.   I can remember him saying that it was evil
to go to the cinema on a Sunday, and I could still hear his voice as
I stood at the bus stop, on my way to the cinema.   This particular
Vicar hid and pretended to be out when we went to his house
Carol singing at Christmas.   He left our Parish when I was in my
early teens, only to be replaced by someone even weirder, I
thoroughly disliked the new one.   He took me aside one day and
asked me to remove my make-up.   My mother was with me and
retorted sharply, "Stella doesn't wear any - that's her natural
colouring." Thank you, Mother.   Vicars! My father always said
that when he returned to earth for his next life he was going to be a
vicar, the reason being that it was the only way to get a really nice
house without having to do a days work.   There's no answer to
that!

My mother's father, granddad Sidney, was awarded the Military
Medal during the First World War for bravery rescuing an officer
from behind enemy lines.   With the sort of things the vicar used to
say about who was and who wasn't going to heaven, (and I don't
think according to him anybody went), it always bothered me that
granddad wouldn't go to heaven if he had fought in a war, and I

11

used to lie awake as a child worrying about it. He was such a lovely kindly old man, and all my friends loved him. If anybody deserved to go to heaven, granddad did.

During the period before secondary school I met Richard, who was one of Eileen's many admirers. I mention this only because his sister Helen, who I met at secondary school, was to become one of my best friends for years. He also had the same birthday as I did, which intrigued me. I thought Eileen was much more attractive than I was, as the boys used to flock around her like bees to a honeycomb. I always hoped that one day just one of them would notice me. She thought me an absolute pain, like all older sisters do. I always hung around hoping I could go with her if she was going out. "Find your own friends" she used to say. I was a bit young at eleven to have much of a social life, whereas she was fourteen months older than I was and at the grammar school, so she had to put up with me. I did come in extremely handy to do her paper round though when she was playing hockey after school. I had my uses. We later both became Girl Guides. I was particularly interested in getting my child care badge, (which I got) as I always seemed, even at that tender age, to be looking after some one's child. I was crazy about babies, and as I mentioned earlier I would race home from school to take one of the neighbours babies out in the pram. I had two babies to take out now because my Sunday school teacher had become a grandmother to a baby girl called Hazel. I could hardly wait to grow up and have my own babies. It seemed sometimes as if it would be forever before I grew up.

Through the guides I went camping, and then I got the chance to go to Scotland Youth Hostelling, which was very enjoyable. My first sight of mountains I will never forget. What beauty! The colours were magnificent. Purple, greens and the white of the snowcaps. I thought it must be like heaven.

I then went to Worthing County Secondary School for girls, and enjoyed it much more than primary school, which isn't saying much, but at least you were treated in a more grown up way. This was when I met Helen, Richard's sister, who was to be my best friend for many years. One particular teacher, Mrs. Thomas, made a beeline for me as soon as I arrived, because Betty had been at the school for five years and had done very well. It was always "Betty this" and "Betty that". I think I disliked that teacher from then on. I was not allowed to be myself. It made me quite rebellious in certain ways with certain teachers who were not very good at controlling classes, and I, along with several other girls, would take great delight in winding them up. One particular mistress who took Religious Education must have quaked at the thoughts of our class. We led her such a dance, poor soul. However, Mrs. Thomas was unfortunately the one who taught English, so there was no escaping her. It seemed as if we had her every day. I had my first panic attack in one of her English classes, although I didn't know it was a panic attack at the time. I only learnt years later what they were. I could not bear having to read out loud to the class, and she always picked on me. It was as if there was an arrow over my head pointing to me. On this particular occasion, I started out all right with my reading, and then became more and more breathless until I was gasping for breath. Mrs. Thomas, instead of leaving me alone, hauled me up to the front of the class, amidst giggles from my classmates, and proceeded to cross-examine me as to whether I ate properly. After asking me what soap I used as I smelt nice, (you can imagine how embarrassed that made me feel, and my classmates by this time were beside themselves), she decided that I did not eat properly (which I might add was not true, as I had a good appetite). In her infinite wisdom she arranged for a teacher to stand over me every lunchtime, to make sure that I ate my lunch.

Fortunately Betty had not been very good at maths, so at least my favourite lesson was relaxing. I also got on very well with the French Mistress, Miss Clarke, who had the most unusual hair. I used to sit there wondering how she managed to twist this lovely black hair up onto her head and stick so many different things into it. She always called me Estelle, which I liked very much, and she wore the most amazing coloured jumpers, it looked as if she used all the bits of wool left over from everybody's knitting. I had a good singing voice, but I was told by the music teacher that I did not smile enough to go into the choir. What!?

Once a year we had a school trip, which was always exciting.

One year the class was to go to London. You can imagine the thrill of being told this; I had never been to London. We were to go first to the Tower of London, and then to the Planetarium. As Helen and I arrived at school that morning on our bicycles, the coach that was to take us was standing there in all its glory. Everybody had their packed lunches with them, and in our freshly laundered summer dresses we got onto the coach, all very excited. When we arrived in London, we sat and ate our lunches outside the walls of the Tower, eager to get inside and explore. Then once inside, to my horror, the class was expected to climb up a spiral staircase to one of the towers. I had and still have a real fear and horror of spiral staircases and I couldn't climb up them. Mrs. Thomas told me that if I disobeyed I would have to go on detention. I was not being difficult. I really couldn't do it. I opted for the detention, this being the lesser of two evils. She didn't back down and I did the detention! Children just wouldn't be treated like that today, thank goodness.

I started going out with a boy called Chris when I was thirteen. He was sixteen. We met whilst I was doing Eileen's paper round. She had to play hockey after school one day, and asked me if I would do it for her, and as I was to be paid, I would. There he was doing his paper round. It was love at first sight. He was a very attractive boy, tall and very blonde. I remembered him from junior school, when he was in the top class and a prefect and I was in the first or second year. He went on to the grammar school. I actually thought he liked Eileen, but no, to my surprise he liked me. His parents were very nice and his sister Carol, who was a year older than me, went to my school. Chris and I spent all our spare time together after school and at weekends we, and a group of our friends, would go to the local recreation ground and play either cricket or rounders. Eileen used to come too if she wasn't doing anything else, and so did Helen. We tried to even up the numbers of boys to girls, which is better for team games, but never managed it! On a Saturday evening just the two of us would go to the cinema. It was all so innocent and charming compared with today. On a warm Sunday afternoon we liked to play pitch and putt, and often Chris would come round with a bunch of pansies from his parent's garden. Oh, I loved pansies. They remind me of pussycat's faces.

I joined various organisations whilst at school, including the Drama Society, and the Geographic Society, and I became a librarian. I used to read a lot and it was during this time that I decided to become a buyer when I left school. I'd always admired beautiful clothes. When I used to go to the pictures I would drool at Doris Day's and Audrey Hepburn's wardrobes. They always wore beautiful clothing. Well, all the stars did, but those in particular had a huge effect on me. So the idea of travelling the world, going to fashion shows etc sounded fantastic. I spent a lot of time designing clothes whenever I had a pencil and paper handy, and making them as well. I was often either sewing or knitting outfits. Clothes were my passion.

I also liked sports of all kinds, and was an extremely fast runner, and was always put last in the relay team, which we invariably won. One of my highlights at school was having the chance to run at Withdean, it was only an open day, all the schools participated. I liked running in particular, so this was a golden opportunity. I didn't win any races there, but it didn't matter, because at least I had donned the spikes and run on one of the most famous tracks in England. Life is like a race. We mostly start off at the same place, in as much as we all have to learn to walk and talk, then read and write. But then some are given a head start, by the choice of schools their parents choose. But it's largely up to us how we run the race; parents cannot after all buy brains or intelligence for their children, so in the end we all have to make our own opportunities. And it's really not whether you win or lose, but how you play the game that matters.

School became more and more uncomfortable for me. I had no idea then what was wrong with me; agoraphobia was a word I'd never heard of. I would dread going to school some days, as my throat would go dry and my chest tightened. I lived in fear and dread of Mrs. Thomas picking on me in class to read. She had even decided to give me a leading role in the drama society's new production about a convent. I was to be the mischievous nun. I wonder why? I just knew that I must leave school as soon as I could. I would have enjoyed school, because I loved learning, and I have proved this by gaining the qualifications I have since leaving school. I was studying for seven o-levels, but no one was allowed to have problems, especially nervous problems. It all became so difficult for me, and I could only see one way out. If only I could have gone to the headmistress and said 'I have a problem', but that wasn't allowed. Children weren't allowed problems. Assembly became a total nightmare, being herded in with hundreds of other girls, gave me a terrifying feeling. I found I needed to keep swallowing, as my throat was always dry, and my chest felt so tight, and when your classmates snigger at you it makes it ten times worse. In the end, I dreaded not only the English lessons with Mrs. Thomas, but also any lesson in which I might have to stand up and read out loud. I didn't seem to have any choice in the end, so I left school, and without any feelings of sadness, I sailed out of the gate on my bicycle and headed for home. Freedom! Chris had already left school and was working for a tile firm in Storrington, so leaving seemed almost natural. It's so different today, thank God. They have child psychologists on hand to help. I could only escape my problems by leaving school.

Chapter 2 - Initiation

My father had made an appointment for me to see the Personnel
Manageress, Miss James, at Bentalls. The books that I had read
at school about becoming a buyer came vividly to mind, and I was
very excited. I passed my interview, and yes, I could go up onto
the fashion floor, and was told that I could start the following
Monday, and that I must wear a black skirt, black cardigan, white
blouse and black shoes. It would be a nice change after the brown
and canary yellow school uniform. I certainly wouldn't miss that!

I arrived the following Monday, feeling very nervous, which is to
be expected with my first job. I had not had many new clothes in
my life so far, and this was no exception. The blouse was new,
but the rest was what Mum had managed to put together by asking
around. My shoes were uncomfortable, and as we were not
allowed to sit down at all on the fashion floor, eight hours of
standing gave me blisters after a few days. Being the youngest of
three girls, I had always made do with hand me downs. Even my
school uniform had been mostly second-hand. I had never
minded. Mum did her best for us, and she was fastidious about
cleanliness. She always used to say 'cleanliness costs nothing',
so we were always sent regularly to the hairdressers, the dentist,
and when it came round, the chest x-ray van. We grew up very
aware of health and looking after ourselves.

I was nervous but very excited. What would life be like in the real world? I was taken onto the fashion floor by Miss James, and introduced to the ladies I was to work with in the dress department. It was all so different to anything I had ever known. Some of the ladies (assistants they were called) were so smart, their clothes were of the best quality, lovely dark suits with fitted waists. Some suits had velvet collars, and they wore expensive looking leather shoes. With their immaculately groomed hair and tasteful jewellery they looked wonderful to me, and they smelt so nice! It appeared that several of the most senior ladies had in their younger days worked in London in large stores like Harrods and Dickens and Jones.

The job was everything that I thought it would be. I learned quickly, and not just about selling, but about fabrics, what different fabrics were, how to clean them, especially velvet. I learned about fur, how to tell real fur from fake (you blow on it and if it goes into a circle its real, if it doesn't its fake). In the spring, clients would bring their furs in to go into cold storage. Some of the coats were glorious. The Duke of Norfolk's family would come in at times, but they would only be seen by the buyer Miss Joyce. The only really difficult thing for me to cope with was when Miss Joyce suddenly announced that we would have regular Monday morning meetings, before the store opened. Oh God! Assembly all over again. We would all stand round in a semicircle and Miss Joyce would give us all a talk on whatever was important at the time. The panicky feeling returned; I found my throat dried up again, I couldn't swallow properly, and my chest would tighten. I thought the feeling would never leave me, but as soon as the meeting was over, it went.

Before long I had one very important customer specifically asking for me. I remember on one occasion the buyer coming over and asking 'Madam' if she wouldn't prefer a more senior sales assistant to see to her. This was, after all, a very valued customer, and one particular senior sales lady was not at all pleased at my dealing with this customer. 'Madam' replied that she wanted me. This was such a feather in my cap. This lady only came to England once a year, as she lived abroad. Her husband, if I remember rightly, was a military man, and she needed to buy enough clothes to last another year. As it was then obvious that I alone was to deal with this valued customer, I was given special permission to go to the evening wear section where the lovely Frank Usher dresses hung, and my customer bought everything she needed for every occasion from day wear to evening wear. She was such a nice person to deal with, and I could only dream of the life that she must have led. I had several other customers that I was popular with, (not in the same league money wise as the last lady, but nevertheless very nice), and one such customer wanted to adopt me! Every time she came in, the question of adoption came up. I was flattered, but declined. I was quite happy with my family.

My sales figures were good, and at the end of the year when totalling up was done, I must have done very well because I was offered my own Department, Sportswear. When the Buyer called me into her office one morning, I didn't realise it was to give me promotion, and I shook. That woman scared the living daylights out of me. What had I done? Miss Joyce informed me that I was to take over the Sportswear Dept. I replied "But that doesn't seem very fair. There are women who have been here a lot longer than I have. Shouldn't they be considered first?" She glared at me. "It's not your place to query decisions. We decide who gets what department." I was by this time feeling quite anxious. This woman was like a giant compared to me. She was a very large person, in every way, and was always dressed in the most beautiful clothing imaginable. "Do you want it or not?" she said. "Oh, yes please," I replied. "Right," she said, still glaring at me, "start on Monday." "Thank you, Miss Joyce," I said, and hurriedly left. I moved to the Sportswear Department the following Monday, and a new chapter began.

I started by buying myself some new work clothes to wear. I bought a very good quality, and very smart, straight black skirt with a kick pleat and an invisible zip with the benefit of my staff discount, and a new cardigan and shoes. I had to learn to do my own departmental displays, which was fun. There was no one telling me how to do it, so I got stuck in and enjoyed myself. Having been very sporty in my school days I enjoyed my new position very much. I also had the chance to do a bit of modelling, which was exciting. "Lift up your skirt," I was told one morning, by Miss Joyce. I didn't dare refuse, so dutifully showed a leg. "Right, you'll do," she said, "tomorrow morning the Daily Mail will be here. You can model a swimsuit." There was no question of asking whether I wanted to do it or not, you just did what you were told. So the next day I, and two other girls, went down to the beach and modelled swimsuits. All in a day's work really! I did quite enjoy it, but I have never been one to show off my body, as I was very modest. When the photos came out I was quite pleased after all to have been asked, as they were not at all bad. Then I learned from one of the girls on the fashion floor whom I was friendly with, that she had been selected for the Buying School in London. The way things were going; maybe I might get selected, when I'm old enough. You had to be eighteen I seem to remember, so I was to have a bit of a wait yet.

I had made a couple of very good friends during my year on the fashion floor. Pat was one, who did rainwear, and Solveig was the other. I'd worked with Solveig in the Dress Department. She was Swedish, with typical very blonde hair and flawless skin. She was always so jolly, and helpful. I liked her very much and picked up a lot of tips from her on life, and about looking after oneself during pregnancy. She had been a nurse before she came to England, I remembered these tips, I thought they might come in useful when I was married.

In the beginning I used to go home for lunch every day, which was nice. I still rode my bicycle and could be home in ten minutes. One of my favourite meals in those days was minced beef and carrots. It sounds like a song, doesn't it? Solveig was most intrigued by this meal, as I used to go on and on about it, and how delicious it was. They didn't have anything like that in Sweden, so she just had to do it for her husband. I just hope he enjoyed it as much as me! Pat, who later changed her name to Tricia, was engaged to Peter, a silversmith, who was to go on to do very well in life. Tricia had real style and knew how to make the best of herself. She was very attractive. We became very good friends, and as she lived quite a long way from me, I would sometimes get the bus to her house in the evening.

20

My social life was very good during this time. I'd grown up so quickly, and I had made friends at work to socialise with in the evening, as well as seeing Chris. I had been going out with Chris for three years now, on and off. Sometimes we drifted apart, but we always ended up back together. We were after all far too young to be very serious. But young love is very intense, and your first love is very important, and is always remembered. He did ask me to marry him, first when I was thirteen, and again when I was sixteen, but I was far too young to consider an engagement. It seems ridiculous today, as the youngsters marry much later than we did, if they marry at all, and they often don't consider having children until their thirties. That was unknown in my day. You were considered on the shelf if you weren't married at twenty-three.

I found Chris's company easy, and fun. We had mutual friends from school days, which was nice, but he did like things to go his way, and it invariably caused problems. I found him very pushy, and we would often start an evening together but go home separately, although he would always be waiting on the doorstep for me when I got home, and we'd always make it up before we said goodnight. He was now a trainee journalist for a local newspaper, working on the sports page, and it was his ambition to get to Fleet Street eventually. I wanted to get to the Buying School in London and we thought we'd planned our lives out. We thought we'd eventually marry, and so did everybody else, we were thought to be an ideal couple. He said something totally out of the blue one day. We were walking along the road, just talking about this and that, when he suddenly asked me if he could be the one to write my biography one-day. I laughed. Why would I ever have a book written about me? What was I going to do? I thought the whole thing so unlikely, and dismissed it. I didn't even remember the remark until years later when my second husband told me I had to write my autobiography. I've often thought about that day, and wondered how Chris could have known then that there was even the likelihood of it ever happening.

We both had Wednesday afternoons off. Sometimes we went ice skating, sometimes to a football match, and sometimes we went into the country to pick wild flowers. Chris had a car now, so it made life much easier, and we could get to the places where the flowers grew. I was always wanting to pick something, anything from lilacs to primroses, from rhododendrons to cowslips. I remember on one occasion at Bentalls the under-buyer coming round with the spring holiday list. "When would you like your holiday Miss Golds?" she enquired. I replied that I must have this particular week in April because the primroses would be out then. She was so surprised, because I must have seemed genuinely distressed at the thought of missing them. She went off, only to come back later having rearranged the list. "I know the importance of this to you," she said, smiling. I thought that was really nice, because I was after all only sixteen and very much a junior.

Chris and I were also film buffs, going three times a week. I grew up like many others with Doris Day, Audrey Hepburn and the lovely Sophia Loren, as my idols. And the clothes. Oh my, the clothes! Chris took me to my first ball, the Journalists Ball at the Pier Pavilion, Worthing. I'd wanted to look nice for this special occasion, and a friend of mine, Mel, from the fashion floor told me that she was also going, and would I like to see her dress. When she showed me, I thought it was so beautiful. Oh, to have a dress like that to wear. "They have others," said Mel, "and in other colours. Why don't you go and have a look?" I didn't need telling twice. I ran round to the shop in my lunch hour. There was a lovely pale lemon one in my size, but how would I get the money in time? I asked Chris if he would lend it to me, but he said 'no'! I asked my father if he would lend it to me, but he seemed very disinterested, and could hardly even answer me. The next morning I told Mel of my dilemma, and she suggested that I got an advance on my wages. "Can you do that?" I asked. "Oh yes," said Mel very knowingly. "It's quite common". I made an appointment to see the lady in accounts and yes, that would be alright, but we do not normally do this for dresses. "It's more for emergencies," I was told. Then she beamed at me, "You've obviously set your heart on this dress, so this time we'll help you, but don't expect us to do it again, and we'll deduct a pound a week until it's paid." I thanked her very much, and with the advance in my hand I ran round and bought the dress of my dreams. Oh! I felt like the cat's whiskers when I got dressed to go to the Ball.

The dress was strapless, with a fitted ruched bodice and then layers of petticoats with the top layer lemon embroidered nylon, ballerina length. Chris's mother wanted to see my dress, so Chris rang up and told me that his father would be coming to collect me, as he himself wasn't quite ready. When his father came to collect me, he thought I looked so nice, he joked with me and said he thought he would take me himself. Ah, how nice! John was a lovely man. Very tall and very handsome.

I then had the chance to go to my first Fashion Show. Jantzen the swimwear manufacturers were having a fashion launch of their new spring collection, and I as head of a department was eligible to go. I declined. I would have loved to have gone but I was unable to think about going all that way on my own. Partly I was too young at sixteen to go to London on my own, but even if I'd been older, I would still have had difficulty coping with all the crowds. The buyer was not amused at my declining the offer. Then something dreadful happened to me, which changed the whole course of my life. It was an ordinary working day, and nothing seemed out of the ordinary. Somebody wanted to try on a suede jacket. Nothing unusual about that, except that suddenly I realised that my entire stock of suede coats and jackets had disappeared. In those days suede jackets were very expensive, and the average person didn't own one. I informed the buyer, and the police were called. I experienced at first hand the dreadful way in which the police can interrogate and treat you. I was called downstairs to the despatch room, to be met by a plain-clothes detective, and was then asked a series of questions. His whole line of questioning seemed unreal. Was I a suspect? I obviously was. I was interrogated for what seemed hours, then told I could go home. I was so scared. I was after all a minor, and when I've looked back at this part of my life I've wondered how they got away with it - me being so young. I went back to my department and looked across the whole floor including knitwear millinery and shoes. Everybody had gone home. What time was it? Didn't anybody wait for me? No they hadn't, I was all alone. I hurried and got my coat as quickly as I could and left. I was crying so much that I didn't feel I could get the bus, so I started walking, sobbing my heart out all the way, and eventually reached home.

When I entered the house my mother heard my cries and rushed to me. I think she thought that I'd been raped, because I could hardly speak. I told her all about it, and she was very cross that I had been subjected to the third degree without another person present. "Your father will know what to do," she said. He was working away at this particular time, but she went into the hall and rang the house where he was staying. "Call a solicitor in the morning," he said to her, "and we'll sort it out." I had to go back to work the next day. I don't know how I walked in there, but although I was very young and very scared, I refused to let them bully me. I hadn't done anything wrong, and somehow I would get through this nightmare. Even at that tender age I had such a strong sense of justice and an inner strength that seemed to come from somewhere. I was cross-examined again, with a sordid line of questioning. "Was I pregnant? Did I have sex? Did I have boy friends? Did I need the money for something?" What he said to me was filthy and disgusting. If my father had been there he would have put a stop to it. I never felt the same about the police again, I thought they were honourable people, but this was beyond my comprehension. I kept saying, "I didn't do it," over and over again, and he eventually let me go back to my department. I was told to wash my face, as it was obvious that I had been crying.

The next day I was finger printed. This to me seemed like one step from prison. My father, who had by this time come down from where he was working in Essex, had been in to see the manager with my mother, and then they came and saw me. They tried to reassure me that all would be well. There was one query my father had. The advance on my wages. "What was it for?" asked my father rather sternly. "For my ball gown," I replied. "I did ask you to lend me four pounds, but you said no, and I wanted to look nice for my first ball." Had the police jumped to conclusions? Had I needed money for another reason? Good grief, it was only four pounds for a dress. The next few weeks were hell. I was watched all day by the store detectives. It was a war of nerves. I couldn't believe that anybody would think I had stolen the coats. Fortunately, the whole of the store seemed to be on my side. I suppose they didn't know if it would be their department next. If something went missing from their departments they would be in my shoes. There was real

24

camaraderie. I wanted to leave, but knew that if I did they would think I was getting rattled. I would stick it out at all costs until they either caught the thieves or decided that I was innocent. It was about two months before the store detectives left. I waited for another two months and then went to the Youth Advisory Centre. I was offered an interview with a local firm of solicitors, Messrs. Bowles and Stevens. I went along to an interview and got the job there and then, and twice the money! I thought that if life in the outside world was so dangerous as to be accused of a crime when one was totally innocent, it must be best to work in the safety of a firm of solicitors. That experience proved one important point to me, and that is, you are guilty in the eyes of the law until you can prove yourself innocent, not the other way round.

When I handed in my notice at Bentalls, my colleagues were very sad to see me go. There had been some nice ladies and girls on the fashion floor, and had been very supportive of me. The under-buyer who had always thought that I had been treated very shabbily was pleased that I had found what she thought was a better job. I was pleased in a way but saddened. My dream of being a buyer and travelling the world was over, all because of a crook, or crooks.

I could hardly believe the collection they had for me. It seemed that everyone in the store had been rooting for me during my problems. Leaving day was lovely. I was presented with a hand painted Wedgwood donkey (they had asked me if there was anything I wanted, and that was my choice), and a silver brooch made by Peter, Tricia's Fiancé, which was an 'S' but cleverly done to look like a swan. I had a card signed by everyone, messages from people in other departments that I didn't even know, and drinks at lunchtime in the Ship pub. I made the most of my last chance of staff discount and bought several items of clothing, including a Jantzen swimsuit. I would model my own swimsuit, have my one-person fashion show. I walked out of the staff door of Bentalls at six p.m. for the last time. I felt terrific, and so glad that the nightmare was over.

My new job was very interesting. Junior clerk and general dogsbody. I had to draw the plans for contracts, (conveyances and leases) to show which parcel of land purchasers were buying or leasing. I found it all quite tricky to start with. I had a funny old ink pen to draw with, and different coloured inks, to denote the boundaries. Sometimes I would be asked to check a legal document with the typist who had typed it. I could recite a conveyance off by heart. I could even read out loud with others listening after a while, without getting that awful panicky feeling. It was a major step forward for me and I was very pleased with myself. I was helped by one of the younger solicitors, who was also nervous, and was never without his packet of polos. It intrigued me the way he constantly got them out of his pocket and popped one into his mouth. He got me hooked on them and it helped to keep my mouth moistened, and also having something to do, sucking a sweet, took my mind off tying to swallow all the time. That's why people smoked I suppose, same principle, and today the youngsters are constantly chewing gum.

I started my day by delivering all the local mail by hand. That was good fun, and if you were lucky it could take an hour or more. I met a lot of interesting people on my rounds. I met the husband of the under-buyer at Bentalls who had been so nice to me. He sold typewriters. I met the teacher that I had tormented at school, who was now working for an estate agent. She was rather sweet and smiled at me forgivingly. Maybe she was happier in her new job? I used to pass the fashion buyer, Miss Joyce, on her way to Bentalls. She used to look at me as if to say, "How dared you leave? Weren't we good enough for you?" Incidentally, I heard, via the grapevine, that a gang of professional shoplifters had been charged with stealing the coats, but no one from Bentalls management had the decency to tell me that they were sorry for the way I had been treated. And I do think that the police ought to apologise to people they have wronged. Wouldn't that be a nice touch!

Sometimes I would be asked to witness contracts. This I found a bit nerve racking, with everybody watching me write my name address and occupation. My hand used to tremble, but I did it. I still had this thing about being left-handed; you would never believe the amount of people who remarked about it. Didn't they know that Einstein and Leonardo de Vinci were left-handed? Sometimes I would be asked to accompany clients to other firms of solicitors to swear oaths, which used to make me feel very important. I used to like the feel of law. I've always had a very strong sense of right and wrong. I liked the people I worked for, especially the senior solicitor. What a handsome man he was. The presence this man possessed was awesome. The earth shook when he walked into the office, and I admired him very much. I liked the way it was in those days, when people respected their elders and betters, and there was none of the calling of everyone by first names like today. You felt that there was something very worth while in striving to do well, because you would then get all the respect back. Oh, isn't life different now, when you ring the bank and the girl answers and says "so and so bank, Tiffany speaking". I think it's so unprofessional. And children call adults by their Christian names today. I don't like it.

One morning, whilst delivering the mail to another firm of solicitors, I was chatting to the girl in the general office and she asked me if I would like to volunteer to do a collection for Cancer Research after work one day. I was only too pleased to help, and was allocated Marlowe Road, Worthing. This was not only where Chris' parents lived, but also Solveig, my Swedish friend, and her husband and new baby Helen, and also the Baptist Minister I mentioned earlier, the 'make-up man'. I thought it would be very interesting meeting them all again and prising as much as I could out of them for a splendid cause. Solveig and I were very pleased to see each other. I saw baby Helen, who was gorgeous, and we caught up on all the news. I then went into Chris' house and met his aunt, and then went on to the vicarage. Mrs. Vicar answered the door and I explained what I was doing. To my surprise she said she was sick of giving to charity, and wouldn't give me anything, not a brass farthing. Well there's no answer to that is there? Charity didn't begin in that house. I suspect actually that the minister was pretty poorly paid, and the poor minister's wife probably needed some help herself.

It was during this time that I met my future husband, who I will refer to as Mitch. Mitch was articled to a local firm of chartered accountants. He used to make me shake with nerves when he came near me. Even if he just came and stood in the office talking

27

to somebody else, I would get nervous and find it difficult to do the simplest tasks when he was there. I became a blithering idiot, with the return of the dreaded panicky feeling, and tight chest. Why was this, I wondered? (It reminds me of the Sophia Loren and Peter Sellers film when she sang 'Oh Doctor I'm in trouble'). I thought Mitch was very attractive, with his brown curly hair, hazel eyes and very long eyelashes, and I thought he looked like Russ Tamblyn, the actor. He was also very smart and very articulate. It was soon apparent that he liked me as well, and came over to the office at every opportunity. He was the epitome of the perfect gentleman. I had never been used to this kind of treatment, having got used to Chris being an hour or two late because he had been held up somewhere, usually the pub. Journalists do like to drink, it goes with the job somehow, and I'd seen enough of the effects of that on my mother, when my father spent so much time at the pub. I also think that if Chris hadn't taken me quite so much for granted, things might have been very different. But at that tender young age a girl wants to feel special, adored, and so this new treatment was glorious.

Mitch and I saw each other every day, (I had by this time stopped seeing Chris). He used to meet me from the bus and walk me to the office every morning, and then we would meet again after work. Sometimes he would just walk me to the bus stop, because he or I had other things to do that night. Mitch was studying for his accountancy exams, and I was doing a correspondence course. Other times he would get the bus home with me, and sample my mother's lovely home cooking, and then we usually listened to music. If it was a nice evening, we would go for a walk. At the end of the evening there was always a mad rush for him to get the bus to the station, to connect with the train to get home. We always saw each other on Friday nights and Sunday afternoon and evening, but not Saturdays because he played in a pop group called The Legends. He was an extremely good guitarist, and could actually have been a professional musician. The group used to play at Butlins at Bognor Regis on Saturday nights. I went along one Saturday at Mitch's request, and was sitting there enjoying listening to the music when he made an announcement, "This next piece is for my girlfriend, Stella, who is sitting in the audience over there." He pointed me out and everybody looked at me. They then played 'A Certain Smile' by Johnny Mathis. It was lovely, and they were very good. I didn't wish to go every week because I would not have wanted to dance with anybody else, and it's no fun watching everybody else dance. So I used to see Helen on a Saturday, and have a girl's night.

Mitch was a quiet, serious young man, entirely different to Chris who was much more outgoing, and of course sports mad. I was undoubtedly, flattered by this charming young man, and I fell in love with him.

I often used to be complimented on my clothing, and I must admit that I spent all my wages on clothes. My mother actually used to take people on tours of my wardrobe when I was out, as she admitted one day. On one occasion one of the secretaries at the office did a 'look alike' of me. It was a weird feeling, looking at her, as she had all the same things on as me. I had knitted myself a Jaeger pattern dress, and I'd worn it several times to the office. She, seeing mine, knitted the same dress, the same colour, and she even did her hair the same way. They say imitation is the sincerest form of flattery, but no one had ever wanted to look like me before. On one occasion one of the solicitor's wives asked who I was, purely because of the outfit I wore. I mention this not for any other reason than to emphasise my love of fashion and design. Having been denied one avenue of design; it comes out later in another form, much later in the book.

I got engaged at the tender age of seventeen to Mitch, much to the disappointment of Chris, who had achieved his ambition and was now working in Fleet Street for the Daily Mail. It was and is a small world, and it turned out that he and Chris had been best friends at the High School. It was naturally an exciting moment for me getting engaged to Mitch. We had planned to do it at Christmas, and I had been allowed to choose my ring, so I chose a ruby, it looked so pretty, and Mitch had made the ultimate sacrifice, he had sold his guitar to pay for it. It was a decision he had made on his own. He had thought that he had better spend less time playing the guitar, and knuckle down to some serious studying and pass his exams if he was to have a wife to support. I suppose one of the many things that attracted me to him was that he was so very charming, and very attentive. He always seemed to be there whenever I needed him. I thought nothing could ever happen to me whilst I was with him. I felt safe at last. He spoilt me, buying me little presents whenever he had any money, which was nice because he didn't earn much as an articled clerk. He used to buy me Pendalfin Rabbits, which were so cute. He made me feel so special, and I naturally loved it. I didn't realise until some years later that when Mitch had asked my father for my hand in marriage, my father had said yes, but had warned him that it would take some man to be able to handle me. I was so surprised when Mitch told me this; I couldn't think why Dad had said that. Again it was many years before I realised my destiny and the powers that I possessed, I firmly believe that my father knew who I was years before I did. It certainly didn't put Mitch off, thank goodness.

Mitch did have a very intense side to him, however, and this resulted in a serious car accident one Sunday afternoon. We had a very minor disagreement, and he lost his temper, and put his foot down on approaching a crossroads. I pleaded with him to slow down, but he made no attempt to do so at all. We hit another car head on, the car left the ground and I can remember thinking that that was it, I thought we'd had it. We were very lucky to escape with cuts and severe bruising. His sister's mini, which he had borrowed, was written off. Maureen came and collected us from the scene and deposited us at the crossroads about a hundred yards from my house. I remarked that I could hardly walk, as my legs were very painful. There were no seat belts in those days, and my legs had taken the full force of the dashboard, but Mitch was in total shock, which was not surprising. I walked like a wooden legged soldier to my house. My mother put me to bed and called the doctor. Mum very rarely called a doctor, so I must have looked awful, she was worried too about Mitch, his ribs had taken the full force of the steering wheel. He assured Mum that he was alright and that he would go to his brother's house which was just a few streets away. My legs hurt terribly and were swelling up around the knees nicely. They were not broken, fortunately, just severe bruising. I also had severe shock. When I went back to work after two weeks, one of the solicitors said jokingly, "What, trying to kill you already, Miss Golds, and before the wedding?"

The whole office laughed like you do at silly remarks. Charming!
I thought. Mitch was always telling me how much he loved me
and couldn't live without me, and I believed him. I loved him so
much.

I sensed a feeling of animosity from his mother. She always
treated me coolly. I wasn't used to this treatment, and it made no
difference what I said or did, there was no warmth for me there.
She admitted years later that she had always resented me, having
lost her husband at quite an early age. She had thought Mitch had
been a gift from God, to be with her in her old age, and I had
ruined that. I had no answer to that. It's sad for a mother to want
to hold on to a child, and it often happens when mothers have
unhappy lives, but to deny your child their own life is quite wrong.
I more than once detected a very unhappy Mitch and although he
adored his mother, I knew he loved being at my home, and he was
very fond of my Dad.

Betty, who was now known as Liz, worked in the Health
Department in the Town Hall, and was our family bookies runner.
She didn't look the type to frequent bookmakers. She looked
more like a librarian than a gambler. It was just a bit of fun
actually. We used to look at the runners for the big races such as
The Derby, The Oaks and The Grand National and then choose
our horses. Liz would then take our bets into the betting shop on
her way to the Town Hall. She was very slight of build, and very
prim and proper, and couldn't see a thing without her glasses. She
was a positive hazard on her boneshaker, which she rode every
day to the office.

Liz met David in the Town Hall and they got engaged. David was
a trainee Public Health Inspector. He was very good looking and
they got married. Eileen had joined the W.R.A.F. by this time and
had been sent overseas to Aden, so was unable to come home for
the wedding. David's sister, Linda, and I were bridesmaids; we
wore long peach satin dresses with peach roses in our hair. Liz
looked exquisite in a straight white lace dress, with her blonde
hair. She was like a tiny little doll. David looked like Jeremy
Spencer the film star. Sarah was born in the following December,
and I became an Auntie. How exiting, Auntie Stella. I could

hardly wait to have my own babies.

I applied and got the position of telephonist and receptionist in our office, as the previous lady had left. Mr. Day, the office manager, had urged me to go for it. I really enjoyed this new position and put my all into it. It paid off, and I was told unofficially that I was the best private telephonist in town. The title was due largely to the fact that I got on very well with one of the senior partner's most important and difficult clients. This man was a property developer of some considerable standing in the town, and when he rang up he only had to say 'Good Morning' and I would reply, "Good morning, Mr Pateman" which of course flattered him, although I didn't do it for that reason. I just knew most voices as soon as they said 'Hello'. He also got me a pay rise because of praising me so much to the senior partner. I very much enjoyed my job, especially the meeting people and chatting. Fancy getting paid to talk, the very thing that had always got me into trouble over the years!!!

When Mitch's articles finished, as he had wasted a lot of time, (in his own words) playing the guitar, and hadn't taken his final exams, he would have to continue studying whilst working full time for someone else. He quickly found a job in Brighton as an auditor for a firm of chartered accountants in the famous Lanes, so having moved away from Worthing, it was suggested that I too, should find another job preferably nearer Brighton, and use my brain. Something, which he didn't think, I used in my present position. I thought he might be right, so I applied to be a company bookkeeper. Let's all be bookkeepers I thought! I had no knowledge of this area at all, but that didn't deter me. I was willing to give it a try. I was a very strange mixture of bravado and nerves. Situations didn't seem to make me nervous, but people did. Off I went to a carpet accessory manufacturer, at Lancing just outside Worthing, and after a very short interview I got the job, to start the following Monday. Feeling pleased with myself, I walked back towards my home along the beach. The tide was out, so I took my shoes and stockings off, and walked along the edge of the warm water, feeling the lovely soft warm sand under my bare feet. I thought about the interview, and how well it had gone, Mitch would be pleased with me. I had told the woman who'd interviewed me, that I was engaged to be married later that year, and as such had kept my ring on, they couldn't have missed a ruby with eight diamonds. In those days it was common for a woman to get married and give up working altogether, so it was a risk I wanted her to know about, although I had every intention of keeping on working. We would need my income at least for the foreseeable future, as we were not going to be well off at all. It wasn't an issue, the interviewer had said, and the job was mine if I wanted it, and I did. The money was brilliant, fifty per cent up on what I had been getting at the solicitors. I can remember Eileen's voice, when on returning home I told her about my new job. "How much?" You jammy devil, that's more than I earn!" Eileen had come home from Aden; she had things to sort out...

I gave in my notice to the solicitors the next morning. I was offered a rise to stay, but declined, stating that my reason for leaving was not money but the chance to learn something new. I was sorry to leave in a way, having been there for three years, but I had to prove to Mitch that I had a brain!

My first morning in my new job was awful. I didn't understand anything. "Pardon?" I kept saying. "You'll soon get the hang of it," my boss said. I was none too sure. I might as well have been learning Russian, but it's the same with anything in life. You can't do anything until you're taught it, can you? I did soon get the hang of it, but Oh Glory, was it boring! Sitting at a desk all day was not me. The only light relief was the trips to the loo, and coffee time.

During this time, as already mentioned, Eileen had come home from Aden. She had been discharged from the air force because she was pregnant. The baby's father was going to marry her, she had said optimistically. There was just one small problem, he was already married, with children, and as it turned out had no intention of leaving his wife. He even denied the child was his. I suppose he'd been a long way from home and totally forgotten he was married with children. These little things are easy to forget! Poor Eileen. It was just the worst thing to happen to her, and not as acceptable as it is today. It wasn't so many years earlier that girls were packed off to a mother and baby home, so that no one knew about the baby. But thank goodness those days were over; it's the last thing my mother would have insisted on. Eileen was such an attractive girl; she could have had anybody she'd wanted, so this was very sad for her. As I said, in those days it was not as acceptable as it is today. It ruined girls' lives. Today's girls would not believe how different life was for us. Women were not supposed to have sex before marriage, but with men being like they were, it wasn't so easy. It was a constant fight to keep one's honour. Men, it seemed, always had one thing on their minds, but if you succumbed to their evil ways and got pregnant, you damned well had to pay for it. I always thought that men should have worn a sign around their necks: 'This man could seriously damage your life if you let him'. I'm only being partly serious. I think today's girls have much more fun, they have relationships with whomever they like, and they are in total charge of their sexuality. It's much easier in many ways for women today. I was lucky with Mitch, we had decided to wait, so there was no pressure on me. We made do with a grope.

I made a friend called Maureen at Cimco. She was also getting married that year to David. She was a real laugh. We sat at desks opposite each other, so it was possible for a bit of a chat if the boss was out. Lunchtimes we would either go and sit in the park opposite, or on the beach, to eat our sandwiches, and on Friday, pay day, we would walk into Lancing and buy something for our bottom drawers. Happy days they were.

 I learnt various skills whilst working at Cimco, the most interesting of which was the accounting machine. It looked really difficult to operate, and when I first sat opposite it, I quaked. When the person who normally operated it was away on holiday, or ill, it duly fell to me to take over, and gradually I learned how to use it. On the whole I found the entire job deadly dull, and I would have used any excuse not to have gone to work. This was very unlike me, as I have always liked my work. Offices I decided were dull places to be.

In the June sadly my grandfather Sidney died, he had been ill with cancer for a while and had been in a lot of pain. In retrospect it seemed an unfair death for such a brave soldier, winning the M.M.

like he did. But who said life was fair? I had, on this particular day, to pick up my wedding dress, and then go into the office. I thought I would be all right, but I was devastated. I thought I could work, but after bursting into tears several times they sent me home. I remember sitting on my bed back at home gazing at my dress, which I'd unwrapped and hung on the door. It was a quite beautiful, pure silk Elizabethan style, full-length dress, with a small fan shaped train. Leg-of-mutton sleeves pointed at the wrists, fastened with pearls. Eileen was at home, but we were not much company for each other. She was about eight months pregnant now, and the sight of my wedding dress was too much for her. She was naturally sad and angry that her life had gone so horribly wrong for her, even though she had had so much going for her earlier in her life. It was a strange time for me because normally everyone would have been so happy, with a forthcoming marriage. Presents were arriving daily, and the two bridesmaids dresses were being made by one of Mum's friends. But the shine was taken away, partly because of Eileen, and then because of my grandfather's death. Oh why did granddad have to die now, and not see me married? So it was hard to be happy in those circumstances for me, and rather a shame. It should have been a gloriously happy time for me, but the atmosphere indoors was awful. To rub salt even further into Eileen's wounds I had not one but two young men practically fighting over me now, because Chris had heard I was getting married and tried to persuade me to call it off. Oh dear! If only Eileen hadn't gone into the wretched Air Force maybe this wouldn't have happened. It did cause a lot of animosity between us, and we used to argue all the time.

After Rachael's birth in the July, I asked Eileen if she would like to be one of my bridesmaids, and she said she would. I thought it only right as she had missed the opportunity of being a bridesmaid at Liz's wedding through being abroad. I wanted her to be a part of my day, and look beautiful. All animosity stopped between us and Eileen asked me to be Rachael's godmother, I was delighted. There was a slight possibility when I was married to Mitch that we could adopt Rachael. That was a lovely thought.

Chris was by now getting quite perturbed at the prospect of my marriage, and was often ringing me and popping round to try to get me to change my mind. He did succeed at one point. I realised Mitch and I had differences, and I was feeling very uneasy. I was missing the social side of life. Journalists are by the very nature of the job sociable animals, and I missed all the social engagements that we'd gone to, the yacht races, the chasing over the downs following the golf tournaments. I missed the dancing; Mitch didn't dance, and had no intention of learning. It wasn't his scene - he would rather play the guitar at one, which was fair enough, because he was so good at it. I also missed going to the pub on Friday nights; Mitch didn't drink, so of course that eliminated nearly all social events. And I missed the flowers. Chris always gave me flowers, usually pansies on a Sunday afternoon - a large bunch that he had picked himself, from the garden. I tried to break off the engagement. I really had second thoughts. Was it nerves? It's a big decision, marriage. Was it all the goings on indoors? That certainly didn't help me. I couldn't think very straight any more. I was becoming more and more uneasy. Mitch was a lovely person, a perfect gentleman in every way, but maybe too quiet for me. I would be the one who would have to change my entire lifestyle. I was afraid that we were unsuited. I was a people person. I liked dressing up, I had lovely clothes and suddenly no where to wear them to. I liked dancing, socialising, and generally having a good time. I liked to laugh, and was a bit of an exhibitionist maybe? I remembered the night Chris and I had danced the Pasa Doble from the Pier Pavilion to the bridge, along the white line in the middle of the main road. We did mad things like that. He was impulsive, Mitch was the total opposite, and it had been just that which attracted me to him. But now I just wasn't sure.

I needed some time to think. I was very confused, but when I tried to break it off, he wouldn't take no for an answer. My feelings were very confused, I knew I was in love with him, but I also knew I felt very sorry for him, and I never knew why. He was a sad soul underneath, and I knew he adored my Dad and the sort of family life that we enjoyed. He had sadly lost his father when he was only seven, and being the last of the children at home, naturally his mother was possessive. And so he found my home a lovely place to be, full of laughter and fun. My mother was also worried about the marriage. She said to me, "You feel sorry for him, but if you marry him he'll have you right there," pointing a finger downwards. I knew deep down inside myself she was right but I only had to hear his voice or see him and I knew I was in love with him. I also know that I still didn't feel quite right about it, so after my last effort to call the wedding off, he said that if I didn't marry him as arranged he would borrow his sister's car and drive it into a brick wall, and kill himself. I knew he meant it when he said it, it wasn't just an idle threat. I thought, however, that it was a bit drastic, and I did feel somewhat pressurised. Of course I didn't realise at that tender age the consequences of someone exerting that much pressure on another person, and it was the beginning of a very bizarre marriage. So I assured myself that I was suffering from nerves or something, I was sure that he must have loved me to distraction to not want to live without me. Oh how wonderful, to be so loved that someone would die for you. So I said 'Yes', but the most strange feeling came over me and it wouldn't go away. Someone or something was telling me that I was supposed to marry this man. Why? That I didn't learn for many years, but there was a definite reason behind it all. I told Mitch about it and the feelings I had, I even asked for a divorce if it didn't work out, he seemed to accept it all quite naturally. What a strange state of affairs this was and no mistake!

We were to be married on Saturday the 11th of September 1965, at a church called St. Peter and St. Paul's, in Rustington village. It was a lovely old church with a lych gate. This was Mitch's parish church. The reason we chose his was that we had been along to my lovely old parish church of Broadwater, as I had been christened Church of England. (We went to the Baptist Sunday school I think because it was nearer.) We had been to see my Vicar, but we'd had a very disinterested interview with a very disinterested vicar. I wanted the new marriage service, but he, without even giving reasons, said 'No'. He didn't like the new service and wouldn't perform it. I regarded marriage as a very serious step, and didn't feel that I could say the word 'obey' when I didn't believe that marriage was about obeying. To me it was a partnership. His answer I didn't care for and neither did Mitch so we ended up at St. Peter and St. Paul's, in Rustington, where the vicar was really nice and caring. He took the trouble to explain the words of the marriage service to me, and when I understood them, I ended up wanting the traditional wedding service. It just goes to show doesn't it? We went for several lessons at the vicarage before our big day, something that was quite common in those days, preparing us for the responsibilities of marriage. We were both very excited about it all, and I now felt totally happy about everything, I'd just been nervous.

On the day of our wedding I had to travel about ten miles along the dual carriageway in my limousine with my father by my side to the church. The sun was shining and I was eager to get there but on the way to the church I passed three funeral corteges. I know we're much more superstitious when we're young, but nevertheless when I saw the first funeral I thought it a shame to see a coffin on my wedding day, but I dismissed it as much more unlucky for the person in the coffin. But then there was another one. I hardly dared look, but you can't help but look with morbid curiosity, and I was really unnerved. When the third passed me I was totally shaken. This had to mean something! I thought brides saw chimney sweeps or black cats, this was horrible and I felt this was an omen! The fact was it was a Friday, and on weekdays there are always funerals. (We had to rearrange the wedding completely from the Saturday to the Friday, because our honeymoon flight had been brought forward twenty four hours), and as I said I did have to travel along the main road which also led to the crematorium going the other way. When I got to the church it started to rain slightly, and who should be there with an umbrella but Chris' Mum. She had waited at the gate to get a glimpse of me, and once again, her kindness was obvious. I felt sad that I hadn't felt I could invite her and John, and I knew she was very disappointed at not having me for a daughter-in-law, but there she was, generous in spirit, right to the last. She and John sat in the back of the church for the service not wanting to miss my day.

After the service the sun came out, and photographs were taken in the churchyard as planned. I had three bridesmaids, Eileen, Helen, and my cousin Yvonne's daughter, Wendy, who was six. Our reception was held at the Broadmark Hotel, Rustington, right on the beach. John, Mitch's brother, was best man. He had a good sense of humour, and made a very good speech, including a reference to g-strings, musically speaking I believed! It was all over very quickly; the time seemed to fly by. Afterwards we left for our honeymoon in Sardinia. We got to the station, only to realise that there was no train. Mitch had got the times of the trains wrong and it looked as if we might miss our plane. I had an idea. I went to the call box and dialled. "Hello, Richard? It's me, we've missed our train and the plane takes off at nine thirty. Can you help us please?" "Where are you Stella?" "Worthing Central." "OK. Will be there in five minutes." I don't know what we'd have done without him. He drove us all the way to Heathrow Airport, and waited around until our flight was called. Goodbyes were said for at least the tenth time, and off we then went to get our plane.

Chapter 3 - Incompetence

I had not flown before, and I was really looking forward to it. We were hoping to fly on the new 'Bus stop jet' the B.A.C 1-11, but it wasn't ready to go into use. Instead we went on a propeller plane. I didn't feel at all nervous. Flying seemed the most natural way of travelling to me. We were very tired after our long and exhausting day, and I hadn't wanted to sleep during the flight and miss something! I don't know what I would have missed, mind you, as there was nothing but blackness out of the window in the middle of the night. I was nevertheless just hoping for a glimpse of something. Weddings are very tiring, what with the build up over months, and all the planning that you have to do right down to the tooth picks. And then it's all over in a matter of hours. It goes almost too quickly to enjoy it.

We were not disappointed when we arrived. Sardinia was everything we'd dreamed it would be, with miles of deserted white sandy beaches and a pale turquoise sea. I expect it's changed quite a bit now, but in the sixties it was still quite unusual to go abroad like they do today. The hotel was lovely, and we disappeared to our room as soon as we could. It was now morning, and we hadn't slept for twenty-two hours. We must have fallen straight asleep as soon as our heads hit the pillows, because when we awoke it was six o'clock in the evening.

We felt very hungry when we woke up so we quickly got dressed.

Well, we did linger a bit. We had just got married. Then we went downstairs, and appeared in the dining room, trying to appear all calm and collected. The waiter wondered who we were, because all the others on the flight had turned up for lunch, and had been allocated tables. Mitch explained that we'd obviously slept through lunch and most of the afternoon, because having got married the previous day and travelled all night, we'd felt exhausted. I could tell the waiter thought "a likely tale", because he grinned, and there were the usual sniggers from other guests. I tried to look unembarrassed, but I did feel my face go a little hot. All eyes were on us, as the waiter showed us to our table.

The next day we hired a car and toured the island. At that time bandits were rife, and we were all advised by our tour guide what we should do if we were held up by them. "Don't try to be heroic" we were told. "Hand over whatever it is they want". We didn't have anything of much value except our rings, so we decided that if we were stopped we would pop them into a little secret place we'd found in the car. Anyway, nothing untoward happened. We went right across to the other side of the Island. We were trying to find where the Aga Khan had his yacht moored, and also where Princess Margaret used to stay, but found neither, but it was a lovely trip through the mountains. The hotel did packed lunches, which were delicious, with lots of cheese, fresh bread and always heaps of grapes. We liked going up into the hilly areas. It was very beautiful, rather as I imagined Israel to look. The temperature was lovely and hot, and I enjoyed the freedom of walking about in a blouse with shorts and sandals. We do it all the time now in England, but in those days it wasn't widely done. We as a nation didn't wear casual clothes as a matter of course like they do today; it wasn't until the eighties that everyone took to jeans and trainers. I still remember wearing little white cotton gloves with summer dresses and white sandals in the sixties. Oh, those were the days!

The area of beach next to the hotel was rocky, with wide flat rocks. We didn't swim from there, but we used it for sunbathing, as we wanted to go back as brown as berries. And of course, I had to wear my Jantzen swimsuit! On one such lovely lazy hot day, we were brought back to consciousness because one of the local lads had caught a squid, and proceeded to chew one of its legs off whilst it was still alive. I was horrified at how barbaric this young man was. Did he think it felt no pain, or did he not care? Probably the latter. Have some human beings really come very far since the days of the cave man? Sometimes I think not. That was my first trip abroad and my introduction to animal cruelty. Since then I have travelled a lot more, and what some people do to animals is beyond my comprehension. Squid was on the menu that evening, and even if I had thought of trying it, I wouldn't after the beach incident. So I declined and stuck to pasta.

We had two glorious weeks in the sun, but all good things come to an end, and we prepared to fly back home. It had been very relaxing apart from one very funny thing that happened. We were on our way down a mountain in the car we had hired; it was all hairpin bends, when suddenly Mitch veered off towards the edge of the road. I knew it was a sheer drop, and I wasn't waiting around to see what he was up to, I jumped out. I jumped out of a moving car, just like in a film. How was I to know he just wanted to perch on the edge of a precipice to enjoy the view? We laughed about it for years afterwards. It shows there's nothing wrong with my reflexes!

On the coach going back to the airport after the holiday, two charming old ladies who had been staying at the same hotel as us asked me if I had enjoyed my holiday with my brother! Well what was one to make of that? I was a bit shocked. Were we so unromantic? You remember remarks like that forever afterwards.

When we got back to Victoria station Mitch informed me that we didn't have enough money for the train fare home. He explained that we'd spent the last of the money the day before on presents to bring back for the family. I replied that if I had realised that it was our train money we were spending, we wouldn't have spent it! Why didn't he say at the time that we were short of funds? What was he hoping would happen when we got to Victoria station? I naturally assumed that he was in charge of the situation. I only mention this because it seemed so out of character for him. He had always been so efficient, taking care of every last little detail. I was a little worried, what with getting the trains wrong going out

42

and then no money coming back. I could hardly believe it. I know he only wanted to be nice and buy little presents for family and friends, but I felt that I couldn't ring Richard and shout "help" again, I was too embarrassed. "Could you sort it out this time?" I asked, and he agreed.

He rang his sister Maureen and spoke to her. Bless her heart, she arranged for us to get the train and she paid at the other end. I was used to being very independent and I found this rather embarrassing. Was this an omen of what was to come? We subsequently arrived at my parent's house to collect the keys to our new home. I quickly forgot the business about the train. I could hardly contain my excitement. I wanted to tell them all about flying, and Sardinia.

We came back down to earth with a bump when we got home. It appeared that due to very heavy rain whilst we had been away, the floors of the bungalow that we were about to rent were very wet, especially the bedroom floor and carpet. So our new home to be, which was very low lying at the foot of the downs, was very wet indeed. My mother said it was not advisable to sleep there until it had been dried out. She said it was unhealthy. We thought about it. It did seem daft to go into a wet place, especially as we had just left a temperature of eighty degrees, so we took up their kind offer and stayed with them. We were a bit disappointed, because naturally we wanted to be on our own. We had lots of new things to take over, all our wedding presents and bits and pieces I'd been collecting for years. We used to have things in those days called 'bottom drawers'. Which was another way of saying, save it for when you are married. People used to say 'Put it in your bottom drawer dear'. I just wanted to start my homemaking as soon as possible.

After a few days the bungalow dried out, and we moved in, and set about making it into a home. It was a nice detached bungalow, fully furnished, with a garden overlooking the downs at Portslade. There were some nice walks, which we took advantage of every Sunday afternoon. The bungalow could have done with some decorating by the landlord, what an understatement. It all smelt very damp, and some of the furniture was past it, but it's amazing

43

what you can do with a little imagination, new bedspreads, a new carpet in the lounge, my lovely state of the art cooker, and most important, a gas fire. I had been used to various things in my life, like heat. Especially heat! I had been used to a very warm family home, and I had always had seven blankets, with an electric blanket as well, on my bed. I was told that I needed toughening up, and smiling at me Mitch said that I would not need all those blankets or my electric one any more, as my blood would soon thicken up. I hoped he was right. I thought it was marriage, not the army!

I have happy memories of packet cake mixture and Cliff Richard singing Maria from Westside Story, when I think of the bungalow, and Helen driving over on a Sunday. Apart from the heat, I missed the telephone and I seemed to spend a lot of time walking up the road to the call box, to ring either Mum or Helen. I've always been a devil for the phone; it's got to be, apart from the wheel, the greatest invention ever.

We had an extremely nice neighbour called Margaret, whose husband was a Captain in the Merchant Navy. She was a bit lonely when her husband was at sea, so I would often go over to her bungalow in the evening and watch television with her, and we would chat for hours about this and that. You wouldn't have thought that we were newly weds, as really, Mitch and I should have been inseparable in the evenings, especially in the early days. Perhaps that's why the old ladies on holiday thought we were brother and sister! Margaret had a little boy called David who was two years old, and I would look after him sometimes for her on a Saturday, she said I could use her washing machine whilst I was babysitting, so that seemed a good idea to me. Mitch didn't mind me going to see her; in fact he positively encouraged me to go. He often brought work home to do from the office. He could have gone with me, but chose not to. I think I got very disillusioned early on.

Looking back, there was not a lot of romance, it was as if we'd been married for years not months. I don't know quite what I expected married life to be like, but definitely more togetherness would have been a start. But I didn't know any difference, and I felt quite happy in my own way. It's much better today, the young expect to have sexual relationships before they settle down. They end up knowing the person they are marrying. Suddenly, my generation went from living with our parents to living with a man we'd never spent a night with. And of course it was the same the other way round, for men. I felt much better, when much later on and having married for the second time, my new husband told me that he'd felt exactly the same way I had, when he'd got married the first time. He'd found it just as strange, the fact he couldn't do as he pleased with hobbies etc any more. How on earth can you know if you're going to be suited or not. It was all such trial and error for us, as it was for all previous generations. I definitely wouldn't like it to go back to being like that. I'm talking now with the benefit of hindsight. I think Mitch and I were both quite happy with the way things were, and we both wanted the same things out of life. We dreamed of all the things that we would do, when he was qualified, and possibly a partner in an accountancy practice. I kept on working full time, and at weekends Mitch would help me with the housework, and then we used to go to Marks and Spencer's in Brighton to do our food shopping, that was when Marks first did food in their stores. We thought it all very trendy, packet soups and all that!!! I'm a born homemaker and I've always enjoyed anything to do with homes and gardens. Having had nothing to compare life with then I wasn't aware of how it should have been, but now having got a very romantic husband I realise just how unromantic that marriage was. If you have no previous experience of life and marriage you just think that your life is normal.

Eileen, meanwhile, married Barry, one of the bosses of the engineering company she was working for. They'd been going out together for a while and she liked him, but she wasn't in love with him. I think he knew that, but was still keen to have her as his wife. Who wouldn't have been? She was an attractive girl. It was sad on her Wedding day. She stood there in her bedroom in a beautiful cream dress and coat with a navy blue hat and shoes, which I'd gone with her to help choose. She looked positively beautiful, but sad, and proceeded to tell me that she didn't love him. I'll never forget the way she looked at me. It was as if our minds touched for a brief moment, and she would have loved any excuse not to have gone through with it. Why was she doing it? I asked, and she replied that no one else would want her as she had a child, and partly to give Rachael a home. Her motives were good, she had decided to take Rachael with her when she was married. Mum and Dad had looked after Rachael since she was born, thus enabling Eileen to be able to work. This was a dreadful wrench for Mum, Rachael was like her own, and so loved by her and Dad.

I really hoped it would work out for her. I was so young and incredibly naïve. In films it always works out, so why not in life. I decided to be optimistic. You often hear of people saying that they got married and love came later. Perhaps that would happen in this case.

 After the honeymoon, they moved into a very smart house in West Worthing. I was glad for her sake that she was settled at last, and Barry seemed a nice enough man, although perhaps a little staid for Eileen, but maybe she would grow to love him. I liked his Mum; I'd have gladly swapped her for my mother-in-law any day. She was a spiritualist and we got on very well.

Meanwhile, my neighbour was moving away to Cornwall. I would miss her so much. She had family down there, and as her husband was away so much it made sense to be nearer them. She wanted my lovely cooker. We always had a joke about it. 'Buy your own' I would say with a laugh. I was a bit of an artist in my spare time and she asked me, before she left, if she could have an oil painting I'd done. I could never part with anything I had ever painted, made or created, so I declined. I regretted it later, because when we visited her house several years later I realised that she had quite an art gallery, and mine could have been hung amongst the rest. That'll teach me!

On one particular Sunday morning I realised something was wrong with me. I was bleeding, but it didn't feel like a period pain, I had such a lot of pain in my stomach. I had been ploughing through the weekly wash by hand in the kitchen sink, including large sheets and towels, when the pain started, and soon became unbearable. It hurt to put my feet to the ground. I didn't know what the matter was, I did think perhaps I had strained myself. I

46

did find doing the washing quite a chore by hand; I didn't have any kind of washing machine. We were supposed to be going out that evening to the cinema in Brighton, to see The Sound of Music, and I seriously doubted whether I would be able to go. It seemed to cause problems me not going, so I said I would go. He thought it would do me good. Oh yeah, like a hole in the head! I saw the film; I sat in pain all the way through. I can remember the agony of putting my feet to the ground, as we walked up to the station to come home. I should not have gone, and if left to my own discretion I would have gone to bed. I did take a couple of days off work afterwards, and I soon recovered after a rest. I must have strained myself. I tell this only to show the lack of interest he showed in me from very early on in the marriage. How different to that attentive young man I had got engaged to, who had wooed me to distraction.

I decided to find a part time job, but before I left, I was asked if I would like to do an advertising photo shoot for the company for some magazines. I reluctantly agreed. Well actually in truth, they told me I was going to do it. It was like Bentalls all over again. I was really too shy for that kind of thing, and I got nervous at the thought of it, but on the other hand who would have thought it, little old me being photographed yet again. I was asked to come in the next day in my best dress and to report to the boardroom. This I did, and to my horror there was a room full of men with lights and cameras. Now, one camera can be alarming to some people, including me, but several was terrifying. I was panic stricken and I shook from head to toe. Some of the directors had to leave the room; they were making me worse. When they left it was a bit easier for me, I had to have my dress pulled in tight and pinned to show off my curves, and I had to stand by a table and look interested in carpet fittings. Not easy at any time, but especially when one is so nervous. The heat of the lights and several cameras flashing was so daunting for me, and I had had no training for this kind of thing. I was not a model, nor had I the slightest desire to become one. The pictures I believe went into House and Garden, Ideal Home and trade journals. Not bad for the awkward, panicky girl. I then left the company. Where next would they want to photograph me?

I enrolled with a job agency in Brighton and waited to see what turned up. Meanwhile, I often used to get the bus into Brighton and meet Mitch from work, and maybe look around the Lanes. I loved looking around the Lanes, with all its little Antique shops. Mitch hadn't made any long-term career plans, until one day he was approached by the firm of accountants he had been articled to in Worthing. We were both asked to go and see the partner and his wife who lived in nearby Goring by Sea. Mitch was asked if he would be interested in running a subsidiary office for them in Rayleigh, Essex, in conjunction with a firm of solicitors, the solicitor being the partner's wife's brother. We were very excited at the thoughts of it, and Mitch would earn enough to be able to buy a house. He said yes without any hesitation, we both said yes. Oh! How exciting! They wanted us to go as soon as possible to have a look at houses. We didn't need telling twice, so the next week we drove up there with the partner, and after looking at several houses we decided on one. I could hardly believe it. It was like a dream. A brand new detached house with garage and garden. Mitch went ahead and bought it. Oh, how excited we were, a lot of what we'd lost in the first few months of marriage came back. This was going to be good for us. The signs were very encouraging.

Mitch also had a company car - a new Mini. I spent all my spare time making curtains, and planning the decor. We were able to choose wallpapers and floor tiles. We bought some new furniture from Bentalls, and with what we already had, we had enough to start us off. Before we moved up there, we went on holiday to the Norfolk Broads. Mitch and I had been two years earlier, when we were engaged, with an older lady from his office and her man friend, but this time we were going with my parents. My Dad was none too sure about it really. He even delayed coming with us for a few days. "I'm much too busy at work," he said, "You go on ahead, and I'll join you later." After a few days he did arrive and to his amazement he actually started to enjoy himself, and started to steer the boat. I think Dad found it hard to relax. He was not used to holidays, but I know he enjoyed that week. Mum loved it and has often said since that she would go again anytime. In my haste one day to get my camera, to photograph a heron, I ran into the top of the cabin door, and slid to the bottom of the stairs in a crumpled heap. My mother rushed to my aid. My head was bleeding and I was quite dizzy. I haven't wanted to photograph one since.

On returning home my mother, who had a thing about hitting ones head, sent me to see the doctor, who in turn sent me to the hospital for an x-ray. They discovered that I have a very thin skull, and said that it wouldn't take much to kill me if I was ever hit on the head. I said I would try and avoid it if possible. I also discovered that I was pregnant. We were thrilled - new house and new baby! We knew things would be tight money wise, but when you are young such things don't really bother you. When Mitch told his mother that she was going to be a grandmother again she insisted that it must be Marjorie, her other daughter-in-law who was pregnant, and refused to believe that it was me. Strange, I don't think she wanted me to be pregnant.

We moved to our new house in Hullbridge, near Rayleigh, and set about putting up the curtains and laying our carpets. I was really happy. The neighbours both sides were very nice. On one side they were Eastenders, and a very friendly couple, the wife Chris, had been trying to have a baby for some time, so she was understandably a little envious of my pregnancy, but nevertheless we got on really well, and we became good friends. She asked if she could share my baby. It must be devastating when couples are trying to have a baby and it just doesn't happen. The couple the other side were from Birmingham. We just loved their accent. They were also a very nice couple, and she told me that she was also pregnant, and the baby was due about the same time as mine. It was quite common in that part of the world to have babies at home, the reason being the lack of hospital beds. (It's not just these days that there is a bed shortage. This was the sixties). We couldn't even get onto a doctor's list. What with all the new building work going on in the area, the one and only doctor's list was full. He couldn't deny me help though, as I was pregnant, so I was an unofficial patient. The midwife was nice and I settled for a home birth.

Mitch, meanwhile, brought home a Basset Hound called Benjamin. We had discussed having a dog, so he had been to the

49

RSPCA kennels and this dog needed a home. It didn't take long before Ben drove me up the wall. He insisted on sitting on my lap, and bearing in mind he weighed forty pounds and I was pregnant, this was uncomfortable. He also insisted on sleeping on the bed at night. We gave up trying to persuade him to sleep in the kitchen because he barked so much. I thought I had better have some sleep in my condition, so he lay right across the bed and me every night. He actually turned my nice house into an indoor kennel. His feet were like saucers, so when he came in from his walk with muddy feet, the pale beige tiles quickly became brown, and he slobbered saliva everywhere. Mitch remedied that and covered the entire floors with newspaper. It looked like a horror film to me. I couldn't imagine having a new baby in such filthy conditions.

On returning home to Worthing to stay with my parents for Christmas, (we took Ben, who had to have a tranquillising drug if we took him on long journeys because he was such a nervous passenger) I went to see my old doctor, as I was still registered with him. Dr. Campbell thought that I ought to have my first baby in hospital, and I readily agreed. He examined me, this was my first experience of an internal examination, and it occurred to me afterwards that I had never had an examination with the doctor or midwife back at home in Essex, and I was six months gone. That was quite a frightening thought. Anyway, the examination was very uncomfortable and Dr. Campbell seemed very offhand with me, telling me that I would have to get used to it. (Mother you never told me about this bit!) It was then decided between us that I would stay down in Worthing with my parents, and have our baby in hospital, whilst Mitch returned home without me, but with the dog.

I was by this time six and a half months pregnant, and it was suggested by Dr. Campbell that I go into the Zachary Merton maternity hospital at Rustington. Neither of us were happy about being separated, but we thought the doctor knew best. Mitch also decided to put Ben into boarding kennels, for three months, I ask you. I wanted him to take him back to the RSPCA because we could no way afford this dog, and I dreaded the thoughts of all that mess with a new baby, but he wouldn't hear of it - all would be fine. So he went home and I took myself off to Zachary Merton hospital the next week, thinking that there would be no problem, and that I would get a bed without any bother. How wrong could I be? This was my first encounter with a Consultant gynaecologist, and what a rude arrogant man he was! Why should he give me a bed? If I couldn't be bothered to book myself in when I first knew I was pregnant like everybody else did, why should he bother? I tried to explain that I lived away, and that I had been unable to get on a doctor's list at home, so I had gone to see my own GP when I was back in Worthing with my parents for Christmas. But would he listen? Oh no, he wouldn't! And after deciding that he wouldn't help me, he then gave me a gruelling painful internal examination. He said it was to satisfy himself that everything was ok. Why should he do that to me when he knew he was not going to look after me? I felt totally humiliated. It was like being raped. I couldn't believe that I would be treated so badly, and I burst into tears. They were indifferent to me, so I took myself off to see my mother-in-law, who lived about a half a mile away at the other end of the village. She was horrified that I should be treated so rudely and was in such a state. She made me tea and got the bus back with me to Worthing, to make sure I was going to be alright.

Then Dr. Campbell sent me off to Southland's Hospital at Shoreham, to see the consultant gynaecologist there, who also wouldn't give me a bed. He said there wouldn't be any extra beds in March. He was full. What was I to do? I asked. I was told I could see the lady Consultant Mrs B. if I wanted to. I thought I had better talk to my doctor on the telephone to see what he thought, and after a brief phone call, Dr. Campbell said, "Yes go with Mrs. B." I went back to the department and I saw the lady specialist, who seemed much nicer, and she also gave me a gruelling internal examination, which seemed to go on for ages, but at least she offered me a bed in return. Third time lucky! I turned up for my first antenatal appointment and it all seemed very relaxed, the nurses were very pleasant and for the first time in ages I felt confident. Everything was explained during the classes, such as what would happen to me when I went into labour, and I felt happy at last. Mitch came down every Friday night and stayed until Sunday night. We enjoyed our weekends, and we were both impatient for the baby to come so that I could go back home. I had a very healthy pregnancy, apart from being sick in the first few months. I walked a lot. My mother and I would go off every afternoon and walk a few miles, so I felt extremely fit. I did, however, at eight months get a very woozy head, and at my next visit to the antenatal clinic was told that I had blood pressure, which would need watching, and if it didn't go down I might have to be admitted. I thought this strange, because as I've said I was a very fit person. I decided off my own back that it was the iron pills that were doing it to me, so I stopped taking them. My blood was actually very good. I had never been anaemic in my life, so at my next antenatal appointment I questioned the nurse as to whether I needed to take iron pills. 'Everybody takes them' I was told, as she handed me another bottle. I didn't take them any more and when I went for my next check-up after having not taken the pills for a month, I was told that my blood pressure was normal. "Strange," said the sister. I never said a word.

It appeared, though, that the antenatal staff and the actual hospital ward nurses had never met. Everything that I had been told about gentleness and reassurance went by the board, and insensitivity was the order or the day. It was Easter, and Mitch was down for a few days. On Good Friday it was so warm that we walked along the sea front at Worthing. There was no need for coats; the sun was lovely and warm. When my waters broke early the next morning I got up woke up Mitch and collected my bag. We were on our way out of the front door when my mother's voice was heard at the top of the stairs, "Why the rush, you'll be ages yet." I explained what had happened and she changed her mind, saying it was unusual for waters to break so soon, but if that was the case to go straightway. I then sat for two days with not a twinge. I was really fed up and worried that my baby was now left without any water to protect him. I repeatedly asked the nurse if she could do anything for me, but for the whole of Saturday and all day Sunday I was ignored. On the Easter Monday 27th March, they informed me that I was to have an enema. I didn't care what they did, I just wanted to get on with it and get out of that dreadful place. Not long after the enema I felt a twinge. Hooray at last! I told the nurses that I had started, but they took no notice. After a short while, the pains were so strong, I was in agony. They ignored me all during visiting time in the main ward, with husbands walking

52

by. Mine was trying to comfort me, with someone else's husband as well talking to me. It was unbelievable, I felt like an animal, with no regard being shown for my feelings. The sister who was a cold and clinical person sent my husband home, saying I was making a lot of fuss. I had hours to go yet, she said, and that she would let him know when anything happened. They had said in the antenatal clinic that husbands were welcome to stay, but they wouldn't let him, so off he went home to my parent's house. They had by this time put me on a drip, the pains were so strong, and I felt very afraid, and very alone. I asked if I could have a nurse to sit with me, because I was afraid. "What a lot of fuss," said the sister, but sent over a Black nurse anyway. I was repeatedly told to be quiet and behave, and just two hours after my pains began I asked if I might have a bedpan. I thought my whole body was going to explode. Then they realised they'd been wrong and that I had had my entire labour in full view of everybody. "Quick get the trolley, she's having it," said the nurse. I remembered singing 'Whenever you feel alone, just hold your head up high, and whistle a happy tune' on my way to the delivery room. What else could I do? I felt surrounded by Aliens, very unkind Aliens. I was only in labour three hours and forty minutes, and then Julian arrived. Because the waters had broken two days previously his skin was peeling off, but he was still gorgeous! My Easter Monday baby. My horror story was only just beginning, though.

I wasn't given Julian to hold. They just put him into a cot. I remember Mitch coming in and being very surprised that it was all over so quickly. It was not at all what they'd told him. He glanced down at Julian who still had the clamps attached to him, lying unattended, and remarked how pleased he was that we were both ok. He wasn't allowed to stay long, as thankfully we were both going to be attended to. Julian was weighed and whisked away to the premature baby unit. "But he's not premature," I said, "he was late!" "It goes by weight," I was told, "he only weighs five pounds five ounces, so he has to go to the premature unit - those are the rules." I hadn't even seen him, but I was too tired to argue at that time, and they got on and stitched me up.

Julian was a long baby - twenty-one inches. He was one of the longest on the ward. I remember dozing in and out of consciousness as they repaired me. There were several of them standing there, chatting away, me with my legs in stirrups, and then the doctor said, "You could have one every year. Built for it - a double-decker bus could get through there!" Weren't they a nice sensitive bunch? He also threw in casually that I'd had toxaemia. "Hadn't I felt unwell?" said the Doctor, "and how come the antenatal staff hadn't picked it up?" I didn't realise the full implications of this at the time. I was just glad it was over. Or at least I thought it was.

I went back to the ward without my baby, unlike everybody else. Julian was across in another building, and Mitch had to go back to Rayleigh. He hadn't held Julian yet. I remembered sitting in the ward with the other Mums, who were afraid to ask me where my baby was in case something awful had happened. One girl who'd had her baby and for some reason had been living in the ward for six months, (she had a heart condition) was able to roam the hospital and go out with a list of wants to the shop across the road. She seemed to know everything that was going on, and asked me if the beautiful child in the premature baby unit was mine. I said 'yes', and she then told the entire ward that she had seen the most beautiful baby there. I felt a lot happier then.

As I wanted to feed Julian myself, I had to go down two flights of stairs, across the garden and into the prem. baby unit in my nightclothes five times a day. On one occasion Richard was half way up the stairs on his way to see me as I was on my way down. "Where are you going Stella?" I explained, and he was horrified. It wasn't very warm out, and I might catch cold, and should I have been walking up and down stairs all day? Shouldn't I have been resting, like the other mums? After seven days of doing this they weighed Julian and discovered that he weighed quite a bit more than they thought. "We think he was weighed wrongly in the beginning." I was told, "You can have him now." I was incensed that I had missed having him with me for seven days. There was a strange nurse on the ward as well. One day she announced that we should all have our holes sewn up. I was so embarrassed. No one used language like that in those days. I went bright red.

On the ninth day I started to become ill, and I developed a

temperature. I'd only had Julian with me for two days so far. I really hoped it was nothing, as I was due to be discharged the next day. I had my examination by the doctor, and he told me that he was not happy with me, and said it was unlikely I would be going home the next day. You can't imagine my horror at being told that. This was a dreadful place to feel ill in. The specialist, Mrs. B., came to see me, and said that in her opinion as I only had a sore throat she would see the doctor in question and get my release. But no, he wouldn't let me go. He came and sat on my bed later that afternoon and told me that I was to be on his operating table the next morning. I was so scared. Mitch was in Rayleigh and didn't know anything about it. I remembered reading the operation form and it saying D&C. or hysterectomy if necessary. Was I scared or was I scared? There had been some afterbirth left behind, so they had to be quick. The next morning I was prepared for the operation and taken down to theatre. When I came round I was glad I was still alive. Mum came in to check on me, and whilst she was there I started to haemorrhage. I then had two or three pints of blood whilst my poor mother was sent off yet again. (I didn't realise just how worried she had been until it was all over). It appeared I'd had toxaemia whilst pregnant, and it was undetected. This caused a lot of blood clots, and was maybe the reason the afterbirth hadn't come away. (I'm not a medical person but it struck me that if my blood had been just about as good as a person's blood should be, wouldn't giving me iron pills cause the blood to react in some way? After all, my headaches stopped when I no longer took the pills. And my blood pressure returned to normal!) And aren't they supposed as a matter of course, to piece together the afterbirth. And if they'd seen blood clots, there would have been even more reason to do this vital task, and weigh it. This was a serious error.

I was put back into the ward, and was then an object of great medical interest. I had a student nurse come and tell me that they were doing a thesis on me at the nurse's school. "How not to treat someone when they're having a baby," I thought. She proceeded to tell me, (this young nurse actually told me) that if I had been sent home I would have died, because I would have developed gangrene within twenty-four hours and collapsed, and died. Oh dear God I thought, I only came in to have my baby and go home.

No one expects these errors in this day and age. Everyone knows the importance of removing the afterbirth. I developed a fever the next day and was told that I had septicaemia. I was convinced by now that I was a goner. Mentally I was beaten up.

I was put into a side ward with a nurse who was to do everything for me. I was very ill, and filled with all sorts of pills. I had now been in hospital for nearly three weeks. I was aware that I was being peered at through the glass windows of the little side room. I was an object of great curiosity and I expect dread by some of the other mums, lest the same things happen to them. When I eventually recovered and got up, I couldn't wait to see Julian, I felt I'd seen so little of him since his birth. I wasn't surprised to discover that no one had bothered to bathe him since he was born. The first thing I did was fill up the big sink in the nursery, and gently and tenderly I bathed my baby son. He was a beautiful baby, his flaky skin was gone and he had beautiful skin and the lightest of hair. This was my Easter Monday baby and an important date in the Christian calendar. I was cross that they had separated us for a whole week, due to an error in weighing him wrongly, and that I had been too ill to look after him, again because of hospital errors. As soon as we could get out of here I would make it up to him. I would spoil him something rotten. I can still remember the sister trying to be nice to me as I was packing to go. "Why are you bothering to be nice to me now?" I said, "I've craved a kind word from you ever since I arrived. Please don't speak to me again, because I am very choosy who I speak to." If I had not been leaving she would have made my life hell again, but as I was going home she had no more power over me. She went bright red, and I ignored her. She was a very nasty cold young woman. I would have loved some kindness during my stay, but now it was too late. Thank God for the nice Asian doctor who overruled the specialist, and insisted on operating on me. To this man I owe my life. Thank you whoever you are.

I dressed Julian in a lovely outfit that I had seen previously in a shop window in Broadwater, and asked my mother if she would pop in and buy it for me. It was a sweet little white suit with little yellow chicks on it. Everybody on the ward thought he was a beautiful baby, and as I finished dressing him, handing him to a nurse to carry out for me, I said goodbye to the other mums and left, thankful to be alive. My Mum and Dad collected us, and took us home. I felt so abandoned by my husband. Surely work doesn't take preference over us? I think he had only been to visit half a dozen times in three weeks. Still he's sure to want to sue the hospital, I thought. He'll go mad when he knows what they did to us. We actually had a perfect case.

We went back to my parents for the night, and then Mitch came as usual on Friday night for the weekend, and we went back to Hullbridge on the Sunday afternoon, having proudly shown Julian to all the family. I hadn't been home for three and a half months, and was naturally excited at the prospect of seeing my house again, and friends. I'd missed three weeks of my baby's life and I wanted to make up for it, starting as soon as possible. I needed to get into a routine with the feeding, as I was making masses of milk, which was surprising when I'd been so ill. My neighbours back home were pleased to see me. They had heard all about my trauma, and I felt surprisingly quite well. Being home was nothing short of wonderful.

The pram arrived after a couple of days, I thought back to when I'd first seen it in the shop window in Worthing, an old lady was looking longingly in the window of the baby shop at all the lovely things. She came up to me and said, "Make sure you have the babies that you want my dear, because I didn't." I felt she was sad. I always remembered that conversation and I think lots of girls today put having babies on hold for career reasons, and maybe leave it too late in some cases, creating a lot of unhappiness for themselves later in their lives. Anyway back to my lovely pram. It was a navy blue coach-built Royal, and Julian looked so sweet in it. It was a very warm April and I had to use the canopy, as it was so sunny. I made myself a new dress with a remnant I picked up at the market, and feeling like the bee's knees, I used to walk into the village, pushing my lovely pram with my beautiful baby in it. Life seemed lazy and more normal than it had been for some time. I loved being a mum.

Then I started getting an acute pain in my lower region. It was acute and burning, and the only relief was to sit astride the loo. It got so bad that I had to see the doctor. I had little faith in doctors as you can imagine, but this man was nice. He examined me very gently internally and found that I had an enormous abscess, which he burst. I felt the relief immediately and I couldn't thank him enough. He put me on another course of antibiotics. I felt so relieved it was nothing more than that. After that, I got on with my life. I was commended at the baby clinic, for the wonderful state of Julian, by the doctor. I was thrilled. Mitch told me that he wouldn't sue the hospital, it wasn't worth it. "Forget about it," he said. Where had my knight in shining armour gone? He'd ridden off. I felt very let down.

Benjamin came back from the kennels. I had tried to persuade Mitch that we could not afford a dog. Money was very tight, and we could not even afford a cot for Julian. He slept in his carrycot. But it was hopeless. He wouldn't hear of it. He wanted him back. I had to plead with him not to have him in the house. Bearing in mind all I had gone through only weeks before, I was still not one hundred per cent well, and was told that it would be six months before I would be really recovered. So Mitch had a luxurious kennel built for the dog (this money could have bought a cot several times over). The only problem was - Benjamin hated it. It really was a work of art, built by the chap next door who was in the building industry, with proper roof and everything, and carpeted. But Benjamin howled so much, he lost his voice, and the neighbours complained. The man across the back said that his wife just had a baby and she needed her rest. Lucky wife! Would he like two wives?

Then Mitch lost his job through no fault of his own. It appeared that the solicitor, who handed him the bulk of his work, and clients, unexpectedly had to close the office in Rayleigh. Mitch thought it would be quite easy to get another job, but it proved very difficult, in fact impossible. Things were very tight. Ben had to go (every cloud has a silver lining), and actually he went to a very good home, with a couple who owned a garage. They had a six-year-old lad who was able to devote all his spare time to him, a much more suitable life for Ben. He needed to be loved, and go for long walks, etc. All the energy I had I needed for Julian.

Things were very tight money wise, and we thought the best thing we could do, would be to go back to Worthing. So we put the house on the market, and arranged that we would live with my parents until the house sold and we could buy another.

Meanwhile, my gran came to stay with us for a week, and one day she spotted a wet patch on the floor. I pulled up the lino, to discover the concrete floor underneath was saturated. It looked as though the pipes under the floor had burst. Mitch asked me to deal with it, as I had more knowledge of such things. So I spent ages going to and from the call box ringing the builder, who denied any responsibility. "The insurance will cover it," he said. "That's not the point," I said, "the house is not yet a year old." It was a total waste of time ringing him; he couldn't have been less interested. So I rang my Dad, who came up the following day, Saturday. There wasn't much urgency now, as it had obviously been leaking for ages. Dad surveyed the situation. It was serious. The radiators would have to be re-plumbed downstairs, it turned out that the builders hadn't used copper pipes under the floor, and as the house had just gone up for sale, this came as a huge blow and setback. Dad arranged for a builder friend he knew, who'd moved to Essex previously, to carry out the work, paid for by the insurance. We had to evacuate the house, so arranged the removals van.

Whilst Dad went back to Worthing and took gran with him, my mother stayed with me, and helped me pack. Mitch's mother and sister came on removals day to help take some of the many things that weren't going into store. I was choked with emotion. What else was going to happen to us? We loaded our mini, with just enough room for Mum in the back with Julian. Maureen loaded her car up to the roof and off we all went. We hadn't got far down the road when our mini overheated and broke down. The AA were called, and we sat there like zombies waiting for the mechanic to arrive. "It will have to be towed into a garage," said the AA man, "I can't repair it here." And so he towed it away! Maureen with Mitch went back to our house in Hullbridge to unload her car; she had to get all of us into her car now. We waited on the grass verge for her to come back for us. Meanwhile, I burst into tears, I fiddled with my rings, like you do when you're down. It was all too much. Nothing had gone right for such a long time. I think I was mentally and physically exhausted. In the heat of the moment, I said out loud, "When I get the chance I'll sell this ring and have a really good night out." My mother-in-law was on me in a second. "You would marry him wouldn't you, you couldn't wait, taking my son away from me...." I sobbed. My mother just put her arm around my shoulder, turning her back on Mitch's mother, and said, "Come along, let's wait over there."

We eventually got home. I was in trouble with Mitch for upsetting his mother. My Mother tried to tell him that it was not entirely my fault. His mother could have tried to understand just a little of how I was feeling. I was ragged. I thought to myself about the last few months. I'd had a baby, then been seriously ill. I'd had to put up with the dog; Mitch losing his job which was not his fault, had meant that we'd had to give up our home, even the job of dealing with the burst pipes had fallen into my lap, but he wouldn't have it. I was never to speak to his mother like that again. I ran out of the house, I didn't want to be with him any more. I ran and ran till I could run no more. Eventually he found me wandering round one of the Avenues and I had to go back. I didn't want to be separated from Julian for any length of time, and I would have gone back home sooner or later anyway. Thank goodness for my Mum and Dad, I don't know what I would have done without them. I was very unhappy with Mitch, very unhappy.

Chapter 4 - Revelation

Mitch went for several interviews for jobs, unfortunately none of
which came to anything, and he was getting very despondent.
Then looking at a newspaper one day, which covered a different
area, I spotted an advertisement for a recruitment agency in
Burgess Hill, and I suggested he rang them. Mitch rang up, and
made an appointment to see someone at the agency to discuss his
requirements, and lo and behold he ended up with an interview
with British United Airways, at Gatwick Airport, in the accounts
department. To his immense relief and pleasure he got the job.
The money was good and we both hoped that now things would
start to look up for us.

We were still living with my parents in Worthing, whilst waiting
for a sale on our house in Essex. We simply couldn't afford to
buy another house until the Essex house sold. Mitch had to
commute every day to the airport, which was about thirty-five
miles away. He didn't mind that at all, in fact he soon discovered
a colleague in the office who lived nearby, with whom he could
share the driving and the petrol expenses. Our house in
Hullbridge, (because of the plumbing problems, and the recession)
took nearly a year to sell. Boom and bust has been a problem for
the country for decades, not just the eighties.

I think my poor parents must have thought we'd be living with
them forever. Eventually, though, completion took place and we
received practically nothing back from the proceeds of sale, just a
couple of hundred pounds. Mitch was all for renting this time. He

didn't want to chance buying again. But I, meanwhile, had been sussing out a derelict Victorian house in the same road as my parents. I had already been to the agents, asked the price, got the keys and looked at it, before I'd even mentioned it to him. He wasn't overly keen. It wasn't at all what he had imagined we'd buy, as it was in a disgusting state, but I assured him it would be very nice when it was done up. An old lady had lived there and hadn't been able to do anything to it for years; even the garden was very overgrown. It needed everything doing, and I fell in love with that house there and then. It actually wasn't fit for habitation, it needed rewiring, re-plumbing, a complete new kitchen and bathroom, timber treatment and complete redecoration inside and out. As I'd said, when I'd first mentioned the house to Mitch he was none too keen, but gradually got more and more interested when my father said he would be able to organise the work for us. Being in the building industry it was easy for him to get the right tradesmen. Dad actually did a lot of the work himself, saving us a lot of money. Because of its condition, and the fact that it was an executor's sale we bought the house for three thousand pounds, which was very cheap.

Mum and I set about clearing out the piles of rubbish, which were left by the vendors, including a motorbike! At that time there were allotments at the back of these houses, and we spent days wheeling the wheelbarrow loaded to the top with rubbish round to the allotment and burning it. Julian used to ride back in the empty barrow and we did this all day for days. We were as black as the ace of spades most days. We found some old love letters in the attic, and we sat and read them. I was engrossed in a bygone era, of romance and gentility. It seemed sad that this old lady, who had obviously come from a very good family, should live to the end of her life in such grim circumstances.

Gradually the house started to take shape. I went to demolition sites and got a fireplace from one house, and a sink unit from another. We rescued an old Rayburn from Mitch's sister Maureen and cleaned it up. Boy! Did that throw out some heat? My father disappeared through the floor in the sitting room one day and I shrieked with laughter. It wasn't funny really, but it did look funny to me. Fortunately he wasn't hurt. That was my first introduction to dry rot.

When the house got up to the wallpaper stage, we decided (as we'd been with Mum and Dad so long) that if we could just get the sitting room and Julian's room papered we would move in. So we did just that and hooray, our own home again! My parents must have been so pleased to get rid of us, and get their house back to themselves again. The thrill of ringing the storage people and arranging to get our furniture back was in itself wonderful. We hadn't seen our furniture for eighteen months, and it was just like Christmas watching the lorry unload our bits and pieces. I was so happy, I loved our house. It was a friendly house. My father had been making a rocking horse for Julian in his spare time (spare time I ask you!), and this was delivered at the same time. Mitch was climbing the ladder of success at work, he always seemed to be getting promotion, and the more promotion he got, the more travelling it entailed. He was travelling the world. Places like South America, the Far East, Africa and America.

We started a completely new chapter in our lives, and one, which I hoped, would make us both happy. My father taught me how to decorate, do wall tiling and floor tiling, and I was in my element. I spent a lot of time on my own, as Mitch was either abroad or working very long hours, so this gave me a purpose and something to do whilst Julian was at nursery school. I experimented with a lot of other home crafts like painting furniture, dried flower arranging, re-covering chairs, and making curtains. I remember Mum telling me that I was obsessed with that house, as I was always doing something to it. It wasn't normal, she said, to be so obsessed with a house. It wasn't that. I needed something to do. I was incredibly lonely. The loneliness was unbearable at times. Sometimes Mitch was away for weeks on end, and although Julian was old for his age and extremely good company, he was only three. So he would be in bed by eight o'clock and I would sit every evening watching television by myself, so I needed the stimuli of anything I could get my teeth into. Once a week Helen would come and see me. She didn't live far away, and I always enjoyed her visits, but she had been seeing someone for some time and they were going to get married. I was pleased for her, but I knew I wouldn't be able to see her as much. Weekends were the most lonely, my friends had their husbands home and so were otherwise engaged. Sometimes my parents would take Julian and me out in the car with them, if they were going into the country. I did spend an extraordinary amount of time alone though. It felt very weird. I was only twenty-four years old.

Mitch seemed to get promotion every six months, but with promotion went more and more business trips, and often he would be away for up to three weeks at a time. One of the perks of Mitch working for an airline was the cheap travelling for the families of staff. We got the chance to go to Canada to see Mitch's eldest sister Patsy, and her husband Peter and their two girls, who I had met only once before whilst they were over in England visiting their respective families. Their visit had coincided very nicely with Julian's christening, so Peter was one of the godfathers. I looked forward to meeting them all again.

Canada was the trip of a lifetime. In the early seventies very few people went across the Atlantic for their holidays. It wasn't like today with all the cheap package deals on offer. We went on what was considered at the time to be one of the best aircraft ever built, the V.C.10, and because of Mitch's position in the company, I was invited up on to the flight deck to meet the crew. What an experience, talking to the pilot and the navigator. I remember looking down over Newfoundland and wondering at the beauty of it, and following the St. Lawrence River. It was a very clear day and I could see so much more from the flight deck. I will never forget that holiday; Canada had such an effect on me. It was like going through a time warp into the next century. When I came home it was as if England was a third world country, a deprived backwater. We were decades apart, and that was the early seventies! There were so many differences, the attitudes of the people; women worked out there as a matter of course. It was an emancipated country. Over here in the sixties and seventies only two types of women worked, the educated professional and the poor. Over there, it seemed everybody worked. Also the attitude towards other races was brilliant. In the average road there were several different nationalities, all getting on, unlike England where it was common to hear the expression whispered 'They're foreign!' The Canadian houses were built for the weather, with very good insulation, and central heating. The windows had fly screens over them, as well as the houses having an inner and outer door. They all had basements, housing all their essential equipment for busy working people. They all had as a matter of course automatic washing machines and dryers. Some had rotary ironers. All had deep freezes. A lot of the houses had children's sitting rooms, with their own TV, and three piece suites. Can you imagine that? One of the houses we visited had a beauty room, (posh downstairs bathroom) with loads of Formica surfaces and mirrors. (You couldn't say toilet as that was considered to be a rude word; you had to say bathroom!) That particular beauty room was fitted out better than most kitchens back home. It was like Hollywood to me.

The kitchens were all wood. Patsy's was made of Cherry wood. I had never seen a kitchen like this before, so many cupboards, and I was overawed at it all. They also had colour T.V. long before we did over here. It changed my attitude to England. We'd always felt that we were the nation that ruled the waves and were therefore superior, but the beauty of travel is that it educates you! There were so many differences, too many to list, and it changed me forever. I have always loved technology, so it was a dream for me to see it first hand. Coming back home to England was a bit of a shock. The average house then did not have central heating, and a lot of the older houses didn't have bathrooms, some didn't even have inside toilets. We've never as a country quite got away from the system of Lord of the manor and the surfs. The haves and the have nots, and as I'm writing this, I'm aware that too many people in this country still do live very meagre lives. How many people in the twenty-first century in this country have dishwashers and bidets?

Helen got married to Mike the week after we came back from Canada. He worked as a stable lad for the Duke of Norfolk, so they moved to Arundel. I didn't see much of her after that.

I continued to do the house up, and it was shaping up well. It was, after all, my first attempt at interior design. I also planted the gardens back and front, planting as much as I could into a relatively small space. Small gardens can be very colourful, and ours was really pretty. My daytime social life had looked up considerably since Julian started nursery school, and I had also passed my driving test. This gave me a new freedom, I had our original mini and Mitch had treated himself to an almost new Rover. This meant that I could now visit Eileen, who now had two children, she and Barry had a son Mark, a little brother for Rachael. They had moved house and were living near Littlehampton, quite near my mother-in-law, so I could visit both on my trips over there. Sometimes Julian and I would go to London on the coach to stay with Liz and Sarah, if David was away on business. David was now working for a chocolate company, (oh, what Heaven) and he was allowed to bring some of it home. I've always been a chocoholic, so that was good news. I was able to look after Sarah whilst Liz was at the office, and then when Liz was able to come home early, we would go to Richmond Park, Bushy park or Hampstead Heath, and of course the shops. The shops were glorious. Sometimes we would go into Richmond and have a wander round. I had always been used to good shops in Worthing, but these were something else. They were more like London shops.

Liz and David's house was right under the flight path for Heathrow, and when Concorde was due to go over, Julian and I would run outside into the garden to see this magnificent aeroplane in the distance coming towards us. What a fantastic engineering feat that was and still is. It reminds me of a swan, a huge metal swan, quite beautiful. I would usually only stay with Liz for a week until David came home at the weekend. It was a break for both of us, and a chance to catch up on the gossip. I liked to go away but I also liked to go back home, although it could be that after a week at Liz's, I still had two weeks on my own

We then went through a very bad patch in our marriage. I wasn't sure what was going on with Mitch; he used to say some dreadful things to me. One evening, totally out of the blue, he told me to have sex with other men, so that I could find more interesting ways of making love. I was so shocked; I certainly would do no such thing I replied. He was like a different person, so cold and so hard. He would go to bed and leave me in a very confused state, and very, very miserable. I would sit on the stairs long after he had gone to bed and cry for hours. Why would he want to say those things to me? I told other members of the family but they refused to believe me. My sister-in-law actually told me I was wicked to make up lies about her husband's brother. I couldn't win. Things got very bad, and sometimes when he returned from business trips abroad, I would make a point of being out. I was often at Eileen's talking to her mother-in-law about just this very subject. I found her good to talk to. I became very nervous of Mitch. Our sex life was very sporadic, and he often slept in the spare room. I was very naïve in those days, people didn't talk like they do nowadays, so you just got on with your life as best you could. It wasn't until years later when I was married again, and in a very loving relationship, that I realised what normality was. I confided in my sister Liz at the time, and she commented on how unnatural it was, not to have a proper sex life. I felt such a failure. I felt it must all have been my fault, I thought if we had another baby he would be bound to love me, but at this rate that seemed a long way off.

As I mentioned previously Mitch used to travel up and down from Gatwick Airport with a colleague, to help share the travelling expenses. Mitch would travel to this chap's house in the morning to pick him up, and drop him off again at his house in the evening. But this chap never came to our house to pick Mitch up. Instead Mitch arranged a pick up point about half a mile away. And he used to walk in all weathers to this particular spot. One evening, whilst Mitch was away in South America, there was a ring on the doorbell. It turned out to be the chap Mitch travelled up and down to the airport with. He had a letter from Mitch that had come through the internal staff mail. Anyway he had decided that instead of posting it on to me, he would deliver it in person. He had thought it odd that whereas Mitch picked him up at his home, he in turn was not invited to see where we lived. He was in fact dying of curiosity. Did we live in a tumbledown shack? He actually told me that he was longing to see where we lived. I laughed and invited him in to see, and he was amazed. Whereas he lived in a modern box, 'Wimpy special' he called it, through lounge-diner, with kitchen, we had three reception rooms and kitchen, lovely staircase, and ceiling mouldings, all immaculate.

He thought it was lovely, and he just couldn't understand why he had never been given the opportunity to see it before. I never knew why Mitch didn't like the house. It was as if he was ashamed of it or me.... Although, he did show a colleague in the office a photo of me one day. I was holding Julian in my arms, and I remember him telling me this story with some unease because the colleague had mischievously asked Mitch to inform him of when he was next away, saying 'She's rather gorgeous'. Was that why he never invited anyone home? I didn't think it was that because...

We were invited to a party by a couple, who worked for the airline and I was eager to meet some of the people he worked with. I bought a pair of black velvet trousers and a cream top, and I'd been to the hairdressers. When we got there, I was duly told not to stay by his side in my usual suffocating way and with that he disappeared. Bearing in mind that I didn't know anybody there I was a bit daunted, and nervous. I managed to get through the evening somehow. The hostess asked me what I did for a living, and I replied that I looked after our son and I cooked and cleaned. She said, "Oh how awful, how boring." I replied that it wasn't at all boring. I thought she was very rude. I hated that Jack Jones record that went something like this 'Day after day there are girls at the office and men will always be men... don't think because there's a ring on your finger...I'm warning you.' I absolutely hated that record, telling us wives to watch out, husbands potentially always on the look out. I digress.

Life revolved around Julian. In the morning he would go to nursery school, and then I'd spend every afternoon amusing him. We had everything in Worthing. The beach, the downs, lovely parks, and friends to do things with. Julian was a tall child for three years old, and rode a two wheeler bicycle easily. He was also very attractive, with pale blue eyes and thick blonde curly hair. He was a bit of a card already at age three, always laughing. During the summer months I would walk and Julian would ride his bicycle up to where his father was still being dropped off, and the three of us would walk back home together. I tried so hard to make things right between us, but I found it very difficult. I was convinced now that he only married me to enable him to leave home, and also because he wanted a father. Also since starting this job he had changed a lot. I felt that I was somehow in the way, but what of? I realised that he was meeting very interesting people now from all around the world, and I think that in retrospect he would have loved to have been a bachelor again. He wasn't loving towards me, and sex was rare. I've often wondered why we didn't split up then, except in those days it was very unusual to get divorced.

Julian was very accident prone as a child. If he wasn't falling down the stairs, he would be walking into lampposts or parking meters. I spent a considerable amount of time in the casualty department at the hospital. Whilst living with my parents he had suffered severe burns to his hand. I am such a careful person, I'm the type who checks the gas is off at least ten times, uses stair gates, child alarm systems etc. I had been ironing and put the iron on the floor in the pantry, where it would cool very quickly. My mother, unaware of the iron, decided to cook, and had the pantry door wide open. Julian was so quick as children are and touched the hot iron, and as a result suffered dreadful burns to his left hand. I was distraught in casualty, feeling as mothers do that it was entirely my fault, and the nurse rightly told me not to show such distress in front of my child. He didn't stop screaming for over three hours, and by this time I was worried about his anxiety level, so back at home I gave him a whole disprin which put him to sleep forthwith. When he woke up, although the hand was still sore he seemed to cope with it.

On another occasion he went to play with a neighbour's child in her garden, only to be brought back a little later covered in blood. I thought he had been knocked over by a car. I was stunned. The neighbour just left him with me and went. I gather he had fallen off a wall onto a piece of sheet metal, which sliced through his head. What was a piece of sheet metal doing propped up against the wall in a garden where children play? I needed to get him to hospital as soon as possible. I couldn't drive and hold Julian, so I rang my friend Margaret, who I'd met through nursery school, her little girl and Julian were best friends. Fortunately she was in, and rushed round and took us to the hospital. Afterwards my father insisted that Julian needed glasses. "He must do," he said, "he's always falling over or walking into something." I made an appointment with the optician straightaway, and Dad was right, Julian did need glasses. He had had the usual eye tests that the health service provided for pre-school children, and his short sight was very good, and because he was so good at reading and writing, and he could do puzzles and Lego I just assumed that he could see. What they didn't do tests for was distance, and so that was why Julian was always walking into things and falling over. Dad always referred to Julian as Sam. He was very fond of his Sam.

The following Christmas, whilst we were staying with Liz and David, I realised I could have been pregnant. Was this the glimmer of hope for our relationship that I had been waiting for? I had virtually given up hope, and I'd decided to foster children for a while. I'd been thoroughly scrutinised by social services, and accepted. I suppose this resulted in me relaxing, and subsequently getting pregnant. The tests were confirmed by Dr. Campbell over the telephone and we were both over the moon with joy, a new life. The baby was due the following September 1972.

We had often talked about moving house, and now Mitch, who was so happy about the prospect of another child, decided that we could well afford it. Our relationship improved and that was all I wanted. A new baby on the way gave us the push we needed to get on with things. We put the house on the market in the spring. The agent came round, he took down all the particulars, put it on the market the next morning, and by the evening we had a purchaser. We made a profit of two hundred and thirty per cent. The house was beautiful, and I thought how different to our last effort at selling the house in Essex. In fact if this purchaser couldn't proceed there was another waiting in the wings, this was a girl I'd known for years. She saw the 'For Sale' sign and knocked on the door one day and was disappointed that it was under offer. She asked if she could have a look anyway, and she loved it. I would have preferred her to have it.

After a nice family afternoon out, and my managing to pick some catkins, which were a bit high up, I noticed some blood when I went to the loo later that day. Mitch called the doctor, who examined me and tried to reassure me that possibly everything was OK, but that I would have to stay in bed for a few days, and then take it easy for a while. I wasn't to do anything at all for the time being. I wished things like catkins didn't excite me so much. If I so much as saw them or any wild flowers, it was as if I'd found gold. I lay about for a few weeks and then was so fed up, I decided that if I was going to miscarry, it was a chance I would have to take. I couldn't lay about forever. I had Julian to think about. So I got back to normal, and went about my business, being very careful with my fingers crossed that all would be OK. Sitting in the lounge one morning having my early cup of tea, what should walk past me but a rat, A RAT....! Bearing in mind I must not get excited, I got very excited, and ran out of the room, making sure to shut the door behind me. I was not even dressed, so hurriedly pulled on my clothes and went down to my Mum's. Mitch was away in the States so he missed all the excitement. When he came back the following weekend lots of floorboards were up and Dad was still trying to find out how the rat had got into and out of the house.

There was a shortage of houses at this time and property was selling very quickly. The house we were hoping to buy was in the process of being built on an estate along the Arundel Road. When this particular phase was ready for release we were told that we would have to queue all night for it, in order to get the one we wanted. I actually wanted a house in Findon Valley, but we had a very 'democratic' marriage and I was told it was the house along the Arundel Road or nothing. Put like that, it would do nicely thank you. The one I wanted needed renovating, and I was game to do another, but he wasn't. We were so different. I looked at a derelict house and saw money, and he looked at it as an embarrassment. He thought people would think we couldn't afford a nice house. So he queued all night with his sister-in-law, and bought the new house. There was an article in the paper about people who queued all night for homes. It wasn't a particularly warm night so they lit a campfire. It all looked very cosy. I wished I could have gone, but being pregnant and having Julian to look after it wasn't possible. When I first looked at the house I was sick in the garden, (which was another omen) and I became ill when my second son was about a year old, and I was ill for the next four years. I hated that house.

We moved into The Close in early summer. It was quite an attractive house for a new one, and spacious. We bought all new furniture, G-plan, and it looked just like a Perrings showroom. The carpets were a thick, shaggy pile, the curtains were all new, and we treated ourselves to a twenty-six inch colour TV with doors. I prepared a nursery for the forthcoming little one, and a proper boy's room for Julian. Landscape gardeners did all the outside back and front with patios etc. and it all looked great.

Suddenly, for no apparent reason, we noticed cracks appearing in the walls. Bit by bit the plaster in every room started to fall off the walls, until eventually we would be laying in bed listening to large sheets falling onto the floor. We even moved our bed into the middle of the bedroom so it wouldn't fall on our heads. It was a living nightmare, a total mess. Bearing in mind I was pregnant and supposed to take it fairly easy, and also that the house was full of new furniture and carpets, this was a nightmare. Where had I moved to? It was my job again to sort it out with the builders. I suppose it was easier for me as my father was one, and I knew more about it all anyway. So off I went large stomach in front of me, to sort out the foreman. I walked down to the site office to find him. He was only a young guy, and he was very arrogant and totally unsympathetic. The whole house would have to be re-rendered and then re-plastered. There had been something wrong with the breezeblocks, and a lot of the houses on the estate were affected, but most not as badly as ours. I asked if we would be able to move out into a hotel and our furniture put into store whilst it was being done, with all expenses paid for the inconvenience caused. He said 'no', or words to that effect! In fact he was so rude I retaliated, and told him in no uncertain terms what I thought of him. I swore at him, and he was quite surprised, I told him he was a bully, and should be ashamed of himself, then left.

Have you ever lived in a house whilst it is being re-rendered and re-plastered? Not just one or two rooms - the whole house! We rolled back the carpets, and covered up all the furniture, took down all the curtains and camped! In moved the plasterers for three weeks and proceeded to knock off all the remaining plaster, and then all the rendering, back to the offending breezeblocks. The mess was unspeakable, but my blood pressure remained normal and I took it all in my stride, made hundreds of cups of tea for the workmen and we got through it. They were very nice guys. It wasn't their fault after all, was it? They were very sympathetic to me and my condition.

The foreman wouldn't even let me choose any different colours for the paint. Can you believe it? It is the same amount of paint whether its magnolia or green. I thought that as some sort of compensation he might say 'choose any colour you like' but no. "It's magnolia you had so it's magnolia you're having." He got the sack later on. I can't think why!?! He must have upset someone important! I've never been so pleased to see someone sacked. "As ye sow, so shall ye reap".

We got the house back to normal and you would not have known that anything had happened, it looked beautiful again. During the latter part of my pregnancy, Mitch didn't go on any business trips. He looked after me very well, treating me like Dresden china, I lapped it up and I thought that maybe things between us would be much better. Maybe having this baby would alter things. We spent a lot of time getting the house just right and treating ourselves to a lot of records for our collection. Whenever I hear the Carpenters I think of that time. I made a lot of friends whilst living there. Maureen was one; she was a teacher and a really nice soul. She helped me a lot through some very difficult times. I tried years later to contact her, when I knew that I was going to write this book. I spoke to her husband Paul only to learn that sadly she'd died. She couldn't have been more than forty-two years of age. If anyone got her wings Maureen did.

Then there was Sandra, who was married to Victor. They lived next door but one. They desperately wanted a child and Sandra had unfortunately had several miscarriages, and was understandably nervous of trying again. It must have been difficult for her with me being pregnant, but she was a brick, and helped me a lot. My next door neighbour Min (I only had one as we were on the end of the row) seemed quite nice when I first got to know her, but after a short while things became tense because she could not control her sons, they would run all over our garden. Not only that, they would ring our doorbell and run away, and throw stones at the cars on the drive. If I mentioned it to Min she just laughed. She spoke with rather an affected voice; I never did know why she felt so posh. I thought they were a scruffy bunch. It soon became apparent that she had no control over her own children at all. One word from her and they did just as they liked. I used to like to have a rest in the afternoon but as soon as I went to sleep, her boys would ring my doorbell. It was most annoying. Then there was Catherine; she lived across the road with Reg and their two little girls. The girls went to the same primary school as Julian, we would often walk back together on a nice warm afternoon. Min's eldest boy Mark would pinch and punch the youngest little girl who was a poppet. One day I caught him in the act and I promptly pinched him hard back. "I'll tell my Mummy about you," he sobbed. "You do that. You are a horrible little boy," I replied. She never bothered to come after me. I expect she realised that he deserved it.

I received a phone call from the school one day. Julian had fallen over in the playground and would I collect him. He was sitting in the secretary's office and I could tell by the way he was sitting that something was really wrong. I undid his shirt and there was a protruding bone in the neck area, "How did he do this?" I said. "He's broken his collar bone." The secretary looked at me amazed. "Didn't you think of examining him? Supposing I had been out?" I remarked. "Would you have just let him sit there for the rest of the day?" He looked so forlorn, my sweet little lad. He was just quietly sitting there. I took hold of his hand and off we went to the hospital. Poor Julian in the wars again.

Chapter 5 - Sickness

I had actually managed this time to get a bed at the Zachary
Merton Maternity hospital, and after my last experience of that
hospital, I wasn't at all sure why I was going there again. Perhaps
the rude specialist had left! I had booked well in advance - Good
girl! This baby seemed in no hurry to be born. I was two weeks
overdue, and it had been a very long hot summer. I had had
enough of being so large and hot, so on my now weekly visit to
the antenatal clinic, I was determined to be admitted. I took my
case filled with everything that I needed, and all the other items on
the list given to me in the antenatal clinic to bring in. It was the
seventh of September, Mitch's birthday, and he had naturally
hoped that the baby would arrive on his birthday. They admitted
me, because I exaggerated and said I wasn't feeling well. Well,
what are you supposed to do? I thought they might have sent me
home again, as I said I wanted to get on with it.

I was put into a nice comfortable bed in a room with other ladies-
in-waiting. I had hardly been there an hour when labour started.
First, a little twinge, and then another. So I had to leave all the
other ladies, whom I was just getting to know, and was whisked
off to the labour ward. I had had Julian very quickly and therefore
thought that this would be the same, because the pains were
coming every couple of minutes. But the baby hung on and hung
on. Afternoon turned into evening, evening turned into night, and

night into morning. I'd had so much gas and air at one point that I was totally 'out of it'. The baby wanted his or her own birthday it appeared. The midwives changed duty, which was a shame. I had built up trust and confidence with the midwife, she had been so nice. She was replaced by a very brusque, young midwife who was not so kindly. I do think it would be better if midwives were also mothers, and have some insight into what they are dealing with. I was going strong with pains every minute and Mitch never left my side this time, asking questions if he felt something wasn't right. We both didn't want a repetition of the mistakes of last time.

Seventeen hours later we were informed that the baby had been the wrong way round, and they had been waiting for it to turn round on its own, and it now had. Thank the Lord. I had so many injections, and gas and air, that I no longer cared what they did. You definitely get to a point where you don't give a monkeys any more, just relieve the pain, that's all you ask. The next minute I was being taken into the delivery room and the sister was counting and then telling me to push. Having had one baby, I knew this wasn't right. You get a normal feeling of wanting to push, and it's a pleasant feeling like going to the loo. I had none of that. She would count and I had to push. Within ten minutes our second son was born, and he was given straight to his father to hold and then put gently into my arms. He had the most lovely black hair and dark blue eyes. He was gorgeous. We were thrilled to have another son, and we'd already decided that if it was a boy he would be called Jeremy.

I still don't know to this day, and Mitch told me that he definitely didn't give permission, but I wondered if they had given me an epidural. There is no other explanation. I had no contractions or desire to push. Even if they thought I'd had too much pain, they still should have got permission to do that, if that's what they did.

After my previous history they made sure the afterbirth was all removed. It was. Phew what a relief. As there was not a doctor to sew me up, (I needed a few stitches), they said I would have to wait until one came on duty. Meanwhile, I was put into a side ward with two other girls. As I was only in for two days, they put me in the Caesarean Ward, where two women were waiting to have their operations. I waited ages to be sewn up, by which time some of the rear end numbness had worn off, and I found it a very painful experience indeed. I would have loved for there to have been just a little dignity with childbirth. I realise, of course, that you can't give birth with your drawers on, but it often crossed my mind after the birth of both my sons, that one was treated like a piece of meat. I remembered saying to my husband afterwards that with all the different doctors that had given me internal examinations, I couldn't for the life of me think why I hadn't had sex with loads of men before I got married. I felt dirty, as if I'd been violated. Both the experiences could have been so different. One could have been allowed a little modesty, surely to God. If men had babies, it would all be changed in an instant.

The girls I shared a room with were very interested in the 'goings on' of the resident doctor (no wonder he didn't have time to see to my stitches). When night came, the girls would put the lights out in our room, and watch the Doctor's flat, which was over one of the wards. They thought he'd had affairs with most of the nurses in the hospital. They could see quite clearly whom he had got up there. They had been in hospital long enough to know what was going on. What did my old gran used to say? 'If a man works with animals it makes him randy, well what did working with women's bodies do'? I think we knew the answer to that! That was why they watched his flat every night. Well you have to have something to do to pass the time when you're in hospital for such a long time! (I was referring to the girls but I could equally be referring to the doctors). I have a saying that is based on the wartime goings on of the American troops. (Over sexed, over paid and over here.) With doctors, is it over sexed, over paid and in the N.H.S?

I was fortunately only in hospital for a couple of days. On the last day, one of the girls looked out of the window and said, "Oh there's a gorgeous little boy walking up the drive, with blonde hair." I knew it was Julian. He was an attractive little boy. But it's always nice to hear someone else say so. I replied that he was my son. She went on to say, "What a lovely car! Is that yours as well?" one of the girls gasped. I felt quite guilty saying 'yes' as if

I'd almost got more than my fair share of things. Mitch had a dark green Rover with cream leather upholstery, which was unusual at his age. They were obviously impressed.

When I was getting ready to leave the hospital, I experienced a really strange feeling. I was dressing Jeremy, getting him ready to take him home. The feeling came over me like a tidal wave; it was a panicky feeling, a feeling of great responsibility for this child. It was so strange; I hadn't experienced anything like that with Julian. It must have been an omen! I took it on board as obviously I had experienced it for a good reason. Only time would tell. Meanwhile, it was our Wedding Anniversary and I couldn't wait to get discharged and get home.

When we got home, Mitch told me that he hadn't been able to get any flowers. It was Sunday and the florist was shut, he said. He purposely hadn't given me any in hospital because he had said I would have had to leave them behind, and it would be better to have them at home. I was a bit disappointed, but I had them the next day. Flowers didn't play a very big part in his life unfortunately. I think things like that are so important to a woman, especially when she's had a baby and it's her Wedding Anniversary.

I went to bed, as instructed by the midwife, and was pleased to be home. Sandra came to see me soon after I got home, and was longing to see the baby. My mother-in-law had been volunteered to look after me by her son. She was so disappointed that it was another boy, and all she did was wander round muttering that she had wanted a girl. She had got four grandsons already in England, and Jeremy made five, and her only granddaughters were in Canada. It took some of the gloss off for me. After all, we were thrilled to have another son. She told all my visitors when they arrived, and when they left, how very disappointed she was, and how I'd let her down. I was so glad when she left after a week to go home.

I had intended to feed Jeremy myself as I had done with Julian, but my nipples got sorer and sorer until one of them bled. Jeremy had half bitten my nipple off. The Doctor said he had never seen anything like it in all his years of practising. And I would have to have my milk dried up. Jeremy's teeth were nearly through, and as a result, I had to put him on a bottle. This made me feel very guilty, as if I had done it to myself. I knew breast milk gave baby the best start in life. He hated the bottle, and he used to head butt me, and get very cross with me. You can't explain to a baby, can you?

It then appeared that the "sex mad doctor" had sewn me up internally with non-dissolving stitches. When my GP found out, he was livid, and he complained to the hospital. It was a cruel and nasty thing to do to me. I had to be held down when two midwives removed them. I cannot describe the pain. When I went for my postnatal examination a few weeks later at my local clinic, I told the doctor on duty. He said it was a lot of fuss about nothing. "If that was so," I said, 'my own GP wouldn't have complained to the hospital." I'd have loved to have ordered this doctor's scrotum be sewn up in the same way! Why, oh why, do doctors think that women have no feeling below the waist? He also remarked that I was still a bit overweight, and my husband would not find me very attractive. What on earth gave him the right to feel that he could say that to me? He was damned rùde, I thought. It was only six weeks since I'd given birth. I asked if he thought he was attractive, if so why? I did at least have a reason for being overweight, what was his excuse? Do men become gynaecologists because they hate their mothers or are they born sadists? I'll be glad when we women have more choice about whether we want to see a man or woman doctor. As I'm writing this book, the women outweigh the men at medical school, wonderful!

When Jeremy was ten days old I went to Holland for the day. Mitch had to go to a meeting of ABTA in The Hague, and asked if I would like to go too, and take Julian. We left on the early 5.30am Bus Stop Jet flight, leaving Jeremy with mother-in-law. Whilst Mitch was at the meeting, Julian and I had a private tour of the city, ending up at the Madurodam model village. It was an interesting day out, but I was very tired having not long given birth, so I was pleased when it was time for us to go back to meet Mitch from the meeting. Julian expressed an interest in the

Mercedes badge from the coach, so the driver gave it to him.
Julian was delighted and clutched it feverishly. Cars were to play
a very important role in his life later on.

After the meeting had finished, the delegates went into the dining
room to have dinner, and we were invited to join them. During the
meal, one of the delegates asked me politely if I had any other
children. I told him about Jeremy, and that he was ten days old.
He looked horrified. Ten days old. What was I doing wandering
around The Hague? Mind you I wondered what I was doing on a
day trip to Holland as well. I was very tired and my right leg was
really painful. On returning home at midnight, we found a very
frustrated mother-in-law. Jeremy hadn't slept since I left the
house at 5.00am and it was now midnight. He hadn't closed his
eyes at all. Ten days old, I ask you. I picked him up and cuddled
him and he went straight to sleep. He never liked to be away from
me. You wouldn't think it possible for a ten-day-old baby to stay
awake for nineteen hours.

When Jeremy was just a few weeks old, I went to get him from the
cot, to discover him lying in some blood. I rushed to the phone,
and the doctor was with me within a very short time. He thought I
was exaggerating, but when he saw the sheet he was immediately
on the phone to the specialist. The specialist came to the house
very quickly, and there was talk of an exploratory operation. I was
beside myself. Why couldn't something go right for us? My
doctor was excellent and tried to assure me that he felt everything
would be all right. In the end, after a lot of talking and examining
of Jeremy, the specialist decided that his teeth were nearly
through, and he had been laying in the crib gnashing his gums. I
suppose we should have thought of this with my mutilated nipple.
So everything was all right thank goodness.

Life continued much the same, with Mitch away more than at
home. I was used to it, and made the boys my life. It was a bit
like being married to someone in the services. When he returned,
I was always showered with gifts. What I craved was affection
and what I got was gifts.

My father, meanwhile, was working at a Convent in

Littlehampton, building an operating theatre and extra bedrooms for the nuns. The nuns adored him and he would joke with them. He had the greatest respect for them. I used to go over there to see him, and he would show me very proudly the work he was doing. As it was for the Roman Catholic Church, money was no object, and the specification was of the ultimate. It's always nice for builders to work with good quality materials. None of that dreadful penny pinching for the church. Dad took me on a guided tour of the work in progress, and I saw things that an outsider would never normally see. I felt very honoured to be in such a hallowed place. The Nuns' rooms were very modest as you would expect, and small, and quite dark. I had quite a yearning as a young woman to be a nun, but I later realised that God wanted me to do other work.

During this time my father would ring me every day for a chat, and sometimes because he was working nearby, he would come and have lunch with me. We were very close. He and Mum had a holiday with Liz and David in Wales. When it was over, Liz rang me and said that Dad had not been very happy on holiday. He hadn't wanted to do anything much, but just wanted to sit all the time. I thought it was a shame that he hadn't enjoyed it, but none of us realised that Dad was actually ill. We didn't realise that until a bit later on. During this period of my life, I saw a lot of my father, we would discuss so many things, and it was such a comfort to me later on in my life when things became difficult for me. I would remember the conversations and moments that we had shared, and it was something that I would look back on with such warmth.

Jeremy didn't like sleeping at all. I think he thought it was a total waste of time, and on one of my trips to see Dr. Campbell, I mentioned it almost in passing. I had actually gone to see the doctor because the pain in my leg wouldn't go away. He thought I was suffering from post-natal depression as well as a touch of sciatica. He put me on a course of anti-depressants. He thought me unnaturally obsessed with Jeremy. Well, after what had happened with the blood on the sheets, I suppose I was over cautious, who wouldn't be? I didn't think I was obsessed, I adored my sons, which I thought was normal, and I loved my home. I was always doing or making things for it. The point was

I had no other life. The children and the house were my life. I
had no sex life, no romance, I never went out, other than with the
children. I was extremely tired. If Jeremy woke up in the night, I
was always the one who got up to see to him. Mitch never
changed a nappy nor did a night feed. He used to say he needed
his sleep because he had to go to work. I gathered I didn't need
much sleep. And that's what I got, very little sleep. Oh, I had
presents, and I lived in a lovely house with everything except the
one thing I needed, affection. Someone to hold hands with and
share moments together. Boy, was I lonely. I only took the anti-
depressants for a short time because they made me very woozy,
and I had to be able to drive the car, and do anything else that was
necessary for running a house with two children, as I was nearly
always by myself. The doctor said it was a shame I couldn't
continue the course because he knew I needed them. I didn't
realise the anxiety that was building up in me, whereas Dr.
Campbell could see which way I was heading. He remarked about
the house being too immaculate, everything always in its place. I
thought it was because I was house proud, but there is a point at
which obsession creeps in. Things creep up on you so gradually
sometimes, and you get so used to living a certain way that until
you get ill, you don't realise the extent of the damage done. Then
it's too late.

Mitch was a strange mixture, on the face of it we wanted for
nothing. The house was beautiful. If I as much as mentioned I
wanted or needed something it was there. We had a large
extension built onto the back of the house, which doubled the size
of the kitchen and gave us a separate dining room. We had all
new kitchen units with peninsular bar etc, all in navy and white, it
was lovely. Whilst it was being done, we went to St. Ives, in
Cornwall for a holiday. I suggested it, thinking it would be nice to
have a caravan holiday as I'd never had one, and it was
inexpensive. With the cost of the extension we couldn't afford
much of a holiday. We saw Margaret, the girl who had lived next
door to us all those years earlier, when we were first married. It
was nice to see her again and chat over old times. She told Julian
that he had verbal diarrhoea, he was such an outgoing child, with
masses to say. Lovely expression isn't it? I remembered looking
at her art gallery on the wall in the hall and thinking that if I'd let

her have the picture of mine she had wanted, it would be up there with the rest. Isn't hindsight a wonderful thing?

When we came back from Cornwall I became ill with a mystery illness. Jeremy was about ten months old by this time, and still hadn't been christened. What with Mitch away such a lot and all the building work going on, there hadn't been the time. I thought first of all I had caught a tummy bug, but it didn't go away, and after a few weeks it became clear that it wasn't going to. I had constant diarrhoea, and was in the loo up to twelve times a day. I was sent to see a specialist for a colonoscopy. That proved negative, and fortunately he couldn't find anything nasty. The same specialist put me on a drug that was for colitis, the condition he said I had, saying that he had never known this drug to upset anyone. I was then to have a barium enema. Not a pleasant experience and that too was alright, thank goodness. My doctor thought I ought to be in hospital really, under observation, but he felt that it would make me more anxious, and he wanted me to be much less anxious. Mitch suggested that I take myself off on holiday by myself. He said I could go anywhere I wanted to, even South America! I wasn't well enough to go on holiday alone, besides which, that's not my idea of a holiday. I think he just wanted rid of me.

During this time, my gran was diagnosed with Cancer of the bowel, and I hated having to visit her at the hospice. I was terrified that I'd got the same thing. I felt really sorry for her; she suffered terribly and would cry with pain. I could see the Hospice from my bedroom window, which didn't help me in trying to take my mind off my own illness. At one point, Gran discharged herself and went to stay with my parents. Mum had a bed put in their sitting room and it was awful for Gran and for Mum. I'll never forget the smell; it lingered for over a year after she died. Gran had to go back to the Hospice after a while; it was too much for Mum to cope with. It was the best place for her really in her poorly state. I hate seeing people suffer like that; it seems so unfair somehow. But whoever said life was fair? There was a lady in the same ward as gran suffering from lung cancer; the noise this lady made in just trying to breathe was frightening. I don't know if her cancer was due to smoking, but I don't know why anyone would want to smoke and risk inflicting that dreadful amount of suffering on themselves. How often do you hear someone say, 'Well you have to die of something'? I always think that is a stupid remark, because they don't just die, they die slowly and painfully over many months, and sometimes years. And what's wrong with dying naturally of old age. Hospices today do marvellous things and can control pain, but in those days it wasn't as sophisticated, but nevertheless, they were brilliant.

Julian then went down with a meningisma, similar to Meningitis, but not as serious, and his temperature soared to 106. It was very frightening. Dr. Campbell came and examined him, and explained to us what it was. Thank goodness for antibiotics, as Julian soon recovered. I did wonder at one point, if our house had been built on the site of something unpleasant, like the grave of a mass murder. This was years before the film Poltergeist came out. I hated the house. If I went out for the day I loathed going back there. On one occasion I had been out with my father, and when he dropped me off he turned to me and said, "You don't want to go in there, do you dear?" I replied that if I didn't leave it soon, it would claim me. I really felt that, I wasn't just saying it. So far we'd had all the plaster fall off the walls, I'd developed this dreadful illness and I was losing weight fast. It was literally dropping off me, Jeremy had given us a scare and then Julian got ill. To cap it all, Mitch wrapped my car round a lamp post. He was ok but my car definitely wasn't. I had my friends in the road, fortunately. Maureen was so kind and would look after Jeremy if I had to go for check-ups. Sandra was pregnant again and doing well, and we saw a lot of each other. There were some neighbours who just gave me looks of sympathy - after all the doctor's car was so often outside our house. On one occasion flowers were left on my doorstep. At one point Dr. Campbell's car was outside every day. He just used to call in on his way home. He used to ask Mitch questions, not about anything in particular, just chat to him. I think he was trying to find out whatever he could in whatever way he could, to see if he could pin down why I was so ill. I couldn't have had better treatment from Dr. Campbell It was totally beyond the call of duty.

One day Mum and I were in Worthing to do some shopping and

we met Dr. Campbell The illness had gone on for so long and I was very depressed about it, and I felt that I looked awful as well. I looked like someone from Belsen. He put his arms around me in the street and said, "I won't let anything happen to you, I promise." Not many patients get that treatment do they? I know he tried really hard to help me, and for that I was grateful.

My immediate neighbour Min was always asking me how I was whenever she saw me, like every day, and this irritated me no end, as it was obvious that I was ill and I didn't need constantly reminding and talking about it. I've always felt that asking someone how they are is rather an intrusion into one's personal life. It's better to just say 'Hello', be friendly, and give the person a chance to tell you if they want to, and then make small talk. I recovered enough to have Jeremy's christening. He was by now fifteen months old.

I had a form of Colitis, caused, they thought, by stress and tiredness. I was all but incontinent, and was offered incontinence pads. I refused - I thought that was the end. I knew Mitch found me unattractive as it was, without using those. He thought I smelt dreadful and would open the windows at every opportunity, making me feel like a leper. I was losing weight rapidly because everything I ate went through me and out the other end the same as it went in, totally undigested. My skin became discoloured and patchy and I felt as if I was dying. I was still going to the loo about twelve times a day, and I ached so much.   Then whilst Mitch was away on one of his trips I became seriously ill. I woke up in the morning and realised straightaway that something was really wrong with me. Not only was the pain much worse in my stomach, but I felt odd, a weird feeling had come over me. I rang the surgery and made an appointment with Dr. Campbell for that afternoon, after I'd picked Julian up from school.   I had previously arranged to go out with my Father on that day to see his brother Bill who still lived in their family home on the outskirts of Worthing, and I wanted to go if I could. I thought maybe it would take my mind off my problems if I went out, so off we went, the three of us, with me driving. I had Jeremy with me and we were to collect a load of apples from Bill, as he grew them commercially. We hadn't been there long, Dad was chatting away to Bill, and we were all drinking tea, when I felt increasingly unwell. I had to ask Dad if we could leave, I wanted to go home. It wasn't like me at all because I loved going up to Bill's. I drove Dad home first and then drove like mad to get home. I could hardly wait to get to the surgery that afternoon. Mitch was due back the next day, and I really felt in need of help. I collected Julian from school, and with both the children I went to the surgery. I could hardly stand up. I was in so much pain, it took my breath away. Dr. Campbell was very concerned about me, and for a busy GP, gave me a lot of attention. All he could say was to continue with the pills. He was sure they could help me. I do not know how I got through the night, after putting the boys to bed. I could only get about on my hands and knees. I crawled upstairs and got into bed, and must have fallen asleep straightaway. I was pretty sure I was going to die, and I don't think I cared anymore.

The next morning I felt a little better. I got up and dressed, and gave the boys their breakfast. Mitch came home mid-morning and I told him I thought something was wrong with me. He didn't think it was anything other than what we already knew about. He thought I should pull myself together. Out of the blue my parents arrived, I thought it was strange as they didn't ever just turn up. Anyway, we were all chatting away in the sitting room asking Mitch about his trip mostly, when suddenly I felt sick. I excused myself from the room, and went upstairs to the bathroom. I was bringing up everything I ate or drank including water by this time, and as I had just had a drink of water I brought it up straightaway. I was sitting on the bed, when my father came into the room. This was very unusual for him as he hated illness and never visited anybody sick. He realised that I was very ill, and I believe they had come over that morning because Dad felt something was wrong. "You poor dear," he said, "you're feeling really rough, aren't you?" I was too weak to answer. I'd had it. I was past it now. I could no longer carry on. He disappeared, and I heard someone on the telephone ringing the doctor. Mitch didn't see me into bed - my mother did, and when the doctor came I was in bed, weak as a newborn baby. He quickly realised that I had been poisoned by the wonder drug, and he removed them from beside the bed, and all the other pills that he'd given me, thirty-six pills a day I was taking, including vitamins. Dr. Campbell wanted me in

hospital, but thought my mental state was too low to remove me
from the children, on the condition that my mother looked after
me, I was allowed to stay at home. I had to stay in bed for three
weeks, only getting up for the loo. Even then Mitch got me up to
change all of Jeremy's nappies. He never changed one, ever. He
even got me up to do the night ones. I didn't mind as he used to
say, "You wanted him, so you look after him," and so I did.

I could only eat steamed fish, and was to have lots of liquids.
Mitch never took any time off, he often went in on a Saturday as
well. He often didn't even take his full quota of holidays each
year. I suppose he did all the travelling he wanted with the job.
He had been everywhere, seen everything. He wouldn't take any
time off to look after me and the boys, so it was left to Mum.
Julian was at school and was taken and collected by Catherine.
Jeremy had to be farmed out between Eileen and Mitch's sister
Maureen every day. Mum was working full time at a bakery, and
she had to ride her bicycle over every day to me to get my lunch,
she was so good to me. My daily ration of steamed fish was duly
served up to me, and I might say, it tasted like caviar to me.
Sandra of course came and sat with me when she could.

Then it was Christmas. It was about this time when Dad and I
were talking generally about health, and he said to me, "You're
not the only one that's ill my dear." I thought he had said it
because I was feeling very sorry for myself, and to remind me that
there are lots of sick people in the world. I stopped moaning
forthwith. I still had diarrhoea, but I had got used to it now. I'd
had it for over a year. I did feel a lot better though in myself, and
the bad effect of the pills had worn off.

But then my eyesight started to go funny next. One moment I
would be sitting watching television, and the next it was like
looking through a telescope with just a pin-prick of vision. It was
really scary, and no one knew what caused it. I plodded on in a
traumatised state. I went from ten and a half stone after having
Jeremy to just six stones twelve. I looked as if I'd come out of
Belsen and I was very embarrassed because everyone remarked
about my size. That's one thing you can rely on in life, if you
have an affliction, someone will always remind you of it. It made

me feel even worse. I went on the Doctor's advice to Yoga classes. He thought that it might help me learn relaxation. I was under the impression that when you first start Yoga you have to be very careful. By that, I mean you can't go straight into the Lotus position. The teacher obviously didn't share my thoughts. She thought my back needed straightening up, and she put her knee in my back and forthwith yanked it back. "There," she said, "that's better." The pain was excruciating, and I knew she had done me a mischief. Needless to say I didn't go back. I was to suffer from this injury for many years. I knew the doctor wanted to help me get better, but this added to my trauma. I used to wake up every morning afterwards with no feeling in my arms, they felt dead, and I would have to work on them straight away to get the feeling back. I was becoming more and more frightened of what was happening to me.

On the first morning of one of Mitch's rare holidays, the phone rang, it was Eileen. "Can I speak to Mitch, please," was all she said. Unusual I thought but I got him anyway. I heard him say 'OK, right, OK, bye'. He came back into the room and told me to sit down. He then said 'I have some very bad news for you. Your father's died'. I sat very still. What do you do or say? I wanted to scream, but nothing came out. He was still talking to me, "They found his body in the car in the car park at work. He had told one of his men that he felt unwell and was going to sit in the car for a while." (I knew that wasn't normal - Dad never sat in the car unless he was driving somewhere). I gathered that he had been gone from the site hut for some considerable time, so one of the men went to find him, but he had already died. They called an ambulance and tried to revive him but to no avail. Mitch was still talking. "We've got to go and identify his body, and bring back the car." He asked Catherine if she would have the boys, and of course she would. It was like having been hit on the head with a hammer, and feeling nothing at all. The day before he had died, he had taken my mother to the place where they had lived when they'd first got married. Funnily enough, Mitch and I had tried to find them that day for a picnic. After finding out that they obviously weren't in when we called at their house, we also ended up at the same picnic spot. We didn't know this until we called in on them on our way back home. I don't know how we missed each other. I'm so glad that they had their last picnic together in the place where they had their first home. It was definitely déjà vu. Dad was tucking into a large plateful of dinner when we arrived, and his last words to me were as he finished the last mouthful, with a grin, "Would you like some Pet?" Ha ha I thought. I never dreamt that I would never see him again. They were the last words he ever said to me. The nightmare seemed never ending.

My doctor was worried that my condition would get worse because of Dad's death, but in a way I felt stronger. Don't get me wrong. I was devastated. We had always been so close, so in tune, but now I felt that if I died I would have someone I loved over the other side, and that gave me an inner strength to carry on. I also felt that he had not left me. I felt his presence strongly at times. Very strongly. But without his physical presence, I felt very alone without him, we were so much on the same wavelength. Eileen told me one day when we were walking through the town that Mum had thought Dad preferred me to her. "That's absolute rubbish," I replied, "the relationship was totally different, he loved her very much, she was his wife, I was his daughter, there's no comparison." I was cross that Mum didn't understand and I tried so hard to explain it to her. Dad had a lot of things that he had to teach me, and as it's turned out he didn't have much time to do it in. I wish you would all understand. But I knew they wouldn't understand. They couldn't understand.

Dad was referring to himself when he had said, 'you're not the only one who's ill'. There had to be a post-mortem, as he had not seen a doctor in ages, and as it was also Easter, by the time the post mortem was carried out, we had to wait for three weeks before we could have a funeral service. I was not allowed to go and see his body at the funeral parlour. They were given instructions not to let me in. My family were so worried that I would have a relapse. In actual fact it had a more damaging effect not seeing him, and I dreamt for years that he had wandered off, having lost his memory and later returned. The Sister Immaculate from the convent in Littlehampton, where Dad had worked, came to see us. 'The nuns were all so sad' she said, and offered our family all their sympathy and prayers. They had all loved my

Dad. Sister gave us courage and faith, in the knowledge that we would meet him again. Sister Immaculate was the sister in House Party, the seventies T.V programme.

Helen came back very briefly into my life. We had seen very little of each other since she got married. She rang me up one day out of the blue. She was quite concerned as to how I was coping with it all. She and her mother would be attending the funeral. I thought that was nice. The funeral was incredible, a testimony to the type of man he had been. The church was filled to capacity. The vicar gave a very good service, and then we went to the crematorium. There were so many flowers and there were men crying as well as the women. He had been an extraordinary man, everybody had loved him, and I had never heard anyone say a bad word about him. What was I going to do now? He wasn't just my father; he was my best friend. And what about my poor mother! It had only been six months since she had buried her mother. She was in deep shock, and she never really recovered from that day. It is necessary to be able to say goodbye to your loved ones. Usually they are ill for a bit and this gives you a chance to come to terms with what might happen. This was a cruel blow.
Mitch's mother was quite cold to me when I next saw her. "These things happen," she said, "that's life." I know she'd very sadly lost Mitch's father at a very young age, but these things are supposed to make you more sympathetic to others in their grief, after all you know what they are going through. It's not supposed to make you bitter. I ended up sitting in the garden crying by myself. Jim, her second husband, was in the garden as well. He looked over at me, he didn't say anything, he just smiled. He had a hard life with her, their marriage wasn't a proper marriage, they slept in separate rooms, and I gather they always had right from the start. I know he felt sorry for me.

Sandra miscarried again. We all felt so sorry for her and Victor. She had got to about six months this time, and everything was looking hopeful. We all had our fingers and toes crossed for them, then suddenly disaster struck, and she miscarried. It was a boy, and because he had lived for a while they had to go through the sad business of a funeral for him. They coped extremely well considering the horror of it all. I really felt for her. I remember bursting into tears one day when my mother-in-law was with us for the day. She had no sympathy in her at all for anybody else, and told me to pull myself together. Sandra was a good friend of mine. Didn't she understand what that meant to me? Obviously not.

My Mother needed a lot of support during the next few months and I was only too happy to do whatever I could for her. After all, she had looked after me for a long time. Now it was my turn. She was naturally devastated with the death of my father. At least if someone is ill you have a chance to think about the possibility of them dying, but when someone is found dead, the shock is indescribable. There are all the things you wanted to say to them, but never got the chance. There is the guilt. Could she have done anything to prevent his death? After all, he did have a pain in the arm, and had complained of feeling unwell for some time. Well, I tried to assure her, no one could have done anything. He had been a very heavy smoker all his life, and there was the fact that he would never go near a doctor, and he hated illness. If he had survived the massive heart attack, he would undoubtedly have been an invalid, and he would have hated that. I believe that he knew he was going to die, which is why he said what he did about me not being the only one who was ill. Also much more importantly, that is why he took my Mother to the place where they had had their first home, the day before he had died. I was glad in retrospect that Mitch and I had not found them that day. At least my mother had him to herself on his last day on earth.

We decided to take Mum to Italy for a holiday. It was her first ever flight, and first ever trip abroad. She was very nervous, and in retrospect, it was too soon for her to enjoy herself. She was very sad at times, and with the benefit of hindsight a holiday in England would have been better, for both of us! It was very hot - 110°, and I was very sick on the beach on the first day, in front of everyone. I felt so very unwell and had to be very careful about what I ate and drank. I looked like a skeleton with skin. My bosom had all but disappeared and I felt self-conscious in my bikini. Because we had Jeremy with us and he was only two years old, I had to eat with him and Julian, and Mitch and Mum ate separately. This was Mitch's idea, I really don't know why. We

91

also took it in turns to go out during the afternoons and evenings. I would stay with Jeremy and the others would go out, and then my mother would stay in with him and we would go out. Very weird. I vowed I would never ever go on holiday with him again, it was horrible. And we never did go on holiday again!

We left Italy a day earlier than planned, we had all had enough. My poor mother - what an awful holiday for her. Mitch would never make love on holiday, and he would never tell me why. We never discussed sex. If ever I started to have a discussion about it he would get very angry and tell me to be quiet. I'd had enough, I decided to leave him, and after a very nasty row I told him I was going. I had somewhere to go now, my mother was alone, I could move in with her for the time being. He thought I was bluffing but soon realised that I was not. He accused me of only being interested in money. Huh that's rich, money was the last thing on my mind. All the years of loneliness I'd suffered, all the responsibility of looking after the boys on my own, seeing to the house, the garden, all the shopping I'd lugged in on my own. And having to be ill on my own, crawling about on my hands and knees. I told him he'd got a damned cheek. "I'll show you just how much I care about money," I said. "I'm leaving right now, you can keep it all." He realised I wasn't joking and started to back track, he got down onto his knees and begged me to stay, apologising for criticising me so much and telling me again how much he loved me. It was all so weird, he was either as nice as pie or vile. There was no in-between with this man. I never knew which one was going to walk through the door, Jekyll or Hyde. He had made me a complete nervous wreck, and I was frightened of him at times. But he talked me round, he always got round me, and I always ended up feeling sorry for him. But I guess he never felt sorry for me.

It was during this time that my mother persuaded me to go to see a man who was an osteopath and a naturopath. Mum had been into alternative medicine and healing for years and was herself seeing a very good osteopath called Leon Chaitow who was helping her a lot. I didn't know what Leon Chaitow could do that my doctor couldn't, but I had nothing to lose, so I went along to see him. It was all very interesting and I felt he genuinely wanted to help me as much as he could. He checked me out physically and also wanted to know everything that I ate. Then he wrote me out a list of everything that I should and should not eat. He was very interested in my condition and like my doctor, I think he thought that there was something fundamentally wrong, but what was it? He asked if I could bring Jeremy to a meeting at his house, he wanted his wife to observe Jeremy and me together. He was going to try to eliminate the causes of my stress one by one. I went for coffee and a chat with his wife while she asked me questions and watched me with Jeremy. Leon came in at one point and as Jeremy had the entire contents of my bag all over the floor whilst I sat quite unperturbed chatting, he therefore decided that it was not Jeremy who was upsetting me. I seemed so laid back and calm with my child, which of course I was. So what was it? I was also beginning at this time to have stronger and stronger feelings that I was in the wrong place, geographically speaking, and a view I was to express many times to my sister-in-law. It used to flow over me. Where was the right place? Where was I supposed to be?

Then out of the blue a job offer came up for Mitch and he decided to give up the airline and follow two other friends who had already left the airline for a travel company in Hastings. One of them said there was a job for him if he wanted it. And he did want it. When Leon learned that I was moving over to the Hastings area he told me to contact an osteopath called Peter Goldman who lived in Bexhill as soon as I'd moved house. Peter would take over my treatment programme, and Leon highly recommended him. I didn't know what to expect or even whether anybody could help me but I was willing to have a go at anything. Mitch was to be the chief accountant for the Travel Company, this meant he would not have to travel anymore and could be with us all the time. He promised me a new life and said he would change. I thought, for the sake of the boys, I would give it a try. He seemed very excited at the thoughts of a new challenge so things were looking good. We had to find a house in or around Hastings and he also had to work out his notice. We put the house on the market and it wasn't long before we had a buyer. We did go over several times to look at houses but everything we liked was too expensive. We had decided to try and get a house in the country, and whereas Hastings itself was relatively cheap, the surrounding areas were very expensive, especially Battle and Sedlescombe. So we were not having a lot of luck.

Whilst Mitch was working out his notice with the airline he had to go on a final trip to the States. I decided, therefore, to go over to Hastings with my sister-in-law to see what I could find myself. Marjorie and I set off, I had never driven that far before, and it would be fun. We looked at several properties to no avail and then we headed for Hastings Old Town to visit one of the wives of one of the other airline chaps who'd gone to work for this travel company. Whilst having coffee with Ann, she suggested going to an estate agent in Hastings Old Town to see what he'd got on his books. I commented that it was not the right area as Mitch and I wanted country areas. She persuaded me that I ought to at least look, so off we went, and to my surprise amongst all the town houses the agent had on his books was a house in Sedlescombe, near Battle. The agent offered to drive us out to the property that afternoon, and so off we went. The house was reasonably priced, because it had been empty for a long while, and the agent had a key, as it was unoccupied. Well, I'll never forget my reaction as long as I live, as I stood at the gate of that house. I'd come home! This was where I was supposed to be. The feeling flowed through me. It was a magnificent feeling. It was an omen. "This is it," I said. "We'll have it." "Don't you want to see inside?" said Mr Thomas, the agent. "Might as well," I said, "but it's academic, I know this is the house." It was really just an ordinary modern house with a half acre garden, which was very overgrown having been empty for so long, but I loved it, I really loved it. I felt so excited. We would soon make it nice.

The sale and purchase went through smoothly and removal day came at last. I'd said my goodbyes to both Maureen and Catherine. Catherine had helped me a lot with the boys during my illness. She was so sweet and kind, also taking the time to spend sitting with me, Sandra had already moved away. She had had quite enough of the Close as well. I told my next door neighbour with great delight that I was moving to a house in the country which was very private in its own grounds, and which had gates to keep out unruly children. It was worth moving just to escape her children.

The removal lorries (we'd been told we needed two) were to arrive after lunch, so I knew I'd have plenty of time to finish packing and be ready for them. But only one turned up, and in the morning. (How did this country ever win any wars?). We explained that we'd ordered two, but as usual they'd got it wrong and it was too late to alter it. We didn't think we'd ever get all of our furniture into one lorry, and it had arrived hours too early as well. I was only half way through packing the kitchen when they arrived. To my horror the removal men were just shoving things into tea chests, some of it quite valuable to me and all of it unwrapped. If we'd had two lorries in the afternoon we'd have had twice the men, and I'd have been ready for them. Right to the last that house was unfriendly. I couldn't even leave it without aggro. When the van eventually left, it was piled high, as they had just forced it in as best they could. They even had the gall to tell us that we had needed two lorries, and at one point admitted that it might not all go in, but with lots of pushing and shoving, and the shed etc shoved in with our lovely furniture they managed. Oh, why oh why are people the way they are, and why would some folk rather die than apologise? God only knows. I cleaned up, and closed the door behind me for the last time. What a relief. We spent the night at Mum's and left early in the morning for our new home in Sedlescombe. I had our sons in my car with me and we followed Mitch on the journey to what was going to be a new beginning, and a new life together, or so I thought...!

Chapter 6 – One door closes

Our new home in Sedlescombe had been empty for a long time, it
looked so unloved and neglected. The lawns had been let go, as
had the rest of the garden. Virginia creeper that had been growing
up one side of the house and across the back walls had got
completely out of hand, and was going in through the upstairs
windows. It was a job to know where to start first, the property
needed completely redecorating inside and out. We knew that we
would have to make do for a while, and do it piecemeal as and
when we could afford it. For the time being, I would spring clean
it from top to bottom. It was also much smaller than we had been
used to, and fitting the furniture into it was a problem, rather like
putting a quart into a pint pot. But we succeeded.

It's amazing how you can fit everything in when you are
determined to. We laid carpets, and I adapted the curtains from
our previous house, so that after a while it began to look and feel
like our home. The kitchen was a fraction of the size of the one I
had left, and the units were ancient, (I'd left a state-of-the-art
kitchen) and there was no separate dining room here. But I was
happy, yes, I was really happy. It felt right, I had such a good
feeling about this house, and Mitch seemed more content too. I
think we were happier at this time, than we had ever been
together.

The house had been built around the same time as the one in

Worthing, but unlike the last one, this had been very well built. The brickwork was superb, and so was the plastering! Oh, plaster that stayed on the walls! The house had secondary double glazing, an open fireplace, and a small conservatory on the back of the lounge. There were also plenty of built in cupboards in the bedrooms and a very large bathroom. Outside although the garden was a veritable jungle, it was, however, very private and we had large white wooden gates. No more neighbours' children running amok over our garden - how wonderful. There was a greenhouse and enormous cold frames. What fun I would have. We went out and bought a really expensive mower, to attack the lawns and I mean attack. It's amazing what just mowing does, and soon the garden was transformed, well nearly!

We had only lived there a couple of days when there was a knock at the front door. When I opened it, there was a very tall, attractive young woman with two small girls standing there. "Hello, I'm Janet, and this is Georgina," she said, pointing to the older child, "and this is Francesca," she said looking at the child in the pushchair. "We live at Two Wells, which is just down the lane on the left. If there is anything I can do just ask, and I thought perhaps you might like to come for coffee one morning." I thanked her and said that I would like that very much, and we arranged a morning the following week. She seemed very nice. I was also lucky with my next door neighbours, Joan and Harold. Joan was very involved with the Girl Guide movement, and was always on hand in an emergency.

As soon as the phone was fixed, I rang Peter Goldman, the osteopath who had been strongly recommended by Leon Chaitow. I explained that he had been recommended to me, and could I please make an appointment. Peter sounded very friendly, and he replied "Certainly ma'am, will tomorrow be OK?" "Tomorrow," I repeated, "what, Saturday?" "Yes ma'am," he said again, "is that any good to you?" It most certainly was OK with me. I thanked him and we agreed a time. I really was so surprised at the speed of the appointment, as normally you would have to wait a week, and osteopaths never usually work weekends. This was so unusual, I liked it. Off I went the next day to Bexhill, wondering what he was going to be like. I needn't have worried, I liked him from the start. He had a very warm friendly manner. I don't know what I felt but I do know I felt safe with this man. All things were possible he said, and he told me he would rebuild me. Music to my ears, and I believed him. What a kind and friendly man he was.

I had to get Julian into school next, and planned to visit the school when I was in Westfield, that being our nearest village. It turned out to be another nice experience. The headmaster was so friendly and helpful, so different to any head teacher I'd ever known. After going through the rules and aims of the school, he walked out to the gate with me, and standing on it, swung on it like a child, and he was chatting away talking about the village and life generally. Life here seemed so relaxed, quite extraordinary. It was unlike anything I had known before. I liked where we had moved to more and more. The headmaster left a lasting impression on me. What a friendly man.

I had to go to the doctors' surgery next which was in the village, and sign on. There was no posh new health centre like I had been used to in Worthing, with all the flashing lights, each colour for a different doctor. This surgery was a shabby Victorian house with a shabby waiting room, full of old chairs destined to give you all the back problems you'd ever want! I would miss Dr. Campbell and I would like to take the opportunity to thank him for all his kindness and support of me over all the years.

My new doctor, after listening to what was wrong with me, said quite calmly, "People in the countryside don't suffer from this kind of illness, (referring to my stomach problems), you'll find it will just settle down." He was so matter of fact about it all that you couldn't help but feel that he must know what he's talking about. And I hoped he was right. I'd still got the problems with my neck and arms from being injured at yoga two years earlier. He suggested I had a neck x-ray, and arranged it. When the results came back the doctor said it was arthritis, and I would have to wear a collar. Funny that! I hadn't had any problems with my neck and arms until I went to yoga. He suggested I wear a collar to relieve the pain. I thanked him but said no thanks, I was thinking that I would ask my new osteopath for his opinion when I saw him next.

I had, by now, been ill for two years. I had not passed a normal motion during that time, it was still just liquid. I felt that my body was a total mess. My arms were still dead first thing in the morning, and I had to shake them as vigorously as I could to get the feeling back in them. It scared me so much. One of the saddest things was that I couldn't pick Jeremy up at all, and hadn't been able to for over a year. How can you explain that to a child of that age? Instead I would sit down wherever I could find a seat and he would climb on me, that way we did have a cuddle. I did ask my osteopath about my neck and he reassured me that it wasn't arthritis. He started working on it, and the rest of my spine to help my arms, and he did something, which was totally new to me, the balancing of the chacras - whatever that meant! I was to learn all about that later. Peter the osteopath and healer gave me hope, and that is the single most important thing when you are ill. I used to look forward very much to having my treatment with Peter. I knew he was special.

I thought at times, that my days of being really active were in jeopardy. For example, I wondered if I would ever be able to play tennis again, it was a frightening thought. I frequently sat with my back against the warm radiator to try to ease the pain in my back and neck. Janet would rub my back for me regularly, she was a very good friend.

Despite the pain, I got very into gardening, although my arms ached it was very good for my mind, it was so therapeutic, and Janet would bring me along various cuttings and bits from their garden. Using the greenhouse, and the lovely cold frames, we grew so much food the first year that we had to invest in the largest freezer we could find. The boys would often say "Oh no, not more strawberries" or "Not more runner beans". We ate very well, I got very into cookery, baking in particular. I was always making cakes, fruit pies, biscuits, and home baked bread. For a bit of fun, I used to put menus up on the wall on a Monday for the whole week, making sure that sensible eating was mixed in with a few of the family's favourite things, followed as well by my thoughts for the day. The thoughts of Chairman Stella! One of my favourite sayings was 'Don't open your mouth until your brain is in gear'.

What didn't freeze very well went into preserving jars. At the end of the year we had a shed full of potatoes, onions and apples, and a freezer full of home grown vegetables and fruit, as well as a larder filled with bottles of tomatoes and fruit, and tins filled with home made cakes and bread. I started to put on weight at last, and I went up to nine stone. I was ecstatic with joy. When we were invited to my mother's for Christmas, I realised that I had nothing to wear that would fit me, as all my clothes were now fortunately too small. Over the years I had bought smaller and smaller sizes, so a neighbour stepped in and lent me a very smart skirt of hers, until I could restock my wardrobe. That is typical of what they were all like in the lane. They were all such nice people, and I think we had all been influenced by watching "The Good Life" on television. Between us, we had cattle, sheep, hens, bees, goats, rabbits and of course every fruit and vegetable known to man. The boys had rabbits, New Zealand Whites, given to us by Janet and her girls. We had half an acre, (the others in the lane had between one third, and four acres) and it was all planted with fruit and vegetables with unfortunately no room for large animals. A cat called Sooty from a nearby bungalow was trying very hard to move in with us, but I wasn't keen. I didn't understand why it wanted to leave its own home and live with us. I was a little nervous of cats because Julian had been given a kitten when he was just three years old when we were living in Worthing. He'd called her Dizzy and she was the sweetest little thing, but it sent me dizzy when I discovered that it was infested with fleas and proceeded to infest our house, resulting in the health department spraying the entire house. I had tried everything including spraying the kitten but when I did, the fleas jumped off the kitten and onto me, and I was covered in fleabites. My neighbour had kindly offered to take Dizzy as she had already got lots of cats. The fleas could jump from one to the other quite easily and not bother the humans! So I was naturally bothered about taking on another cat.

I was in my element with the house and garden, and the boys were able to roam the fields and the woods all around us and have a very natural childhood. I didn't realise there were snakes in Sedlescombe, and when Jeremy came in from the garden talking about 'nakes'! I thought he meant the garden rake. "No," said my neighbour Joan, "you probably have adders in your compost heap." Snakes! I was horrified. Thank goodness he had wellingtons on. I thought this was Sussex not Africa!

Jeremy went to play group for a short while, but he disliked it so much that one day he asked me if he need go any more. Could he stay home with me and help me in the garden? I readily agreed, because I was outdoors all day. I knew he wouldn't get too bored, and it was no bother to me having him digging alongside me. He used to load up the trailer behind his tractor with the weeds and take them to the bonfire. He would soon be going to school anyway, so I could enjoy him a while longer. I never could understand why parents were in such a rush to get their children off their hands. They grow up so quickly. I used to love the school holidays. I would listen to some of the mums groaning about what they were going to do with their children for six weeks or more, and I would be revelling in the fact that they were going to be at home. Whilst I was waiting for Julian one day, I met Pat outside the school gates. She had a son only a few months older than Jeremy who'd been able to start school in that September but Jeremy, because his birthday was in September, was denied starting school until the next year. I ask you what sort of intelligence was there in denying a child entrance to school because of a few weeks? Children needed to go to school earlier, not later, and do now. But in those days...! Pat and I were to become very good friends, and are still good friends today, she and Gavin are salt of the earth type people and have helped me so much over the years deal with various things, and I thank them for that.

Mitch, without a doubt, had a very odd streak. One day he decided that the boys and I should help him move the greenhouse down the garden a little. Our garden was on a slope, and he wanted the greenhouse moved intact without removing any glass. I dread to think what the weight of this was. It wasn't one of the modern aluminium greenhouses, it was a wooden one. I asked if we might not get involved in this because the boys were much too

101

young, and my arms were still very painful, and I didn't need that extra strain on them, but he insisted. I urged him to think again, saying that it was much too dangerous for the boys, but he wouldn't listen. He really thought it was a sensible thing to do. He somehow got it up onto railway sleepers, and the boys and I had to stand on the lower side to make sure it didn't slide down the hill. It weighed a ton, and during this exercise we were spotted by our next door neighbours. They could see how dangerous this was, and without asking if we needed any help they leaped the fence. They were not young, but they could see the folly of this action, and took over from the boys. They told Mitch that he was very foolish to attempt such a thing. He hadn't changed. He was either as nice as pie or vile. There was no in between. I think the rare nice moments carried me through the vile ones. Did I really need to move a greenhouse in that state? And why involve little boys?

My mother sent details in the post of a famous healing centre in Westfield, called Benskins. I read it with interest, and when I mentioned it to Janet she asked me if I would like to go. If so, she would go with me. I replied that I would try anything to ease my pain. We set off the next Sunday afternoon, as there was a meeting on that day, only to discover one of our neighbours playing the piano for the little church service held before the healing ceremony. I wondered why she hadn't mentioned it to me! People can be strange about mentioning healing, and in those days it was akin to witchcraft in this country, so maybe that was why she hadn't said anything. Anyway, I was glad I'd gone, it was such a friendly place and I'm not quite sure what Benskins did for me, but Mitch was positive that I had completely changed from that day. I think there was some truth in the fact that I was changing fast. After years of unhappiness, I was climbing back to some sort of normality. Because of all the drugs I had taken for my stomach problem over the years, my hair was prematurely grey. As a result, I lacked confidence dreadfully. Anything that could help my road to recovery was to be looked into. But I think it was Peter who must take the credit for my gradual return to well-being.

After the garden was tamed, we turned our attention to decorating the inside of the house. I always liked to do my bit, in fact I think I had always done more than my fair share. We had decided to start with the lounge. One Sunday morning, Mitch woke me up and told me to get up as we had painting to do. I didn't get up immediately as it was Sunday, so the next thing was, he physically pulled me out of bed, me and covers all landed on the floor. I told him my arms were hurting but he took no notice and proceeded out of the room telling me to get downstairs to start painting. He would get the paint and brushes ready. Every stroke of the brush was painful for me, looking back it seems quite ridiculous that I didn't retaliate, but I think I was afraid of him. We painted all day, and finished it, it looked good. I hung the curtains, hoping that was the end of the painting for the time being.

Mitch frequently slept in Jeremy's room, telling him to sleep with me. I had got used to this over the years, we so often slept separately it became normal. It was during just such an occasion when he was sleeping in Jeremy's room, and Jeremy for a change was sleeping with Julian, that I was awoken because my room was suddenly filled with light. I always liked to sleep with the curtains open, because I love to see the sky. But this was strange, it was like broad daylight, and there was an unusual noise like sonar. What on earth was going on? I went to the window and looked out. Nothing on earth could have prepared me for what I saw. Just above the trees at the bottom of the garden was a ball of light, hovering. I blinked. Was I dreaming? No I wasn't. Was it the moon? No it was too low, and it did not resemble the moon at all. I had seen the moon a million times and this definitely was not the moon. It was a space ship!!! I was terrified. I ran into Jeremy's room and tried to wake Mitch up, to no avail. He would not wake up. I ran into Julian's room and I tried to wake Julian and Jeremy, but without success. No one would wake up. I couldn't understand what was wrong with them. I prodded and poked, and shouted but it was no good, they remained asleep. It was not normal. They have never ever not woken up before. Still terrified, I crept back to my room hoping it had all been a dream, but no, it hadn't been a dream and my room was the same, filled with light, and still with this strange noise, like a submarine. I looked out again in disbelief and horror, what was a space ship doing in our garden, and why wouldn't the others wake up? I pulled the curtains tightly and jumped into bed, pulling the covers way over my head. I don't remember how long it lasted, and eventually I went back to sleep. The next day when I told the family at breakfast, Mitch said it was the moon, or my imagination. The boys however were excited. A space ship, wow! They bet no one else's mother had seen a space ship. "Wait till we tell them at school" they said. There were reported sightings of a space ship in the newspapers the following week, and afterwards I felt a twinge of excitement. I could afford to then, but at the time I was really scared to death.

When I rang my mother that morning and told her about it, we had a strange conversation, she said, "You'll have to move, they know where you are." I replied, "There's no point - they will know where I am wherever I go." It was said so spontaneously, that it was uncanny. I was to become friends with two separate people years later who had each independently seen or had reason to know about the spacecraft. A woman called Mary with whom I was to become very friendly years later, had spotted it in the sky over Sedlescombe on her way home from the hospital where she worked, she told me it had scared the living daylights out of her. The second person was a farmer, who I got friendly with later on. There were reports of the spacecraft landing on one of his fields, but he himself didn't see it. I only later learned that they'd both known about it when I talked to them individually about my experience. Isn't that amazing? There were reports of sightings of the space ship in the local paper the following week, several people had seen it in the sky. I met fairly recently, 2001, a psychic called Karen, who proceeded to tell me that my last few lives hadn't been on this Planet but on another Solar system. It confirmed what I'd always thought, and joked about to my sons for years. That I was an Alien! Were they checking up on me? Karen also told me that one of the reasons I didn't feel quite right within myself was because I vibrated at a different level to other people who hadn't come from another Solar system. This she explained was something that I would have to cope with as best I could, and after all I had coped all my life so far. Nevertheless as I got older she said I would be even better at coping with it.

I continued to see Peter, and going from strength to strength, my arms were now much better. I had got back to my normal weight, about nine stone, and I found Peter very re-assuring about my health generally. He always assured me that I would get better, and during my visits we had very interesting conversations about life and our beliefs, and there was a lot of common ground. I hadn't ever been able to talk to anyone so frankly before, about my beliefs, apart from my Dad of course.

It was five years after I first became ill, and I had just got home after having taken the boys to school. I went to the loo and oh what joy! I passed my first formed motion in five years. You cannot imagine my happiness. You would have thought that I had won the football pools. To me it was better than winning the pools. My body was returning to normal again. Oh, thank you dear God. I was finding life more and more enjoyable.

It was about this time that I met Vivienne. Her sons went to Westfield school as well, and I met her at a mutual friend's house one morning whilst having coffee. I didn't take to her right away. She came over as rather hard, and very, very sarcastic, whilst sitting in Beth's kitchen puffing away on a cigarette. But when I got to know her better we became inseparable. I gathered a lot of strength from knowing Vivienne, we had such a lot in common. I'd been lost for so many years, lost and unhappy. The spirituality that I had been born with had been more and more repressed by my various situations and unhappy lifestyle, and just as with Peter, not since Dad had been alive had I had such wonderful conversations. I found myself again through our endless conversations about life, God and re-incarnation, and how we are all part of a master plan. I knew Mitch got worried about my friendship with Vivienne. He said she had changed me, but actually her help was invaluable. Little did I know then just how invaluable it was going to be. I was getting my confidence back fast and I could now stand up to Mitch. I had some wonderful spiritual experiences at this time of my life, and when I told Mitch about them I could sense the distance between us getting wider and wider. I was revelling in my joy at being alive and learning all I could about whatever I could. Then I experienced something so incredible it changed my life forever.

It was a day much like any other. I had taken the boys to school, come home and gone out into the garden to survey the beauty of it all. I was standing by the sumac trees, (known as the burning bush, because of their lovely dark red leaves in the Autumn), and I was suddenly aware that I was experiencing the most incredible sensation of the purest love that you could ever feel I could feel it pouring into me as if I were a human vase, it literally poured into me and filled me up. I knew it was the most beautiful feeling that it was possible to experience outside of Heaven and I was ecstatic with happiness. To experience pure love like that was wonderful, and I knew I was lucky to have been chosen, very lucky. If only people knew of the love of God - it's pure, it's unconditional and it lasts forever. I was to tell the Vicar about this some time later and he remarked that people didn't realise who lived in Moat Lane. I wondered what he meant. Who did live in Moat Lane? Who was I then? The Vicar was to help me a lot later on, and we became very good friends.

On another occasion I was standing at the kitchen sink looking at the sky through the windows. I was fraught with tension, and life was getting difficult again with Mitch, my head ached so much and I was feeling very sad. I don't remember if I was praying, or just talking to God, but suddenly all my pain went, it completely went. I rushed to the phone to share this with Mitch but he was getting very jittery. I often tried to share my experiences and thoughts with him but to no avail. He was horrified at the change in me. We were not getting on well at all.

Mitch had often mentioned how he had regretted giving up his previous job with the airline. I suggested that he ring them and try to get back with them. I felt that if we moved to a bungalow with two acres that had just gone on the market three houses down the lane, I could do my self-sufficiency and he could globe trot and come home when it suited him. We would both be happy then. All I had ever wanted was for us to be happy. He said that there was not much chance that they would offer him his old job back, and anyway, everybody that he had known then had left, but that we would try and move to the bungalow down the lane. So we put our house on the market.

I had a premonition about the sale of our house. I was standing on the pavement in a street in Bexhill with my neighbour Barbara, we'd gone to do a bit of shopping. Suddenly, I knew that someone was about to buy our house. I couldn't wait to get back home. Sure enough when I got back home the telephone rang. It was the agent. "We have been trying to contact you Stella. I have some people who want to view your house." We were lucky and managed to sell our house very quickly, and our offer on the bungalow was accepted.

We moved ourselves, with the help of one of Mitch's friends from the office, who had a van. The bungalow, called Hedgerows, was a truly fabulous place. The two acres of land were split up into a formal garden, which was full of every flower imaginable (the lady who had lived there previously had been into flower arranging). There was an orchard, a pig sty, a strange arrangement of sheds, and then a paddock which ran down to a stream. Heaven or what?

Sooty, the cat who had tried for so long to live with us, was now doing so. It seemed to be one of the conditions of the sale! The owner did not want to take her with them. Charming! And the other alternative for the cat was not an alternative to me. I was not really keen on having a cat, but I certainly did not want Sooty to be put to sleep. She soon became a family favourite and we discovered that she could climb ladders in a trice. Julian, who'd surveyed the roof for his steam train layout, found that as soon as the loft ladder came down, Sooty was up there. It was fascinating to watch her, with her little furry feet so adept on the rungs. Better than most humans. It was at this time that Julian changed schools, he was now going to Claverham College in Battle. When I first heard the name I thought it had to be private, but no, it was a comprehensive school and a very good one at that.

We set about doing various things to our new home. Again funds were very limited, and I knew that we would not be able to do much to start with. There was a lot that needed doing, but we would do it piecemeal. The garden was like a park, and I was in my element. My love of flowers just got stronger and stronger, if that was possible. The bungalow was double fronted with two

107

very large double glazed bay windows. There were three large bedrooms, an elegant sitting room and best of all a thirty foot conservatory. And of course the kitchen, bathroom and separate toilet. Who wouldn't be happy with that? The roof was spacious and ideal for Julian's train layout, and we boarded half of it out in anticipation of running the trains at long last. Some had been in boxes for years.

We soon discovered that there was woodworm in the bungalow, a lot in the roof, and loads in the hall. It also became apparent why the windows had always been open when we viewed the property. Drains! Oh boy, what a smell. Fortunately, there was a builder working next door, building an extension, so when one day the loo filled up to the top and we couldn't use it, we shouted help. He came straight round and inspected it. We knew when we bought it that the property had septic tank drainage, and we had every intention as soon as funds permitted to go onto the mains in the road. The builder said it would have to be done now as a matter of urgency, as it was a health hazard. He used our phone, and rang the local Building Inspector's office and explained to them that we could not wait for planning permission, it would have to be done now. It was dangerous having children in the house and sewage spilling over. The building control people let the work go ahead as a matter of priority, saying that the plans could go in afterwards. So the builder started work on them straightaway. My neighbour Barbara was not very pleased because he had stopped work on her extension, although she did appreciate that this was a matter of some urgency.

The builder was a nice man, and I took a great deal of interest in the drains as they were being done, all carefully laid on beach with the fall being very important. All the earth that he dug out then went to fill in the septic tank which was down by the orchard. He was a very gentle man, very caring and community minded. During his couple of weeks with us doing the new drains, I was aware that I had a problem with my neck. Sometimes Mitch would grab the back of my neck. I had got used to it and didn't even take much notice anymore, and I always recovered, but this time it was different. I started to get very light headed along with the pain. I tried to get hold of Peter but he was away on holiday and I didn't know who else to ring. The builder was concerned and told me to ring an Indian osteopath that he himself went to. I did so and got an appointment the same day. After careful examination, it was diagnosed that there was a problem and therefore, not enough oxygen was getting through to my brain. I had to go along to see this particular osteopath every day for a week, and it cost an arm and a leg. But it was necessary, and I got better.

I decided to do my self-sufficiency, and in order to do this I needed a calf, for the milk and the meat, and I would need hens for the eggs. Julian was friendly with a boy at school whose parents had a farm at Crowhurst and they knew where I could get a calf from. I was very excited at the prospect, and when the little calf arrived I was over the moon. It was only a few weeks old, and I had to hand rear her. I used to get a milk bottle and put a rubber glove on the end to make the teats. I obtained the proper animal milk powder from a farm supplier in Battle and was all prepared to do my stuff. Feeding took place several times a day just as with a human baby. I named her Meesha, and she was very pretty. I kept her in the old pig sty.

The boys were in their element with so much space to play in. They swung on an old tyre attached by a rope to an enormous oak tree in the field. Sooty used to sit on the wall of the pig sty and watch all the goings on with great interest. She was a happy cat now. When it snowed the boys would toboggan down the slope of the field. These were very happy memories for them to carry into adulthood.

Friday night was Sainsbury's night. At six o'clock sharp, the boys and I had to line up in the hall for our inspection to see if we were clean and tidy. Usually one of us was sent to the bathroom to re-do our hair or clean our nails. We always had meat pie on Friday nights, meat pies and chip sticks - our habits were as regular as clockwork. We always watched the same programmes on TV, ate at the same time and went to bed at the same time. It never altered. Mitch loved football. He was always glued to the TV on Saturday evening and Sunday afternoons when the football came on. If it was hot I would take the boys to the beach at Hastings.

Mitch never once came with us. I enjoyed taking them, so it didn't matter, but I know that they missed out generally on family life, and all the things that boys do with their Fathers. I think it was probably due to the fact that Mitch didn't have a natural childhood himself, but he could have made some effort.

Then one evening, Mitch had a telephone call from his brother John. I could tell by his voice that it was bad news. He informed me that his mother had died. He would not let me comfort him at all, he wanted to be by himself. I wanted so much to comfort him, but he shrugged me off, and said I had never liked her. He wanted to go out for a walk, so out he went into the night. The next few weeks were awful. He would just run off, literally. He would run miles and miles, and come back exhausted. The great wall was up between us, and he would not discuss her with me. I felt as if he thought it was my fault. I tried to tell him how fond of her I had grown over the last few years, which was true, she used to come and stay with us and we had become friends. I begged him not to shut me out, but he took no notice and the divide grew wider. All he would say was that I had never liked her. I think in retrospect it was or had been the other way round, but certainly in the last few years I got on very well with her. I felt he was in need of some professional help and I tried to get help for him, but he wouldn't see the Vicar and he would not see the doctor. He was fine he said. The doctor wanted him to go to the surgery. 'But he won't come to the surgery' I explained, and as the doctor would not do calls either, the situation was never resolved. Life became unbearable. Six months went by, and I was always in tears. I still tried to think of all the things that might make him happy and I suggested that he go back to the airline. He wouldn't bother. He had given up.

Life became a living hell. I used to be told to go and bath, or to go and wash my hair, just as if I was a child. Mind you, I think I had stopped taking an interest in myself. In retrospect I was showing early signs of depression, but it wasn't picked up. I wish it had been, then maybe I wouldn't have gone down the very painful road when my agoraphobia returned with a vengeance later on. I didn't care what I looked like, as no attention was ever paid to me. I was told by him, after I'd visited the dentist and I was feeling

110

that my teeth were nice, that my teeth were discoloured. This distressed me because I felt sure they were one of my last remaining assets. I was told to get rid of my hair parting, as he didn't like it. I'd had it for thirty odd years - what was I supposed to do? I was told frequently that I smelt and he would come in and open all the windows. He would say that I needed psychiatric help as I was schizophrenic. It was bizarre. You read about situations like these, but when it's you it's a different ball game. I tried so hard to get help, but to no avail. People closed their doors, and didn't want to get involved. I was ringing all our family and friends to try and get some help. His brother told me not to make up stories about his very clever brother. I was totally and utterly beaten. Mitch continued with his never ending washing and spraying of all parts of his anatomy, insisting that I do the same. Christmas Day was strange, he kept popping out. He said he had to test the car, as he had got a problem with it. I was unaware of any problems. "Did they have to be dealt with today? Could we come?" I asked. "No, you can't," he replied, "I won't be long." It never dawned on me that he might be up to something. I just thought it was part of his strange behaviour since his mother's death.

If I hadn't had so many sane friends I might have thought that it was me who was mad, but they constantly reassured me that I was fine. I hoped they were right. I had my first major panic attack at this time. I had been suffering from a bad headache for several days and had been taking it easy. One minute I was sitting in the armchair, and then I knew something horrible was coming over me. I leapt up out of the chair. What was happening to me? I couldn't describe the feeling. It was overwhelming. It seemed to creep over me like a kind of paralysis. It was so horrible. I couldn't get my breath at all. I thought I was having a heart attack. I ran out onto the drive to get some air, and somehow managed to breathe again, but I was sweating and terrified, my heart was racing and I was in a total state of panic. I saw my neighbour's car on the drive, so I rang her and asked her to come round. To my amazement she said that she had just brought in some fish and chips and she would come later. What could I do? I rang Janet, and luckily she was in. She came straight away, and after I had explained what had happened she sent me to bed and called the doctor. The doctor told me that it was a panic attack, but was quite irritated at being called out. Glory me! She should try having one, and see how she gets on with it. She did say I needed rest, so I was to stay in bed for a few days. I did so, hoping desperately that that experience would never return. During one of my days in bed I had my arm hanging out of the bed, and the most lovely thing happened, someone got hold of my hand and just held it. Oh, was it my Dad? I hoped so.

In desperation I pleaded with John to help his brother, so he and Marjorie came and stayed a weekend to see if they could find out what was going on. Although I was very tense, the weekend seemed to be going quite well. Then what was meant as a harmless remark from one woman to another, Marjorie took as an insult. We were taking food out of the oven for supper, and she said something to me, I can't remember what, but it was about how I was handling the food. I just said in my normal jokey way "I feel sorry for your future daughters-in-law', and laughed. I didn't for one moment think that she would take offence, and didn't think anymore about it. She went out of the kitchen and I carried on with the food, taking it out of the oven. John came storming into the kitchen and really went for me. "How dare you talk to Marjorie like that." He went on and on and on, and on and on. It was incredible. I was bereft and totally exhausted anyway, living with his brother for so long, and felt as if my world had ended. I felt again surrounded by enemies. I ran to the loo and locked myself in and sobbed myself into a totally exhausted state. They left me in there. No one cared about me in that family. They went home thankfully the next day and I was not sorry to see the back of John. On departing, he said that Mitch had something to tell me, and left it at that. We said our goodbyes. I was sorry if I had upset Marjorie because she was the only one of the family that I had ever liked. I had many remarks made about what sort of mother-in-law I would be like as my sons grew up, and I'm happy to say that I didn't react in that way. I just laughed.

Two days went by and nothing was said by Mitch. I rang Marjorie to see if John had managed to talk to him. "Hasn't he spoken to you?" she said. "What about?" I replied. There was a deadly silence, then she said, "I'll get John to ring tonight." I had to wait until the evening before John rang. They spoke for a minute, then Mitch came into the room and sat there. He sat staring into space, with tears rolling down his face, and told me that he had been having an affair with a woman at work. I quickly realised which one. The French woman, the one who needed the locks changing on her door, the one who needed help with English to understand the divorce papers, the one who had rung up asking to speak to him on business. We had even gone to a park in Hastings, parked the car, and had a run round with the football so that she could have a look at his children. It still never dawned on me. Wasn't I a fool of the first order? But wait a moment. Hadn't this woman got cancer? Had he been making love to her and me? Although we hadn't had sex regularly for some time, we had nevertheless had sex so I realised that this affair and me must have overlapped. I was sick to my stomach. Although I was now quite well I'd previously been ill for five years. Did this man think so little of me that he would risk my life? I felt dead inside, but under the circumstances I think I handled it very well. "Do you love her?" I asked. "Yes," was his reply through floods of tears. "Do you want to be with her?" I said. "Yes," he said, sobbing into his hands, "but she doesn't want me to leave my children, we want to die together." Wasn't that sad, he wanted to die with her, he had talked about dying all the time we were married, it was all so miserable. Well the decisions weren't hers to make, I told him. Either he left or I would have to leave. The marriage was over. What a joke. What marriage? We'd never had a marriage. I had tried so hard to make him happy and now I would no longer have that responsibility. The pain seared through me. If one died of heartache I would have died many times over the past fourteen years. I felt old, unattractive, unwanted. Even someone dying of cancer was more attractive than me.

He agreed to leave the following day but to my horror he didn't. He came home as usual, and made no move to go. I couldn't bear him to be there anymore. Why wasn't he going? I asked him and he replied that he would go tomorrow. I don't know how I got through the evening and the night, how could I carry on as if nothing had happened? I felt dead inside, and physically very sick. The next morning we separated, after years of anguish. I never understood why I hadn't left him before now, goodness

113

knows I'd had lots of reasons to leave. But love is the strangest thing. I'd always felt I loved him, but it was so intermingled with sympathy, that it was difficult to differentiate sometimes. On the one occasion when I was ready to leave, he got down on his knees and begged me to stay, telling me how much he loved me. I think I must have been a very confused person, for years. If I'd said white he'd have said black and then I would have thought I was colour blind. He played games with me like that all the time, even trying to convince me that I was schizophrenic. I suppose I thought, and rightly so, that I might not get custody of the children if I left. And judging by what the solicitor was about to say to me, I was right not to have left, as I might well not have got custody. Anyway, it was all done for me now, she'd given me the key to the door, and I was released from the insane life I'd led for so long.

Chapter 7 - Divorce

I had arranged to go to Vivienne's house whilst Mitch was moving out, just for the morning. Whilst I was away from home, he and his new partner would be packing all his things and moving him out. I didn't much like the idea of her in my home, but so be it. The sooner it was over the better. My mother was going to stay with me for a few weeks, and would be arriving later that same day. I needed her help to enable me to get my head around it all and to help me sort things out. When I stopped and thought about it, I had only known about his affair for three days, and there we were separating. No wonder it felt so unreal and I felt so ghastly, unlike Mitch who'd had a long time to think about it.

So first thing that morning, he dropped me off at Vivienne's house. Strangely enough I wished him a happy life. I never once in our marriage wished any harm on him, even though at times he'd been so cruel to me, and he'd hurt me more than I ever thought anyone could. But the worm had turned. I was no longer going to endure it, anything would be better than the life I'd had. I went into Vivienne's, feeling dreadful. She was a marvellous friend to me, and although I felt sick to my stomach and fearful of the future, she made me look on the bright side. She uttered something unrepeatable about him, and added 'Good thing he's gone, let's hope he stays gone'. That was her way of dealing with things, always made a joke about it.

At midday, Vivienne drove me back home. "Let's look at the bathroom," she said, giggling, "I bet it's empty." And it was. All the sprays were gone, the shelves were clear, just my lonesome toothbrush, toothpaste and flannel. The place seemed strange, but it must have been in my mind, because apart from his clothes he had only taken his books. Vivienne wished her husband would go as well! That was her sense of humour, but I felt lost, totally lost, like a sheep who had wandered off from the flock, and couldn't find the rest of them. I think shock took over, and I was unable to be alone at all without having a panic attack. My head was sore and very fuzzy. It was the most frightening feeling, and the start of years of agoraphobia.

My mother arrived in the afternoon, much to my relief. I know I couldn't have got through it without her. She was an absolute brick. She stayed with me through all the process of sorting things out, finding and dealing with the solicitors, along with all the practical side, getting the property into a saleable state, which involved finding and dealing with the decorator, choosing and buying wallpapers. What a horrible job, choosing papers for someone else. And the gardens were getting into a mess. I had been so unwell that there had been little inclination for gardening. Mum would be out there sometimes digging for hours. She never minded what she did, as long as she was useful and busy.

My calf, Meesha, went to live with a neighbour across the road. The family already had a cow, so it seemed sensible for her to go there. It all seemed unreal, all the years of building up a life together, all the loneliness I'd endured over the years when he'd been working abroad, in the hope that one day things would be as I'd always wanted them to be, and that we'd be happy. All gone now.

The first solicitor that I saw in Hastings was quite indifferent to me. I think I bored him. Another divorce. Oh, how tedious. He told me that I might not get a share of the matrimonial property, as I had never worked. Damn cheek! Never worked? I felt utterly insulted. Being married to my husband was like being married to someone in the services. He was so often abroad and when he was, I had to do everything, and from the moment we all got up

116

until we all dropped into bed. I raised our sons whilst my husband was working all over the world. I carried on with the solicitor saying 'But who found all the homes and decorated them, who made loads of curtains, who did the gardens, thereby accumulating assets? Is that not worth a lot of money? Supposing we'd had to pay professionals to have all that work done. It would have cost a fortune. My husband would have been happy to have rented a house'. The solicitor wasn't interested in anything I had to say, and I blew a valve. I knew I was onto a hiding to nothing with that man, it simply wasn't worth continuing the conversation. I thanked him for his advice, and left.

Years later, we would pay the price as a country for the non-importance awarded to family life. In my opinion, this has been the singular most major fault with our society, and the cause of the breakdown of our society today, the unworthy way society regarded and still does, women at home. The running of a home and the raising of good citizens has been regarded as menial and insignificant work. How much better it is thought to shove the kids out to child minders and go and sit in an office or behind a till in Tesco's. I'd had remarks myself about being a full time mum, 'How dull' one pompous woman had said, 'All that cleaning and washing. How do you cope with such a dull life?' Well I speak for all the mums out there who don't want to compromise their families. Staying at home until your children are certainly of school age is a caring thing to do, and I think it's essential, especially up to school age. Children learn more in the first seven years of their lives than they do in all the rest. And they learn discipline and manners from a good family background. There's a lovely Chinese proverb it goes like this:

If there is light in the soul, there will be beauty in the person.
If there is beauty in the person, there will be harmony in the house.
If there is harmony in the house, there will be order in the nation.
If there is order in the nation, there will be peace in the world.

It reminds me of the saying 'The hand that rocks the cradle rules the world'. We have a situation now where many of the hands that once rocked the cradles have left their posts, due to pressures on them to work outside the home. The children are either with relatives or child minders. Also many of these same women aren't married to their partners, so maybe have little or no financial security. I go fully into this later on in the book.

I relayed the story about the solicitor to my farmer friends, Mike and Sue. They were cross as well, but told me not to worry as they had a friend who was their solicitor, and his offices were in Tunbridge Wells. They would contact him on my behalf. Later that day, their solicitor rang me at home and made me an appointment for me to see him the following week. He told me over the phone that our family home would undoubtedly have to be sold, and the proceeds split, but he emphasised that I would get my half share. Oh, the relief at hearing a solicitor say that to me was so reassuring. But afterwards when I was thinking about the home having to be sold, I was very unhappy. This was our sons' home as well as ours, and they loved living there. They loved the field leading down to the stream, where they tobogganed in the snow, and the pig sty's that had been made into a camp where Julian and his friend LLoyd slept in the summer. They liked swinging from the tyre hanging from the oak tree, and all the pets they had. Julian had spent ages laying out the train layout in the roof. They were happy lads. I was worried for them as well as me. The solicitor also told me that if my husband wanted custody of our sons, I might have a fight on my hands. After all, he had a readymade home for them and a new mother for them. What was I hearing? Could that be true? Could I really lose them when I had done nothing wrong? It was my husband who had reneged on the marriage contract not me. And why should she get her hands on my sons? He told me to calm down. He was telling me purely to warn me what could happen if we weren't prepared. But we would be prepared, he said. I didn't think it was at all likely that he would take our sons from me, but the very fact that the law would allow him to have them made me so wild. I remember standing on the railway platform at Tunbridge Wells station after the interview with the solicitor. I was thinking about what he said, and what could happen. I looked at the track longingly and wondered whether to throw myself onto the line in front of the next train. "Stand back," said my mother, "you're too close to the edge."

We eventually got back home, and I sat down and began to think. Divorce is always sad, however you view it, even when it's a necessary step to take. For the solicitor to have told me that the family home would inevitably have to be sold, thus enabling my husband to take his half share out, if he so wanted to, was crazy. So in effect the law would allow him to take his share of the roof off from over his son's heads. Leaving me in the position of having to buy a house for the three of us with my half share, whilst living on maintenance until I'd found a job. It seemed more like a punishment for our sons. For it to have been even feasible that my husband could have fought for custody is even more ridiculous, whatever else I was, I was a good mother. No wonder people did silly things. At that precise moment I could have done something silly. But I had more pressing worries to deal with. I had very little money, so off I went off to the D.S.S., to see if I could claim any benefits. I explained my situation to the woman behind the desk, only to be told that I lived in a too expensive house, and so didn't qualify. "But we can't eat the bricks," I told the indifferent woman, "I haven't got any money, I am looking for a job, and my home is going on the market." 'Sorry," she said, "I don't make the rules." Why do people say that? 'I don't make the rules'. They might not make them, but they are only too happy to carry them out, aren't they? It's the same as saying it's not personal, when it's all extremely personal to someone. So I left, again feeling totally bewildered.

Next, I went to the job centre. I had not worked in the outside world for fourteen years, so getting a job was not going to be easy. Understatement! Getting a job was going to be impossible. "You are unemployable," said the young woman. "You might have been a company book-keeper once, but that was a long time ago, and systems change. You have never dealt with VAT, and anyway no one will employ a woman with two dependant children." What a state of affairs to be in, to be told I was unemployable because I had two children. It certainly wouldn't happen today. Anyway off I went again. As I said earlier I had no money of my own, just my half share of the home.

I really needed to find a job. Any job would do as a start. I had a very unreliable old car, but Mike and Sue knew a mechanic who would keep it going for me. I was so worried about losing my sons, and I told them about the situation. They both said they wanted to stay with me at all costs. They both said, and rightly so, that they hadn't really ever done much with their father. It was always me who took them to the beach and on the trains, so they wouldn't miss what they'd never had.

My divorce was my first insight into the injustice of the legal system of this country, which did not and does not recognise the holy vows taken in church. 'Wilt thou love her, comfort her, honour and keep her, etc, etc'. Why doesn't it recognise them? These vows mean a great deal to some people. When I made my vows I made them with every intention of keeping them until death separated us. Divorce was something I never thought would ever be an issue. Having said that I'm also a realist and marriages do break down, but my point is that surely the family that's left behind has a legal right to be financially supported until the partner that's left at home, (be it the wife or the husband that's left), can support themselves. Which is what the marriage vows are about, you might not be able to live with your partner anymore for whatever reason but there is still a duty of care for your wife or husband if he's left, and certainly for your children. Marriage seems to be the only legal contract that you can walk away from. I felt incredibly let down by the system. It might be different today but I'm writing this from my experience of it. After nearly fifteen years with my husband I was told by the first solicitor that I might not get anything. That was never right. To be told that mothers don't do proper recognised work is insulting, and I didn't like his attitude anyway. And then I was told by the second solicitor that I would get a half share of my home, after the mortgage was settled, leaving me with a devil of a job to find anywhere to buy with what was left, for me and my sons. I would inevitably have to get a mortgage on whatever I bought. Surely my sons and I had a right to expect to be looked after financially for as long as was necessary, or at least until I could make adequate provision for us.

By now my conscience was bothering me, and so I had to go to the church and see if it was alright to get divorced. My vows meant everything to me. I discussed it with the Vicar at length, and he agreed that a divorce was necessary for me, for one very good reason, and he proceeded to read me a passage from the bible relating to divorce, which was about "the sword that separates". He thought the passage related to my situation, as he knew I was a very spiritual person. Also, if I married again I would have to get it right that time. And I wanted to get divorced now. I was very surprised at how much I now wanted to get divorced. Mitch was not so keen, and told me so. A legal separation would have suited him, but I know that if the tables had been turned, he would have wanted a divorce. It wasn't just the affair. I could have forgiven him that. If we'd had a happy marriage I would not have ended it, but after the contemptuous way he had treated me over the years, all the loneliness and sleeping alone, this affair was the final insult to my intelligence. Plus he disliked the Spiritual side of me, I think he was afraid of it, and it was growing stronger and stronger in me every day.

Divorce is inevitable for many people, for a variety of reasons. It's inevitable that people change as they get older, and many just grow apart. If you marry when you're young this is more likely to happen. Perhaps one or the other falls out of love with the other, and it is very sad, but unfortunately that's life. But should a marriage be dissolved without the right financial support for the injured parties, wives, husbands (they get left as well) and the children? I think not. There is no other legal contract that the courts will allow you to renege on without huge penalties. So marriage is something where you just put on a pretty dress, and nice suit, get a couple of bridesmaids and some flowers, say a few words at the altar that are not recognised in law, and then later on a husband or wife can simply leave a marriage, demand the home be sold and the proceeds split, and then the one that's left has to cope with very little money, probably maintenance payments. So this is how the law looks at marriage, a non-important institution. But what about the children? Should they lose a parent and their home? I don't think so. I believe children should always come first in a divorce, and that the parent who leaves, whether it be the husband or the wife, should forego any financial pay-outs until the children are of age or have left secondary education. Or until the parent that's left can make adequate provision for themselves and their children, or they marry again. This would enable the family

121

to remain in the family house and cushion the blow a bit for the children. It would also stop the party that leaves from going off and maybe making another family, when his or her first responsibility is to his or her original children. And maybe then we wouldn't need the CSA to chase absent parents. This just seems like old-fashioned common sense to me.

I believe the law on divorce to have been written by men with little or no thought of the effects of divorce on the children. I have been proved right, because as the last twenty years have rolled by, we now have huge numbers of dysfunctional children in our country, the majority from divorced homes and many from homes where the parents won't risk marriage at all. Some couples see marriage as an unnecessary risk. Perhaps they have seen the effects of divorce on their own parents, so are fearful of making a legal commitment to each other. Well, I think that if you can't make a commitment to each other, you definitely might have a problem making a commitment to children, and you can't divorce yourselves from children. They are forever. You are a parent until the day you die. What a thought! We are responsible for our children for a huge amount of years, not just until they are eighteen or twenty- one. After all they wouldn't be here if it wasn't for us. We ought to have car stickers along the same lines as 'A dog is for life not just for Christmas' but saying 'A child is for life not just for eighteen years'. So it comes back to the legal system that allows divorce so easily, and doesn't make sure that financial commitment carries on after separation. In fact, as I'm writing this book twenty years later, Lord Irvine has confirmed that he was dropping the plans under John Major's government to introduce no blame divorce. We must take the blame for our actions in this life, and we must reap the consequences then of our actions, or else admit mental incapability.

My main concern was for our sons. I had to try and make sure that they suffered as little as possible, and that everything at home stayed as normal as was possible, with them seeing their Dad every week. I was fortunate to have a lot of good friends whose help was to prove invaluable during the following months and years. Music as well had an enormously good effect on me. What would I have done without Roger Whittaker's music after my Dad died? And again throughout my divorce, he was played over and over again, I must have worn a groove in the record. Also Cliff Richard, who had been my favourite pop singer from the age of eleven, had a fantastic effect on me. If I watched a video of Cliff's when I was sad, it made me feel as high as a kite, with happiness. He's my happy drug.

It was during this time that John rang me out of the blue, and told me that I had been right, Mitch did need psychological help. I replied that it was a bit late. He had ignored all my cries for help, and now Mitch was all his. After all my pleas for help over the years I could hardly believe it now. I knew I'd tried really hard to keep my marriage together, but it was now well and truly over. I was going to have a go at rebuilding my life.

The bungalow had to have some necessary work carried out on it in order for it to sell for a reasonable price that would be able to be split three ways, the building society, Mitch and me. It wouldn't be put on the market anyway until the divorce petition was heard, which was months away. I was grateful for the fact that Mitch was prepared to pay for the work to be done. I wasn't vindictive. I just wanted the opportunity to obtain a nice suitable home for our sons and me. The builder who had earlier carried out the work for us on the new drains had got a brother-in-law who did decorating, and he thought he might be available to help us. I contacted him, and he was available. He carried out all the necessary work, putting coving up in the sitting room, and then decorating it, and then decorating the kitchen. It was strange choosing wallpapers that were to be for someone else, and carpets. We even had wall lights put up in the sitting room, as all this would enable us to get a much better price when the time came for the property to go on the market. All during the time when the decorator was with us I was suffering from acute stress. I was unable to be left on my own at all, as I would have a panic attack, with all that entails - sweating, palpitations and breathlessness. Little did I know that I was to suffer from agoraphobia and the dreadful sentence that goes with that illness for years to come.

The solicitors for both sides were still negotiating the terms of the divorce, so for the time being we were able to carry on living there. Mitch was finding keeping two homes going extremely hard, and I was still job hunting. We discussed the custody issue, and although I knew in my heart he wouldn't take the boys from me, it was nevertheless a relief to be told that it would not arise. He was, however going for joint custody, but he would allow them to live with me. Well, I tell you, I felt like the criminal in all this. Joint custody I felt was wrong. He didn't deserve it. I should have got sole custody, with him having visiting rights. I had no say in anything, it seemed. He was still in the driving seat, even though he no longer lived there. He wanted the house sold, so therefore it would be. We would receive maintenance payments agreed by him and the solicitors. Great! Let's all go out there and be thoroughly irresponsible, shove all the homes on the market, the judges don't care. Why don't we just stick all the kids in care and be damned? I was so cross I was wild.

My mother stayed for three months, during which time the divorce proceedings were under way and I was feeling a lot calmer, and was back in control. The garden was tamed and we had acquired another cat! How did I let this happen? Another mouth to feed, and me who had sold her engagement ring to help with the finances until a job came along. Well how did I acquire another cat? I put an advert in the local paper to sell Jeremy's bicycle, and a woman rang up and explained that she wanted to buy the bicycle as a present for the little boy next door, and would I deliver it? I was happy to do that small thing, so with Mum coming with me, I loaded up the bicycle and set out for the town. As it turned out this very nice and very kindly woman had MS and was very ill. Around her neck she had a Burmese cat sitting like a collar. I commented about the beautiful cat and asked her name. "Her name is Serena, and she's two years old," she replied, and then enquired, "Where do you live my dear?" I answered her 'Sedlescombe'. Her face lit up. "Will you give my cat a home please?" she asked me, "only I'm too ill to look after her now." 'I'm afraid I can't,' I explained, "I'm having difficulty managing to look after and feed what I've got now." I went on and explained my situation, but she was adamant. The next minute I was standing outside her flat with my mother who had a cat under her coat. "What are you doing? I don't want another cat," I cried. Mum looked helplessly at me. The woman had shoved the little cat at Mum, and Mum didn't feel she could do anything about it at all. When I got back home I was hysterical, "How on earth can I go out to sell a bicycle, in order to get some money, and come back with a cat? It's ridiculous. It could only happen to me." But actually it was one of the best things that ever happened to me. Serena, whom the boys called Sweeney, was a fantastic cat. We grew to love her so much, and she was with us for fifteen years, making her seventeen when she died. I'm quite happy to wait and see if she reincarnates again in my lifetime, because she's the only cat for me.

The time came for Mum to return home, "Just for a while," she said. "Then I'll come back again." Mum was now living with my sister Liz and brother-in-law David in London, which didn't seem too far away, but they were thinking of moving away to Devon. Perish the thought, but I would have to deal with that when the time came. I was daunted at the prospect of being by myself, which is funny really bearing in mind all the times I'd run the house and looked after the boys by myself when Mitch had been abroad. But this was different. I wouldn't have anyone else coming home. This was it. I would have to handle everything myself. I was naturally daunted at the thought, but knew that the time had come for me to cope totally on my own, and I would do it. I was able to drive, I was feeling much better, and my anxiety level was nowhere near as high as it had been.

There had been a certain amount of gossiping about us in the lane, it's inevitable, and it was another thing that I would have to cope with. It was embarrassing being left for another woman. My confidence nosed dived, I'd felt less than human so many times. This was just another one of those times to get through. Mitch had always come across as charming, clever and eloquent, and me the nervous wreck. Vivienne was smashing. She always put everything into perspective and made me laugh at it all, which I did.

As our home would be going up for sale, I started looking around to get a rough idea of what I would be able to afford to buy, and was pleasantly surprised that I could at least afford something. It would have to be a lot smaller but that didn't matter, and whatever it was I would make it nice. During all this time Mitch was calling three times a week to see the boys, which I thought was way too much. They needed to settle down into a routine, I needed to settle down and not have my nose constantly rubbed in the fact that he was going home to someone else. But it always seemed to be the night that Dad was coming, and naturally it caused friction for me to deal with. They naturally got excited when he came and then sad when he went, so I felt after a while that it was more to satisfy him than to make the boys happy. I couldn't get my life back together because he always seemed to be there.

Divorce is a kind of bereavement for the partner that's left. The one that goes has usually had plenty of time to think about everything, and is sometimes with the person they love, and that's fine, but the one that's left has so much emotional baggage to carry for themselves and for the children, that it is just impossible in certain situations to cope with it all. It is a tricky situation, because children need to see their Fathers or mothers and vice versa and there are no right or wrong answers. In the end it must be what suits all parties. I'd felt all the way through that I was over-ruled. It came to a head one evening and I felt I had to ask if Mitch would not call so often. After all I was trying to make a life for the three of us, and his coming so often caused so much friction all round. He used to march in as if he still lived there, he never knocked on the door. I had no privacy, he still went into my bedroom. He used to say that he still owned half of it and had every right to do as he wished. "Even tenants have rights," I said, but he didn't listen.

There was only one thing to do. I picked up the phone after he had left one day and very nervously dialled his flat number. My heart was racing, but I was going to do it. She had got her way, and now I was going to have mine. A voice answered. "Hello C." I said "This is Stella. Tell me. How often does your ex-husband call on you?" "Never," she said, wondering what was coming next. "Why?" "Well mine is always here, and I'm not very happy about it. Do you think you could keep him at home a bit more?" I put the phone down, trying hard not to explode into laughter. 'That should do it' I thought. She probably didn't realise he came so often. After that he came twice a week which was better, taking just Jeremy if he was going to the flat. Julian refused to go to the flat at first to meet her, he was still angry at the way everything had gone, and although he was only eleven, he was old for his age, and realised where his loyalties lay.

I was changing fast, back to my old self. I had grown my hair and had it coloured. It had always been naturally black, but it had gone grey with all the drugs I had taken when I had been so ill. A friend in the lane did hairdressing, and she coloured it for me. It was now a very dark brown, and she also lightly permed it to make the ends curl. I felt so much more like the old me. Now I needed something nice to wear, to cheer myself up. I had still got my account with good old Bentalls, so we took a trip up to Tunbridge Wells, and after careful consideration by myself, my mother (she was staying with us again) and Jeremy, I bought a very nice two piece which they thought was very flattering. Jeremy who was only seven, bless his heart, was convinced that somebody would fall in love with me if they saw me wearing this suit. How sweet! I also bought some strappy shoes with high heels and a very smart raincoat. I hadn't worn anything like it since before I got married. The friend who had been doing my hair, Anne, and her husband, saw me in the lane wearing these clothes and they could not believe their eyes. She told me afterwards that it was like having seen a chrysalis turn into a butterfly. She said it all became so clear to them then what had been going on and what I was really like. No wonder she'd looked at me weirdly when I'd told her I'd previously done some photographic modelling for the Daily Mail and magazines. She must have thought I'd been fantasising. Anyway, I was returning to my normal sociable self, with friends, including a man friend who helped me a lot, some lovely clothes, including two knitted suits that Mum had knitted for me. I felt more attractive again, but I still had a lot of ground to cover. I was very lacking in self-confidence, and still having occasional panic attacks, although not so often now.

I joined Gingerbread, the society set up to help and advise single parents. It was good to meet others in the same situation. Most of them seemed to come from the council houses. This didn't worry me at all but it bothered them. I was asked politely at one of the meetings if I would mind leaving. The girl in question said that as I was so good-looking, well spoken and had a very nice home it made it difficult for them to get any of the men's attention. "You would grace the arm of any man," she said, "and it makes it impossible for us to get noticed." I understood, but it was ironic. I was not wanted anywhere. The only other member who didn't seem to live in a council house was Charles, so he left as well. Charles was nice, much older than me, rather distinguished with a lovely daughter, called Julie. He asked me if it was possible for us to be friends, as I didn't want to get romantically involved. The age gap was too much. He was 21 years older than me. We decided that we would just be friends, and it was lovely having a man friend to ask advice of. My mother asked him to keep an eye on me for her as she worried about me, as if I needed a minder at my age! Well perhaps she was right. I was incredibly naïve. Charles was like an uncle to me. He would get exasperated with me at times. For example, when I met someone, Charles would ask me all these questions about the man, and I would not know the answers to all the questions. He would throw his hands up in horror at me. "What do you mean you don't know? He might be a mad axe man. You should be more careful, Stella, and you should definitely ask a few more questions about them." I knew he was right, I was silly. But I was also very lonely.

A job came up at last, working for a doctor's wife called Muriel. She insisted on coming round to see my home first. Was I the type of person who could look after her lovely house and clean it properly? Yes, I was, in fact my home passed the test. I had always been very house proud. I was elated - a job at last. Never mind what it was, it was money, badly needed money. Muriel was a task master, but she was very kind to me, and I became very fond of her. When I had to go to court for the divorce she came with me, and afterwards she took me for my very first Chinese meal, a celebration she said. I enjoyed working for Muriel and her husband. They were very kind to me. Sometimes on a Saturday we would go shopping. Muriel knew all the shop owners. Her friends were like a page out of 'Who's Who', and included Miss Dolcis, who we went to tea with one afternoon. I was so impressed. Julian used to mow the lawn for Muriel and the doctor on Sundays. It was nice. I felt that we were part of a family again.

Then one particular Saturday they proved what good souls they were. Mitch had come round as usual to collect Jeremy. He wanted Julian as well, as he was going to take them to the flat to meet C. Julian would not go. His father got very angry. Of course he was going, and he would show her the respect she deserved as his partner. A fight broke out, and poor Julian was dragged out crying. I'd had it, he really was the end. What hope had I of trying to build a life for the boys and me with this mad man destroying everything? I wasn't thinking clearly at all. I was so disturbed. I wanted the horror over finally. I wanted out, I just couldn't take anymore. I didn't seem to have any rights, I couldn't make any decisions it seemed over anything in my life. I wanted to die.

I didn't know what I was doing when Muriel rang the doorbell, but she did. She took one look at me and told me to stay put, and she would fetch David from the car. He was so nice, I was going out with them to dinner. He said, "Get a coat. It'll be chilly later." I had a lovely evening with them. They went to David's daughter. She must have thought it odd with me there but she made me very welcome. I knew I'd lost it that evening, and that's a very frightening thought.

I worked for Muriel for about a year, then I saw an advertisement for an office job. I applied and got it. The job was with an insurance agency, doing part-time bookkeeping. I was very rusty but very keen to prove my worth. Muriel was very cross with me for leaving, and would not stay friendly with me afterwards, which was a bit sad. After all I needed much more money than she paid me. She had everything, and there was I fighting to keep my head above water. But I was sad to lose her friendship. I had become fond of her, and I was grateful to her for giving me a job. I wrote to her afterwards, but she never replied.

It was at this time that Julian did some designs of cars, and sent them to British Leyland, as he wanted to be a car designer when he grew up. The drawings were good for an eleven year old, and to his surprise they replied, saying that when he was grown up maybe he could write to them again. They also sent lovely coloured brochures of all their cars for him. He was so thrilled. He was a person who always knew what he was going to do, he never lost sight of his goal.

I enjoyed my new job for the insurance agency very much, and by this time I had a fairly respectable car, thanks to my new boyfriend Leif who just happened to be a car salesman. He got me a good deal on a Mini Clubman estate. I was elated at the thought of having a car that was reliable at last. It was so important to be able to get to my new job. I was responsible for the accounts and doing the banking. At this time I was making a good circle of friends and my social life was good.

I met Alex whilst waiting outside the village primary school. We were waiting for our children to come out, and we became friends. She lived in the village in a very nice house with a swimming pool, and the boys and I would sometimes go round after school for a swim, which on a hot day was wonderful. Alex ran a smart second-hand clothing shop, and as most of her friends were well off, doctors and dentists wives, their expensive cast-offs ended up in Alex's shop, and subsequently some of them in my wardrobe. I was becoming very smart again, and Alex would ring me and say 'I have just the thing for you'. We also played tennis together. I hadn't played since I was a teenager, and before I got married, but it was a game that I'd always enjoyed and we were well matched. When I had suffered with the pains and loss of use of my arms a few years earlier, I never dreamt that I would ever again be able to pick up a tennis racket, let alone play tennis, this was nothing short of a miracle for me. I was feeling more and more like a human being. Her husband became our dentist, and he was a huge improvement on the one we had been going to.

The bungalow was now up for sale, but no buyers yet! I didn't know where we would end up living. I looked at various properties around Battle, thinking that was where I would like to live, but I needed to sell first before I could make any plans. I wanted to get on with it. Why didn't it sell?

Leif had asked me to marry him, and I'd accepted. I found him great fun, a bit over the top at times, but so different to Mitch, but when his mother died leaving him some money, he left me. I was dreadfully hurt, but more embarrassed than anything else that I could have behaved the way I did, taking everything on trust again. He had not been entirely honest with me right from the beginning about his domestic arrangements. And it was really too soon for me to have gone out with anybody anyway, but to have my feelings torn apart again was ghastly. Many years later, when I met the man to whom I was to be married, I was very grateful to Leif for not marrying me, although I was grateful to him for several other reasons, as he had encouraged me to experiment with makeup and wear clothes that I wouldn't have thought of wearing. Also I had wanted to make a patchwork quilt, and I'd got all my Laura Ashley material ready to go, when he insisted that we went to Tunbridge Wells to buy some scissors. He bought me a very expensive pair of scissors and I got cracking with cutting out the first of hundreds of hexagons. The quilt was to prove to be a very important part of my spiritual training programme, and entailed one and a half million hand stitches. I mention it in greater detail later on in the book, because it was very important. Also during the period that I had been going out with Leif, I had been trying without success to get my wedding ring off. My decree absolute had come through, and I wanted to take the ring off. I thought it would have to be cut off as it was so tight. Then one day whilst getting ready to go out, it fell off my finger. It was very odd. The ring was so tightly on my finger one minute, and the next it fell off and rolled across the carpet. It was strange, but I knew it was an omen that that part of my life had well and truly come to an end.

Meanwhile, a girl at the office had a friend who was setting up a dating agency, and the agency was short of middle class women. Would I be interested in joining? I said I would. It so happened that the agency had a farmer from Sedlescombe on its books, and no one to match him up with. This particular farmer had an aeroplane. Oh how exiting. I was definitely interested. Living where I did in Sedlescombe, a small village, everyone knew everyone. I knew who this farmer was, I had often watched him take off and land, muttering 'Poor farmers, they must find it hard to cope'. Little did I know then that I was going to be introduced to him. On our first date he took me to the De La Warr Pavilion in Bexhill. I did find him a little conceited, especially when he said, "You must know who I am. Everyone knows me." I answered mischievously, "No, who are you?" I thought however, that he was a rather nervous man, but very good looking, with a touch of the Robert Redford about him. He walked with a bit of a limp, which he said was a back problem. We had an enjoyable evening, and we agreed to meet again.

My job I thought was going well, and just before Christmas my boss said he was very pleased with me, and I was happier than I had been in a long time. Christmas was good. Mum was staying with us, and Rachael was with us. Since Eileen's divorce we'd often had Rachael to stay for weekends from the children's home she'd been put into by Eileen. Rachael was only supposed to have gone to the home for two weeks, because of one or two things that had happened, social services said that she had behaviour problems, and a holiday would do her good. But it turned out to be three years altogether. Poor girl, she was just a crazy mixed up girl who'd had a very sad time. She wasn't the only child whom social services had told they were going on a holiday, only to stay for years. If adults can't tell the truth to a child what chance have the children of any normality. I had asked Social Services if it was possible for her to live with us but their answer was that as I was on my own with two dependant children they didn't think I could cope with three. What nonsense. We had Rachael as often as we could, and that Christmas we all had a thoroughly good time.

Just before Christmas, I had bought a new television set on the strength of my job. We had been managing for six months, with a little black and white portable set, which was actually Julian's, so this television was well received by the boys. And I was going out with William. All seemed too good to be true. It was during this time of my life that Mum told me that she thought I'd got healing hands and would I work on her arm, which I did. It seemed to work, I was amazed and thrilled, who could I work on next?

The phone rang just after New Year. It was my boss. My services were no longer required. "Why?" I cried, "you said you were pleased with me." It appeared that Mitch had gone to the Inland Revenue on a tax matter. My name had come up, and where I worked, and the Inland Revenue had become rather interested in my boss. He had thought that I had gone to them. Why would I? I would hardly jeopardise my job, would I? And anyway I had no idea that things weren't on the level. I was no longer required. I was sacked. I just couldn't believe my boss would do that to me, the Devil.

Whilst I was on the phone talking, Mum had popped out to the shop, and by the time she came back, I had run off. Without thinking about my agoraphobia I just ran and ran. I ran about two miles across the fields, into Westfield, sobbing all the way. I was so desperately unhappy. No money again, and back to square one. What a rotten thing to happen to me. Was there never to be any let up? Of course when I got to Westfield I realised that I somehow had to get back. I turned to walk back the road way, which was slightly uphill. I started to have a panic attack. Oh, God no, please don't let me have one out here. There's no one around at all to help me. I turned to go the other way towards the Church. I was by now having a full blown panic attack, sweating, palpitations, the full works, and still crying, when around the corner came Anne in her car. She stopped, jumped out, could see I was in dire circumstances, and after comforting me, she told me that she just had to take her sons to a birthday party round the corner, and then she would run me home. My poor mother was going out of her mind with worry, and was so relieved to see me getting out of Anne's car. Anne took the car home, and then came back to see if I was alright. I didn't know anymore what alright was.

That evening William rang and asked me out to dinner. I had almost forgotten it was my birthday, and I said 'yes'. "Is there anything wrong?" he asked. He could tell by my voice that something was up. I told him what had happened. He was so calm, and laughed a little. "You worry too much," he said, "everything has an answer to it, we'll talk about it later." I think it was probably only our second date, and I wasn't very good company. We went for an Italian meal in nearby Rye, and I explained what had happened to me, and how worried I was about finding another job. And I couldn't rely on getting a reference from the Insurance agency either. William had a way of making problems seem somehow less important, he thought everything could be sorted out. "You just have to find which way to go," he said. After discussing various jobs, none of which was suitable because I had to think about my sons, he suggested I have my own business. I laughed, "With what?" I asked. "You have a half share in a property," he said, "and that is good collateral for the bank. We'll think about it," he said. "There's no rush." He didn't mention it again for several weeks. Meanwhile, we had a lot of fun. He took me and Jeremy to the Boat Show at Earls Court. It was spectacular. I've always loved boats, and some of them were 'out of this world'. It was definitely millionaires' playground. I wasn't used to being with somebody who could take time off whenever they liked, this was a whole new ball game for me. I had been so used to a husband at work all the time, this was terrific. William would ring me up in the morning and we would plan where we would go that day. Ours were simple pleasures, walking, eating fish and chips in a little restaurant on Hastings sea front, and a couple of times we went to see the Val Doonican show in Hastings. We took his mother as well. She couldn't believe the difference in him. I gather he had been a bit impossible and now he was happy. When spring came and weather permitted he took me up in his aeroplane. It was such fun, and although I was panicky, I went. I'm glad I did. The exhilaration of being up there, looking down at the beautiful countryside, and going out over the sea was magic. Aeroplanes have always figured largely in my life. Strange that!

This man changed the course of my life. He used to tell me that long before he met me, he would sit in Moat Lane in his car. He had a feeling, he said, that there was someone there he should know. He said I was to be my own person, and that until I was, I would never be really happy. No man could just give me everything, I needed to get it for myself, then I would find myself, and only then would I be able to feel right with someone. I knew he was right, he was spot on. Men and women are like two trees, side by side, both need the light, the sun, the shade and the rain. Neither must take from the other. Unfortunately in life, too many times one partner takes from the other, and leads to the other one being starved of necessary choices. It can lead to a very unhappy old age, when realisation sets in, because opportunities are lost, and it's too late to change it.

It's a strange thing to say but I'll say it anyway. I think that I have never felt like I imagine most other women feel. I say that because at times they said such strange things. Things that I don't associate myself with. Many are so naturally subservient, which goes back to what I said earlier about the way society viewed and treated women, as very second class citizens. And too many women allowed that situation to continue. No wonder the younger women are rejecting it, it's no wonder we now have girls who won't marry and who want to have babies and a life without men. I can't blame them for feeling like that, but that can't be an ideal situation either, because they don't know what life has in store for them. Supposing a girl gives birth to a child that is disabled. That's tough enough for two parents to cope with, but for one parent, it's incredibly hard work. And of course a girl might on the one hand be a career woman, financially independent in her own right with a house and car, be a mother and cope beautifully, until she gets a serious illness, which prevents her carrying on. She might go from being the career woman and mother to living off the state the next minute, and end up envying the married mother next door who has a husband supporting her. So it's alright to be a lone mother if you're young, healthy, well off and if your kids are healthy but life just 'aint' like that. Besides which it could be very lonely later on, when you're old. Which is why I really feel that it's intended that children are brought up in a marriage for the safety of a woman and her children, in cases where either are ill, you need someone to lean on. Marriage is also a financial arrangement for the well being of all parties, as it's not just for the safety of women and children it might be the man who needs looking after. It is possible however to have a real partnership marriage, I know, because I now have one and it's smashing. Women should always feel the equal of men, and a real man, a confident man will treat a woman as an equal. He will realise that one sex cannot exist without the other, so therefore accept and want that they should be equal partners in life. Many women never had the chance to be themselves years ago, they lived their husband's life, either forgetting about or not being allowed their own incarnation, when it really is just as important. Men and women's lives are equally important. I've heard many bitter women say 'When my husband dies I'll sell the house and have a good time, perhaps I'll go round the world'. How sad. How much nicer to go round the world together. Why wouldn't a husband want a happy wife, and therefore a happy life? I realised William was right about me, and my need to do things. I repeat 'Men and women are like two trees, side by side, both need the light, the sun the shade and the rain. Neither must take from the other'.

William did a super thing for us one day. The boys and I had got used to not having much food in the house. We managed more or less on a day to day basis. He took me to Sainsbury's and told me to put everything I wanted into the trolley. I was a bit hesitant, so he did it for me, saying, "Would you like these, and these," and then the trolley was filled to the brim with lovely goodies. When Jeremy came home from school his eyes came out like organ stops at all this wonderful food in our pantry. Then William gave me a hundred pounds. A hundred pounds, I ask you. That was a lovely thing to do from one human being to another.

William had previously suggested to me that I have my own business, and after discussions about what kind of business I could have, he then suggested we do a flat conversion together. I remarked that I had no knowledge of how to do this, and he reminded me that my father had trained me in many aspects of the building trade. I had often talked about my Dad, and now William said I was to put all that knowledge to good use. How very déjà vu all this was. All that ear bending about footings and drains from Dad was not for no reason then. William told me that I had to find a suitable property in Hastings. He wouldn't help me. This was my test. It had to be suitable to convert into four flats, and I was to deal directly with the agent. I was really thrown in the deep end. William was not always an easy person to get on with. He understood what he was talking about, and he expected me to understand straightaway. Some of it I understood, but some of it was like Arabic. I have never ever been a lazy person, but this man had such energy. What a job I had to keep up with him, but I learnt quickly about so many things. I also taught him some important things, as nothing in life is one-sided. I taught him about the spiritual side of life. On a more practical level he needed an osteopath for his painful back. He also needed a local solicitor, as his was in London, and a dentist. I recommended mine. I call that fair exchange.

I found not one but two properties in St. Leonards which met the criteria, and he was most impressed. It was fun, but incredible hard work. Firstly we needed an architect, and we found a good one. His name was Basil and he did all the necessary plans and planning applications, and then we were ready to go. We needed some good tradesmen, and after various recommendations we got a team together, and the flat conversions began. It was fascinating to watch the little units take shape, and before long one house was four flats. Most of the really large Victorian houses are far too big for one family to live in, and this seemed an ideal alternative for them.

The first block sold very quickly, much to our pleasure. A sweet old lady called Mrs. Wallace lived next door to this block of flats, and one day she came out and spoke to me as I was carrying a bathroom suite from the van up the garden path. "You're not a horse my dear," she said, "I've been watching you from my window, I think you ought to be careful." I laughed, but knew she was right. They were heavy, but I was expected to do my share, and I did. Mrs. Wallace and I became very good friends over the years, in fact the boys and I became very attached to her, she had a terrific sense of humour. She didn't have any family locally so we treated her like a member of our family. She'd retired to Hastings from London, after her husband had died. I used to do bits of gardening for her, and at Christmas, Julian and I used to run her down to Portsmouth to stay with friends. Everybody should adopt an older person into their family, and help make some ones life a little easier.

We decided to let the flats in the second block when they were finished. They would be let furnished so it was deemed my job to go to the auction rooms and buy all the necessary furniture. I had never been to an auction before, and at first I found it terrifying. People look at you when your bidding, blind panic would descend

137

upon me, and I would hyperventilate, but after a while I became a dab hand at it. I even replaced a lot of the furniture I had at home, so that was beginning to look good as well. I learned such a lot about so many things. I think it alarmed William what a quick learner I was. I learned a lot about business acumen, as well as how to round up sheep, and wheel out the aeroplanes!!! I even had a flying lesson or two. On Sundays when the weather was good we would go flying, and on the return flight he would fly low over my garden so I could wave to the boys. Sometimes they would go with him. It was a good business relationship but it wasn't a particularly loving one. We were good friends more than anything, and we learnt a lot from each other.

During this time the bungalow had been taken temporarily off the market, because William had taken it upon himself to speak to Mitch telling him about the flats and how it made good sense for me and the boys to remain in the bungalow for a while longer. The reason being that if the bungalow was renovated properly, we would all get the benefit of a higher price for it. Mitch agreed, which he didn't have to, so that was nice of him. So at last the boys and I relaxed, a thing we hadn't done for over two years. After that Julian was often to be seen carrying buckets of papier mache up into the roof, where the most amazing train layout was underway. We all shared in Julian's passion for trains, and when it was finished it was wonderful. Several trains at once all going over bridges, through tunnels under mountains, a sight to behold. He was to go on to be a remarkable engineer. All sons should have a train set.

I was able to do lots of things to the bungalow. In went a luxury bathroom, (when we ordered the bathrooms for the flats, William told me to add on one for me). I updated the kitchen, and the sitting room furniture had mostly been replaced by pieces bought from the auction rooms. It all looked very posh. Lastly I did my bedroom. I had never ever had a nice bedroom. When I was young and at home I had shared a room with Eileen, and when I had been married our bedroom was always the last room to get done, consequently it never ever quite got done. So this was bliss. I wallpapered it with anaglypta, then painted it very pale creamy yellow. The carpet was a pure wool, cream shaggy pile, the furniture was all Stag Minstrel and the bedding was Laura Ashley green and cream. To finish it all off, the wall-lights had pink shades. I had copied the colours of the honeysuckle and it looked absolutely beautiful. I felt like a princess in there, revelling in my new bedroom, and I didn't have to share it with anyone. I never dreamt I'd ever have felt like that, but it was the first time I'd had a room all to myself. Space to be myself, and think, I loved thinking. And of course all of this would get me a better price when we eventually sold, but for the time being thanks to William I had a breather.

Next I decided to get a gardener, as the garden was getting too much for me and Julian to do. Julian used to doing a lot of the mowing at weekends, and I would do all the digging and flower beds. It was like a park, and quite beautiful, but it was too much to cope with, and what with me doing the flats and everything else, and Julian studying, I decided to place an advertisement in our local shop. Lo and behold along came a man called Basil, another Basil, and equally as nice. It was such a relief to have someone who could hedge and ditch and do all the really heavy work. He made me a new vegetable plot on the other side of the field, and much larger. We grew a lot of food.

He had a sweet wife who unfortunately had a nervous breakdown and had to be admitted to a mental hospital. I went with him on one occasion to visit her, and I was not impressed at all with the facilities for the mentally ill. They seemed to be left very much to their own resources, which was not why they were there. They could be left on their own at home. All the doctors seemed to be doing crosswords or reading, and the patients were just sitting and staring into space. Somebody had some knitting wool, and didn't know what to do with it. I asked if she would like me to show her how to knit, and before long, there were several patients round me, all wanting to know how to knit. I wandered through into the games section and there was a table tennis table. Someone came over and we started to play, gently pinging it to each other. Others came and joined in. What sort of a place was this, with no stimulation for the patients? It was early afternoon and not evening, and these people needed something to do. They didn't just want drugging and ignoring. It was a shabby, dreary, ugly

place, not the sort of place that encourages one to get well. I
thought how nice it would be if there could be music gently
playing, if there could be flowers everywhere, and beautiful
pictures for the patients to look at. Basil and I took his wife out
for a while. She was very sad. She was convinced that Basil and I
were having an affair. That was her biggest problem, total
insecurity. It took ages to convince her that we were not. I had a
boy friend, I told her. "I promise you I am not having an affair
with Basil. He is my gardener." On the way out I switched all the
lights on in the building, then stood outside and surveyed the
scene. What people need is love and then more love, not pills.

Basil brought down the power cables one day whilst sawing a tree
down in my garden. The entire area was without power for hours,
including a battery chicken farm, and several other farms. I was
not popular, as you can imagine. How did I know he was going to
do that? I had live cables strewn across the road on the same
afternoon that the local private school was coming back from it's
cross country run!!!

During this time Julian was very ill with chicken pox. What a
ghastly illness that can be. Poor Jules. We couldn't put a pin
between the spots. He had them internally, up the nose, in the
mouth and in his ears. I have never seen such a ghastly sight, and
every time he lay down they burst. He cried so much with the
discomfort of it all and not being able to sleep that I called the
doctor. Julian needed anti-histamines and something to help him
sleep. The doctor was no help at all, in fact, she attacked me
verbally in the kitchen, telling me that I worried too much about
my children. "In fact," she said, "I've watched you in the village,
and you are much too nervous altogether." I couldn't believe what
she said, that she had watched me in the village. "Pardon me?" I
replied, my hackles rising, "Do you know me well enough to
criticise me? Do you have the slightest inkling of what I've had to
go through in my life? No, of course you don't. You're not
interested in me. I've had to endure an unhappy marriage and a
ghastly divorce. I've had times when I've had no money, and
when I haven't known which way to go. You with your great big
house, two doctors' salaries, how dare you criticise me madam."
She turned tail and fled. I was really cross. A moment later there

140

was a knock on the door. "Could you help me?" she said, "only I've driven into the ditch!" I've often thought about that day, and a doctor admitting to me that she had watched me in the village, and thinking how nervous I was, without offering me any help or even a friendly smile. She seemed about as far removed from my doctor in Worthing as she could possibly be. He who had cared about me so much, and she who judged me.

Julian had sometimes said he wanted to die. For any mother to hear her child say that is horrific. The reason was he said, because he'd had a lot of illness in his life so far, and that he was aware that certain of his friends felt sorry for him. No lad wants to feel that. It was true that he'd had a lot to put up with, brittle bones leading to several fractures, diseased knee joints when his father left, short sightedness and trouble with his teeth. And he seemed to have every childhood illness much worse than anybody else. I tried to comfort him, because I knew he would come through it all. I told him that one day he would grow into a very strong and healthy young man who would do very well in life, and then the tables would be turned and his friends would all be very envious of him. "You're just saying that," he replied "because you're my mother." "You just wait and see," I said. I knew he was destined for great things in life. And he was!

During this time some new neighbours had moved in to the house opposite. I heard mowing one day, and as the house had been empty for a long time I went over to see who was there. 'Hello', I said and we introduced ourselves. Her name was Lizzie, and we hit it off straight away. We got on like a house on fire. I invited her over for coffee the next day, and we talked as if we'd known each other forever. Her husband Derrick was in the prison service, and they had two daughters. Lizzie was a very keen horsewoman, riding with the hunt. Not that I agree with hunting, but she did look fantastic in her hunting clothes. She had two lovely horses and two Jack Russell dogs, which was the start of my obsession with Jack Russells.

The time came for William and I to part company. It was really difficult for me, after all I would be all alone again, and I was very fearful of being alone. I knew I had to do it, and that it was the

141

right thing to do. I was sad though. I had been really fond of him, but we were as different as chalk and cheese. Things that were important to me would have been swept aside, and I think he would have destroyed me. He was too dominant for me, and he didn't understand about my agoraphobia, which meant at times I had trouble driving any distance. I loathed having the illness, and he just couldn't understand my problem. He had nevertheless played a very important role in my life, and I will be forever grateful to him for that.

My agoraphobia returned again with a vengeance, triggered off by the stress of feeling alone again. Was I never to be without the feeling of panic? For a brief time I became a prisoner in my own home. I had up until this time been able to control it to some extent and live with it. For example, if I had been going on a journey I would always go the way I knew, and always past familiar places in case I needed to stop. I had always fought to overcome it, but for a brief time I was unable to go out and henceforth became a prisoner. The dreadful fear I experienced at that time fortunately didn't last long, partly because I refused to give in to it, and of course I had two sons who needed me. They were brilliant to me and helped me a lot, as I say nothing in life is ever one way, it does children good to feel important. So I had to drive, we lived in the country. I did find that if I woke up in the morning and felt even slightly better I would seize the moment and go out. So it wasn't long before I was out again. It is a bizarre illness. I'm such a logical person, and to me it was a totally illogical illness. I always likened it to walking uphill in treacle. Very difficult, but not impossible. I was lucky that I had the car and lots of friends to support me emotionally.

I had put the bungalow back on the market at a much higher price and it sold quite quickly this time. I must just mention that one of the potential buyers who'd viewed it, had been a Bank Manager, who had been looking for a retirement home where he could grow Christmas trees. He was being replaced at the bank by a man who, little did I know, was going to be very important to me later on. Meanwhile, I went back to the dating agency, and had one or two more introductions.

That's where I met Nick. I agreed to meet him in a pub at Three Oaks and I must say if I'm honest that I found him very hard going and very sarcastic. It was not a very relaxed meeting, and I don't know why I agreed to meet him again. Except that I always thought it was me, I thought everyone else must be alright and that I must be the difficult one. My lack of confidence showed itself constantly. Nick told me he was going to work in Devon, and so I thought that as my mother and sister and brother-in-law had already moved down to Devon, and I was going to stay with them after the sale of the bungalow went through, I would meet him down there. I didn't think it would do any harm, in fact I thought it would be rather nice. Foolish, silly me! Oh what a lesson I was to learn.

The bungalow sale went through very quickly this time, and I had managed to find a nice home for us. I had become very friendly with an estate agent and his wife, and on a visit to their office one day, Sid showed me the particulars of a five floored Listed Grade Two house in St. Leonards. A Decimus Burton house. "I can't afford that," I said laughing. "Of course you can," he said, "I know the Manager of Barclays Bank up the road, and I'll put in a word for you." This would make a splendid home where we could live quietly whilst Julian was doing his A-levels, and then afterwards I could convert it into five good sized flats. I couldn't tie up the selling of Hedgerows and the purchase of Anglesea together, so I had no option but to let Hedgerows sale go through first so as not to lose the sale. The people that bought it agreed a price with me in the beginning, then at exchange of contracts said they would not exchange if I didn't reduce it by a further £500. That represented a twelfth of the sale price, a huge amount of money to me, but they wouldn't budge. If I didn't reduce it they said they would pull out of the purchase. I couldn't risk it. They knew my circumstances as a divorced mother with two sons. I thought that was a horrible thing to do to us. Some people! I don't know how they sleep at night. After completion I played them at their own game. I stripped the place. I didn't leave anything that I could remove. I even took the bucket off the well. Served them right. I would have left all of it if they'd been honest with me. In goods value, I took much more than £500, so they were the losers in the end.

When moving day eventually came, four years after my divorce, I was ready to start again, and rather looked forward to it now. When everything was loaded into the lorry and it drove off, I felt an enormous sense of relief as it disappeared down the lane and round the corner. We went inside and cleaned the basins and sinks, cleaned the loos for the last time, vacuumed all the floors, and left it. I do believe in leaving houses nice and clean, even if you have sold to people who aren't very nice. There's nothing worse than other peoples' dirt. Lizzie was waiting for us with a superb meal, beef casserole and dumplings. We were all so dirty and tired, and this food was very welcome indeed. She was such a thoughtful friend, and I knew that moving wouldn't affect our friendship at all. We were too close for that to happen. Afterwards, my sons and I wearily made our way downtown to the flat I'd rented. We made our beds up, washed and fell into them. Tomorrow we were going to Devon for a well-earned holiday with my mother, sister and brother-in-law.

Chapter 8 – New beginnings

Whilst on holiday I contacted Nick, as agreed, and we arranged to go out for a meal. I was feeling a lot more relaxed than when I'd first met him at the pub in Three Oaks, and we spent a very pleasant evening at a country restaurant, chatting and getting to know a bit more about each other. He seemed very nice, and good company, and I thought maybe I'd judged him wrongly on our first meeting, and that after all he was really rather nice. At the end of the evening he dropped me off at Liz's and to my surprise told me that he had to come up to Hastings the following week, and asked if it would be possible to see me again. I readily agreed. I would look forward to seeing him again.

The boys and I continued our holiday with my family. We indulged in simple pleasures, like going out for walks or just playing in the ford with the dogs. Jeremy used to sit in the chicken house, and if he was ever missing at meal times we always knew where to find him. He would often be seen walking about with a chicken under his arm, the chicken looking totally unperturbed. We called him Dr. Dolittle the second. The taste of a new laid egg is like nothing you buy from the supermarket, and the yolks are a lovely deep orange, so breakfasts were divine. My sister's house was very large, with barns and a water-mill, surrounded by lots of fields to run around in, and great fun for the boys. Inside there were three staircases, with lots of nooks and crannies to play hide and seek in. All good things come to an end, though, and soon it was time to come home. I didn't much like leaving my family behind. They were such a long way from me now, and the feeling of aloneness would envelope me. It wasn't until we got nearly home that these feelings disappeared, and I felt back home where I belonged. And once I'd made contact with my friends I would be fine again.

The flat that I had rented for us to live in, until the purchase of the house in Anglesea Terrace had gone through, was on the top floor of a four storey block of flats, with no telephone. My agoraphobia was in remission during these few weeks, and the freedom I felt was amazing. I felt so light, I felt as if I was on holiday, and I got fairly fit for a while as I was constantly running up and down the stairs, and up the road to the call box. I needed to speak to my solicitor almost every day, to see how the purchase of our new home was progressing. It seemed a long drawn out business, that at times I wondered if there was going to be a conclusion. The people in the house I was trying to buy from had experienced great difficulty in finding somewhere to buy, but in the end they found a house, and we exchanged contracts. I could hardly believe it. At last I could arrange a moving day. It was lucky that our stay in the flat had partly coincided with the school holidays, and as I'd said it had seemed like being on holiday, as we'd gone to the nearby beach nearly every day. But I knew my sons needed to have their own home again as soon as possible. They must have found it all very strange after having lived in such a lovely home in the country, to then find themselves living in a top floor flat, but they were such good lads, they never complained, and I was a lucky mother to have them.

Out of the blue I received a letter from Nick. A very romantic letter with poetry in it, all about me. Bearing in mind that I'd only really had one date with him, I was surprised and very flattered. He said in the letter that he would be contacting me again very shortly with a surprise, and yes I was surprised when I found out that he had given up his job in Devon to come up and be near me. I was very flattered and very excited. Fancy doing that for me! The danger signs were all there, but I ignored them, as do most lonely people. We even got engaged. He took me off to

Liverpool to meet his sister. It all happened so quickly, and in retrospect, I was so caught up in it all I couldn't see the wood for the trees. He stayed with his mother near Eastbourne whilst he started job hunting, and I had to come back down to earth, and get on with the job of moving into our new home. The new school term was about to begin and I had to get organised.

I'll never forget moving day, our removal lorry arrived, we were all very excited at the prospect of seeing our furniture again. There was one major hiccup. The previous owners were still moving out, and as a result my removal men didn't want to unload our furniture. I was adamant that we were moving in, and an argument ensued. The house was mine, and after a heated discussion with the previous owners, who should have gone the day before, I found a solution. It was such a large house and there were several empty rooms that could be used to store our furniture. The removal men agreed, they weren't happy but they agreed. So they went ahead and started to unload. One of the men was the spitting image of Norman Wisdom. He kept bursting out laughing just like Norman, and we kept expecting him to say 'Mr. Grimsdale' at any moment. He would be carrying something quite heavy upstairs, laughing himself silly. Jules and I laughed ourselves silly too, until our sides ached. We were to laugh about that day for many years afterwards. It was also great to be in our own home again.

It was lovely to have such a large house to live in, just the three of us, with fifteen rooms all to ourselves. Well, to start with there were more than three of us, as the last people were still moving out two weeks after we'd moved in. It was ridiculous actually. You can't imagine the amount of furniture they had accumulated over many years, and they hadn't bothered to use a removal company!!! They thought they could do it themselves, with a van! What a joke. We'd be sitting there in our lounge, and they would arrive in the morning and wander through and take as much as they could that day, for days and days. I had to remind them in the end that they no longer had any rights to come in. They would even use the loo. Talk about bizarre. So what did they do? They threw all the rest of their furniture out of the windows, from whatever floor they were on at the time. Wardrobes and chests of drawers flying through the air landing on the front garden. The wife wandered about crying all the time. Well, so would I in her shoes. It was a ridiculous situation. Then they finally went. Hallelujah! The amount of rubbish left on the premises filled twenty-two skips! Julian, Jeremy and I did nothing for weeks except fill skips with rubbish. It is amazing how people live, and the rubbish they are happy to surround themselves with. Please don't anybody tell me that the French are filthy. The English take the biscuit.

Julian, who had up until the fifth form been at Claverham college in Battle, had decided to go into the sixth form at William Parker school in Hastings. We had discussed this, and both agreed that this would be a good move as we would be living in the town anyway. Then one morning, only a couple of weeks after he'd started at the school, he broke down, "Please don't make me go there anymore," he asked me. This was out of character for Jules, and I could see that he was genuinely distressed. "Why? What's wrong with it, tell me what's wrong?" It turned out that he found it very aggressive, and one of the masters in particular he found very aggressive. He also said that there was a lot of vandalism. "I'll go to the school today and see if I can get you changed over to Bexhill College," I said. "Don't worry, I'll sort it out." He breathed a sigh of absolute relief. I had no idea he was so unhappy, and in such a short time. I went to the school that same day and saw his tutor, who to my surprise said he didn't like being there much himself. Well really! What a good advertisement for the school he was! The tutor also thought that as Julian had been used to a co-ed school, he would find life in an all-male school very different, and much more aggressive. Also being brought up by his mother he was used to a more gentle life. Anyway, whatever the reasons, we agreed that Julian should be moved to Bexhill College. As I came out through the school building I noticed that a lot of the blinds were broken, and just left hanging by threads. It was very run down, with a general feeling of unkemptness. No wonder he hadn't liked it. I rang Bexhill College straightaway, and luckily there was a place for Julian. He started the next day.

Then one day I received a phone call from Nick, his voice sounded strange, could he come over and speak to me, as a matter of some urgency. "Of course." I told him, and arranged a time that same afternoon. When he came over he seemed very agitated, and I knew instantly something was very wrong. He proceeded to tell me that the engagement was off, he had been to see his sister in Lewes, and had been discussing me with her. I was horrified. Engagement off? I could hardly believe what he was saying. I hadn't even met that particular sister, so I couldn't imagine what they could have talked about, and anyway hadn't I got on very well with his other sister in Liverpool? Hadn't she been so thrilled with the engagement that she and her husband had thrown a party for us? But Nick seemed very angry, totally off his head, saying ghastly things about me, things that weren't true, hateful remarks, spewing pure venom. My head was reeling. What had I done? Yesterday, he had been fine, but today, what had happened? The things he said weren't just unkind, they were vile and untrue. And then he was gone. I was so traumatised by this outburst I didn't know what to do. How could I repeat any of it to anyone? It was slanderous. None of what he said made any sense to me. He'd had a real brain storm and it was quite scary. I was beside myself with grief. But inside myself I felt a strange feeling of knowing what had happened, but he would never have understood what had intervened in our destinies. I felt there was so much more to this, but I didn't know precisely what, or care much at that moment. All I knew was that at this precise moment in time I felt devastated.

Then something dropped into my mind that had been said to me a few years earlier by Muriel, the doctor's wife that I had worked for. She had told me about a fortune-teller who was married to a local doctor and who operated from the pier. She had told me that this woman was brilliant, and I needed desperately to see her. I would go and see if she was there that evening. If someone had jumped on my heart it couldn't have ached more. I looked longingly at the sea as I walked up the pier towards the buildings. I was also very embarrassed again at my behaviour. Fancy getting engaged to a man I hardly knew. What was the matter with me? Charles was right, I needed locking up. I knew nothing about him, or why his wife had left. Well, I had a good idea now of why she had left, if what came out of his mouth was any indication of his personality.

The fortune teller was there, much to my relief, and thank God for her. She was to tell me things that were incredible. I was asked if I wanted the Crystal Ball, the Tarot Cards or a hand reading. I wanted the Crystal Ball, and I sat while she got the Ball out, got herself ready, which took a minute, and was ready to begin the reading. She looked into the ball and the first thing she said alarmed me, and I felt myself get on the defensive. "Why does your ex-husband hate you so much?" she said. "What did you do to him to make him hate you so much?" I began to answer, "What did I do? I did nothing!!!" She interrupted me. "No, no he doesn't hate you, its love, this man loves you very much, what on earth happened?" She was very interested in what she was seeing. She could see that it was destiny, but nevertheless very sad. She went on and told me things about my family that she couldn't possibly have known unless she was truly clairvoyant. I believed the things she said, and years later, much of it has come true. I'm waiting for the rest of it to happen now, as the prediction was spread over my whole life. She told me that the man I'd been seeing had been totally wrong for me, and that I would meet a man who as yet hadn't moved to Hastings. This man she said was well worth waiting for, but it would be another year at least. She told me that the man I was to meet had led a very restricted life, and had never been able to be himself. How interesting, I thought. With me, she continued, he would learn to feel his wings, and fly. She also said that no one realised who I was, not even my parents. What a funny thing to say. Who was I then? She didn't answer that, but just kept repeating that no one realised who I was. She was one of three people who were to say that to me. Apart from that strange remark, which un-nerved me, I found her help invaluable. I was so glad that I had gone to see her. Incidentally, on another occasion when I was talking to the wife of a hypnotist, whom I'd taken Julian to see at his request, she looked at my hand draped over the back of her sofa and saw something in my hand that really shocked her. She grabbed my hand and looked closely at it, asking me who on earth I was. She told me that most people are born again for a reason, but that I had come for a specific purpose. "What have you come for?" she asked, saying all the time "Who are you?" I found that quite scary.

150

When I got back home after seeing the fortune teller on the pier, one of my neighbours was talking over the fence to Julian. We spoke for the first time. She seemed so nice, and I immediately felt I could trust her, so I told her about Nick and what had happened to me. She was an absolute brick. Her name was Sally. She was so kind and genuinely concerned about me, and she adored the boys. I went round for tea and sympathy, and she turned out to be related to the Queen Mother's Equerry.

I started to convert the basement a few months after moving in, using a builder who Charles had recommended to me. This builder had done work on Charles' house, and recommendation is so important with building work. Ken was his name, and he was a very amiable chap, and with his small team of workers, they started to turn the basement into a charming garden flat. I had obtained all the necessary planning permissions consents etc, to convert the whole building, but for the time being, I just wanted to convert the basement. And I'd decided to use Basil, the same architect that William and I had used when we'd converted the flats.

There was a strange incident one day. I needed an electrician to put in some extra power points in the main house. Ken recommended one to me called Doug, the same one who he would use to wire up the garden flat when it was ready. Ken told me that he had arranged for this man to call in on me on his way home from another job, on that same day. He wasn't quite what I'd expected, I'd imagined a rather tired, (it was the end of the day) quiet sort of chap, but no, in tore this young man. He stood there spluttering expletives. He was so angry. I shouted at him, "What is the matter with you, get a grip, don't come in here talking like that." He was incredibly angry, not at me but at life in general. "Do you know what this fucking life's about?" he said, looking at me eyeball to eyeball. "As a matter of fact, I do," I replied calmly. "It's about the journey of the soul. It's about the tests we are given and how we deal with them." I explained why we have the tests and how we grow spiritually and how we re-incarnate. He stood there totally gob-smacked. "No one has ever said things like that to me before. I'd thought some of those things, but I didn't

151

have anyone to talk to about it, no one would have known what I was talking about. I thought I was going mad, I really did think I was going mad. I've never met anyone like you before." I could tell the immense relief coming from this young man, as he stood there watching me. He did quite a bit of work for me after that, mostly on the basement flat, some in the rest of the house, and it gave us the opportunity to speak more about life. There are a lot of people like Doug out there, but unless they know where to go to get the information they need, they feel very isolated and very lonely. I'm sure a lot of these people are the ones who commit suicide, because they don't feel that they fit in. There had been a series on television around that time called 'Woman of spirit', Doug had watched this and he told me that the woman reminded him of me.

He asked me if I would like to go to the spiritualist church in Hastings with him. I said I would. I had never been to anything like that before, so I was curious. We were seated in the church, watching a healing session with interest. Afterwards, a woman stood up on the rostrum and proceeded to give out messages to the congregation. She went along every row of people, and seemed to have a message for nearly everyone there, from over the other side. When it came to my turn she told me I was to go on a journey. I would not particularly want to go on this journey she said, but I must go, as it was very important. Ooh er, I wondered, what journey could that be? It was very interesting listening to all the messages coming in for most of the people there. Doug was a very deep man, who managed to calm down a lot when he realised he wasn't mad. He liked writing, and I thought he should have pursued that avenue, instead of being an electrician. But it isn't as easy as that when you have responsibilities and bills to pay.

It was about this time that the window cleaners that I had used for years, whilst living in Sedlescombe, had come to clean all my windows. That was a massive job, bearing in mind the house was on five floors. I told them not to do the top two floors, for obvious reasons, as they were not working from ladders. They thought I was being rather over cautious as they were so used to heights, but nevertheless I warned the younger one who was determined to stand on a window sill, to be very diligent. I left them to it and went indoors. Suddenly, there was an almighty crash and smashing of glass, followed by Jeremy running into the sitting room to find me. "Mum there's been an accident, the window man's laying on the path." I ran out of the room into the kitchen. What a shock to see this young man laying in a crumpled heap. He'd fallen off the ledge on the second floor, and landed on our little raised patio area outside the kitchen door. He was unconscious. I checked to see if he was breathing, and fortunately he was. His feet had gone right through the glass back door. I ran to ring the ambulance. Meanwhile, the other window cleaner wanted to move his friend, but I said no, not to touch him, he might have spinal injuries. The police and ambulance arrived more or less together and took him off to the hospital. It's amazing what you can do in situations like that, how you cope, but afterwards, I felt sick to my stomach. The older window cleaner came round in the evening to see if I was alright. He said, "You went as white as a sheet. I just wanted to check that you are OK." "Never mind me, how is your friend?" I asked. Unfortunately, he had sustained serious head injuries, as well as other serious internal injuries, and although I knew it wasn't my fault, I felt responsible because it had happened on my property. I had said to him only moments before it happened 'Be careful please' but he was so used to jumping about and heights, that he laughed at me. The policeman came back the next day, and several times after that, pretending that it was police business, but it was just an excuse to get to know me. His name was Bob and he seemed quite nice, but I was very wary of men by this time as you can imagine. We did go out for a while, however. One of the things that he took me to was the Christmas dance at the police station. It was great fun. The police certainly knew how to party. I remember saying at the end of the evening in a loud voice aimed at the bar, "I hope none of you are driving home." Knowing full well that they had to get home, who pulls over the police and breathalyses them? Looks of horror came back to me, and Bob was a bit embarrassed, as some of them were his senior officers. Well they certainly wouldn't break the law, would they?

We found an amazing mural on one of the walls of the basement flat. The flat had been completely stripped out of all fixtures and fittings, and the old wallpapers had been stripped off. In the hallway, underneath the paper, we found a portrait on the wall. It was amazing. The painting was the spitting image of Bob! It must have been three feet high and beautifully drawn, and quite an old drawing. I had no way of finding out who did it or who it was. I had no option when the time came round, but to get the decorators to wallpaper over it, as we couldn't remove it. So I guess it's still there today.

Meanwhile, Ken had to dig the new drains for the entire block of flats. The architect's plans had positioned the bathrooms such, that the soil pipe came down inside the building. They would then have extractor fans venting to the outside. If we were just converting this flat we could have left the bathroom as it was, but as there were four other flats to be converted in the not too distant future, we couldn't very well sell this flat and then go back later and ask if we could dig up their floor in the hall. I don't think they would have liked that much. So there was Ken, digging this enormous hole to house the new drains (I loved drains, they were and still are my passion). You have never seen so much earth! The mound was massive, and every time I went to see Ken with tea or coffee, he seemed to be disappearing into this hole. I would peer over the edge, and call out 'Are you going to Australia Ken?' He would laugh. He was a very easy going man, taking everything in his stride.

Another thing I had been asked to do quickly by the planning department, was to re-instate the front wall. When I purchased the house, the front wall had already been knocked down by the previous owner to make a run in for his car. Perish the thought! All the other houses in that grand terrace had their walls intact, this house was the only one whose wall was missing. Bearing in mind this was a Grade II Listed building, he shouldn't have done it. Not long after I'd moved in, I had a letter from the Council telling me that I must replace the wall as soon as possible. As I hadn't been the one who knocked the wall down, I was angry at the tone of their letter. It had been down for years. Why hadn't they approached the previous owner, and told him to re-build it? They had no answer to my question. It was going to cost me a lot of money, so I approached the Decimus Burton Society for a Grant. They agreed to pay a proportion of the costs, but when it came to paying up, they reneged on the deal. So I had to pay the entire bill myself. Ken re-built the wall to such a high standard that you would never have known it wasn't the original wall. He had to make a mould, because all along the top of the wall were shields. It was a work of art, and looked as if it had always been there. I think that a lot of these skills will eventually die with the craftsmen. Apprentices have become a thing of the past. If you want to learn a skill now you have to go to college. How can that possibly be as good as working with the craftsmen themselves on site for several years?

When some of the floors were up, Sweeney somehow got nailed in under the floor. I could hear meowing but couldn't find where it was coming from. The boys and I searched the entire house, opening cupboards, calling her name, but all we could hear was her meowing. I then realised where it was coming from, and with my ear to the floorboards called 'Sweeney'. This much louder reply came back. We pulled up one of the floorboards, and it was so funny, when out jumped this bedraggled cat covered in cobwebs, looking very angry. Sweeney had quite an air about her, like royalty. She looked disdainfully at us as if to say 'how dare you do that to me'. I apologised most profusely. Then we all hooted with laughter.

Several months had gone by, when out of the blue the doorbell rang. When I answered it, to my horror it was Nick. Could he come in and talk to me? he asked. He was just about the last person on earth I'd ever wanted to see again, but he said it was important, and I had a feeling I knew what it was anyway, so I let him in. I felt much more in command of the situation this time, as he stood there asking for the engagement ring back. Knowing what a nasty piece of work he was, I stayed politely calm. He was trying to be nice, but I thought it must have been an effort. I gave him the ring back. I didn't want it. I most certainly would not have worn it. I would, however, have liked to have biffed him, right on the nose. He didn't deserve to get away with what he did to me. After he'd gone, the strangest thing happened to me. I was aware of this voice saying to me 'You didn't listen, you ignored all the signs, and there were so many of them. You ploughed on regardless, and of course you have been hurt. You will not get

155

involved with anyone else until the time is right'. Well, I was so
shocked. I had acted foolishly and I had paid for it. I would listen
more to upstairs in future.

Anglesea was a very busy house. We took in German students,
almost from the first month we were living there, and at one time,
we had thirteen of them. At the beginning, I had no kitchen to
speak of in the main house as it had been stripped out ready for a
new one. I had to cook in the basement on a camping stove for up
to thirteen students at a time, then the boys and I would carry it all
up the outside steps across the garden up more steps and through
the house. I don't know how we managed it all, but we did, we
needed the income. As all the students were German and we were
great fans of Fawlty Towers, Jules would say jokingly 'Don't
mention the war, Mum' and we would crack up laughing. We had
many very nice groups of boys. Some would write to us regularly
after they'd gone home. I only had one unpleasant group. From
the moment they set foot over the threshold they were unpleasant,
and I could tell they were going to be trouble. I suppose they
thought here's a woman on her own, we can do what we like.
How wrong they were. I was awoken one night by the most
dreadful noise coming from the students' quarters upstairs. I
grabbed my dressing gown and with my heart thumping, I made
my way upstairs to their floor, the top floor. They were wrecking
the furniture, trying to get the doors off the wardrobes, and
jumping up and down on the beds throwing whatever came to
hand. I asked them to stop, but they took no notice and continued
to shriek in German to each other, laughing at me. I raised my
voice to a pitch that they could hear and shouted at them to stop
immediately and added, "Right, pick up your belongings and get
out now!" I said. "You can sleep over in the park, you disgust me,
how dare you treat my home like this." They stopped dead in their
tracks. There were several of them and only one of me, and with
my heart thumping, I said, "I'm not afraid of you, you are dreadful
people." They were somewhat surprised at this little woman
standing there in her nightclothes telling them exactly what she
thought of them. They could tell I meant business, and one of
them apologised profusely asking me not to throw them out into
the night. "Alright then but clean up this room now, and in the
morning I want to speak to your leader." They didn't want me to

156

speak to their leader that was obvious, so they set about clearing up the room somewhat sheepishly. Little did I know that Jeremy had crept up the stairs to see what all the commotion was, and he'd been watching me from the landing, and very proudly he said, "Mum, I didn't know you could shout, I've never heard you shout before. Well done." I needed a cup of tea, it was true, I never shouted.

I had been brought up in such an anti-German household that I wanted to prove to my sons that people were just people, no matter where they came from. That luckily was an isolated incident, as many of the students would write to us afterwards thanking us for our warmth and hospitality. We have many happy memories of that house and even today recall happy times spent there.

The house was haunted by a little boy who used to come down from what would have been the servant's quarters on the third floor. Jeremy would line up all his star wars toys at night, only to find in the morning that they were all over the place. First of all we thought it a coincidence, but eventually Jeremy saw him, and described him in the clothes of the period, with one of the big caps that boys used to wear in Victorian times. He also liked mirrors, because I would frequently find the small mirror from my dressing table on the floor, and until Jeremy told me about the little boy, I would wonder how this kept happening. I would talk out loud to this little boy, never quite knowing if he was in the room or not at the time, as I strangely never saw him. I used to tell him that he was welcome to look at my things as long as he put them back afterwards. After that, my mirror was never on the floor again. He was also told that he could play with the Star Wars, but again could he put them back as he found them. What would a child of that period make of Star Wars anyway! From then on it was tidy.

One very hot afternoon during the summer holidays, the boys were going over to the park to kick the football about. They asked me to go with them, as I was having a bit of a down day. I was having one of my panicky times and I used to get so fed up with myself, although this illness never affected my ability to make decisions or make money. I felt I always had to be strong for the boys, but they in return knew that I needed some support, and as

157

far as they could they helped me as well. So I accepted their kind offer and went to the park with them, and promptly sat under a tree, looking across at our lovely house. How grand the houses must have been when they were built, and still were, built by Decimus Burton, the famous Victorian architect. Ours had been owned originally by a Lord and Lady, and I was imagining how lavishly some of the rooms would have been furnished. Staff would have occupied the top floor, with nurseries underneath. I was daydreaming of a bygone era when suddenly, from out of nowhere, a little man appeared.

He was incredibly unreal looking. "Hello," he said. I was so intrigued by his looks, and staring at him I replied, "Hello." This little man had extraordinary eyes. They were so pale, the palest I have ever seen. His hair was long and plaited. He was like an elf, and he had a dog with him. He proceeded to sit down and talk to me, and I knew it was no coincidence that he'd come. He asked me about myself, and I told him how I wanted to be more 'normal' like other people were, how I wanted to live a quiet life, earning my living and looking after my sons, away from the madding crowd that I always seemed to attract. And I told him how I'd had this problem with panic attacks for so long and I was weary of it all. He spoke to me for two hours, sitting on a tree stump opposite me. He told me things that I knew he had come to tell me, and I listened with great interest. "You will always be surrounded by people," he said, "wherever you are, there will be lots of people wanting to listen to you." "Oh dear, really?!" I exclaimed with a certain amount of surprise. He continued, "You have a lot of information to pass on, and that is what you must do, and you'll enjoy it." He said lots of things. I was fascinated by him. He was surreal, and quite amazing. Then he disappeared as quickly as he came. The boys came over to me. "Mum you didn't play football with us. Why were you talking for so long to that man? Who was he?" I just smiled at them, "Sorry." I did see this man again briefly when he called at my house and told me he was on his way to Glastonbury. I do believe that there are angels here on earth who appear when you need them, and he was one of them.

After having had students for a year, I decided to turn the rooms into bed-sits. The money would be more regular, and I wouldn't

158

have all the cooking to do. I went to talk to the estate agents to see what rents I could command, and to see if it was a viable option. Whilst I was there discussing my options with Beverly, a man came into the office. He was a rather large, rather shabby man. Beverly suddenly said to me, "Stella, you must meet Mr. Pierpoint. He was the country's hangman." He turned to face me, and a chill went right through my body. He said to me rather proudly, "I've topped over four hundred people, including Ruth Ellis." I couldn't believe it. There was this man who to all intents and purposes looked like any other man. He was like any other man, except he wasn't, because he had been the British hangman. I was in deep shock, and when he held out his hand to me to shake hands, I pretended that I didn't notice, I couldn't bear him to touch me. I could hear myself saying 'father forgive him for he knows not what he's done'.

I am totally against capital punishment, the whole thing sickens me. I'm glad that we don't have it anymore. It never stopped murder, and it wasn't a deterrent. I personally believe that if we had an education system that was brilliant for all our children, we wouldn't have the wide social divide between the haves and the have-nots. The majority of people who commit murder have not had the benefits of a good education, and subsequently do not go on to college or university. They are nearly always from abused and battered backgrounds, uneducated families, and families living in poverty. In America on death row, most of the murderers awaiting execution are black. That must tell us something about our unjust and unequal society, mustn't it?

Mr Pierpoint then invited me for a sherry one afternoon. It turned out that he lived around the corner from me. It would be like drinking blood, I thought. I thanked him very much for his kind invitation as I backed out of the office and fled. I had only gone into the office for some advice on rents. Oh my God.

So I did my rooms out as bed-sits, with all the necessary furniture and each equipped with cooking facilities. Then I placed my advertisement in the local newspaper. All but two rooms were taken very quickly, and those two weren't quite ready, so I didn't mind. Then one day, a couple turned up at my door enquiring about a room. I explained that the rooms weren't quite ready. Could they come back in a few days time? With that, the young lady all but passed out on me. She was obviously not at all well, and both of them looked so forlorn. "Please can we stay with you?' she begged. "We don't mind where we sleep. We won't be any bother, please don't send us away." I couldn't turn them out, I could see that they were all in. "I have a little room," I said. "There's not much furniture in it but you are welcome to stay there until your room is ready." She thanked me repeatedly. It turned out that they had been in a mental hospital, in fact they had met in a mental hospital and fallen in love, they were such a sweet couple. They idolised each other, and they were to stay with me for a year altogether.

It was such a happy house and I think it rubbed off onto everyone who came into it. Julian had by this time passed his driving test, and it was an exuberant young man who ran all the way back from the test centre, into the dining room at Anglesea where Lizzie and I were having coffee. It was nice to see him so happy, and on the strength of passing his test, I bought him a Triumph Dolomite Sprint in British racing green, with wire wheels. This car was the love of his life, and he started to become more and more confident as the months went by. He had a good friend called Ross who he had met at Bexhill Sixth Form College. Ross' mother, Mary, and I became friends as well, and we used to have glorious Italian evenings. We all shared a passion for food. I would make a huge lasagne, and serve it with salad, lots of lovely tomatoes, and crusty garlic bread. This would be followed by sherry trifle, not very Italian but very heavenly. We would then all sit there drinking the wine that I'd accumulated from the German students and thoroughly enjoy ourselves. Jeremy, not being old enough to drink much, had a little taster, so as to not be left out, and he used to giggle such a lot afterwards. Mary remembers the evenings and the happiness we shared as if it was yesterday. She worked in the local hospital, and many's the time she would fall through my door in a state of complete exhaustion. I would gently put my hands on her head and she would fall asleep. Mary was the other person who had seen the space ship years earlier. She had been on her way back from the hospital in the early evening when she saw it hovering over Sedlescombe. She got quite close to it, and she

160

told me that she actually said to herself 'Dear God, please let me get home to my son'. Strange that I should get to meet two other people who also saw it. Still they say 'Nothing in life is a coincidence'.

Sally would frequently pop in and out of our house. She found the goings on quite exciting. 'Never a dull moment in this house, is there my dear?' she used to say. In the summer, Sally used to go up to her late husband's family estate in Scotland after meeting the Queen Mother's Equerry in London. Sally was a brilliant neighbour, a little removed from reality at times, and still living in the past when she was obviously very well off. Her situation now was not at all what she had been used to, but she was a Christian and therefore, always cheerful. On one occasion, she came round very distressed and asked me to help her. She had been going to the dentist and had undergone extensive treatment at great cost, without realising it. When the bill was given her she was amazed and horrified that the bill was so high. "What shall I do, my dear?" she asked, "I can't possibly pay it. Oh dear, I'm so worried, what shall I do, my dear?" Poor Sally. She was so out of touch with prices, she hadn't thought of getting an estimate like the rest of us. She still lived in the days when she could have had anything done. I rang the dentist and explained the situation to him, and asked if he would very kindly take instalments. He agreed. The relief was so great to Sally when I told her it was alright. (She could keep her teeth). "Oh, thank you, my dear," she said with enormous relief, "what would we all do without you?" Sometimes she would come round and instruct me to ring someone up, making me feel like her staff. I used to ask her what her last slave died of. There would be a pause whilst she collected herself, and then she would come back down to planet earth, and laugh. I liked Sally very much. I always rang whoever it was for her, as I enjoyed helping her.

Although Julian hadn't liked the William Parker School, I nevertheless let Jeremy go there when he reached the age for secondary school. He wanted to be with his friend who was going there, so I agreed. I thought it might suit him better than Julian, after all, there were hundreds of boys going there, and some of them must like it. And it did, after all, have a very good record of exam results. Jeremy had never been very good at liking school, so it was important that he liked wherever he went. He hadn't been going to the school for very long, when he told me that he had been sent to see the school psychologist. I had just picked him up from school in the car, and he told me very quietly about it, taking it in his stride. I knew he found life very hard, and he'd suffered very much from the divorce. It was during this period that I'd been converting the basement flat, so there was a lot going on and that probably made it tougher for him to cope. Children suffer much more than we realise, they often don't bounce back the way we are always being told they do. Things became difficult when one day he refused to go to school, and one of the masters had to come and fetch him. I almost begged Jeremy not to upset the boat, insisting that he had to go as it was the law, and I would get into trouble if he didn't go. If I could have afforded it and we had lived nearer I would have sent him to one of the Steiner schools. But we didn't live near one, and to have made him a boarder would have in my opinion made him worse. So I had to try and make things as nice as I could for him.

When he'd been at the infant school in Westfield, Jeremy had written a poem called 'Stonehenge Awake'. At first I couldn't believe that he'd written it, as he was only seven, but the teacher confirmed that he had. I knew then that he was not going to be like other children, this was a very serious soul with a high degree of sensitivity. I mention that just so you can understand what sort of child he was.

Then as if seeing the counsellor wasn't bad enough for him, he suffered a punishment at the school, which was hardly going to endear him to the school, and made my blood boil. On this particular day, I picked Jeremy up from school as usual. He was very sombre. "My back hurts so much Mum, can you carry my bag for me?" he said. I picked up the bag for him wondering what he had done to injure himself. My poor little lad looked so forlorn. "I'll have a look at it when we get home," I said. Jeremy continued, "I was punished today in the gym lesson, and I had to climb the ropes in the gymnasium and stay there for ages." I said, "What, they did what?" I could hardly believe my ears. What had they done to him? When we got home I took his shirt off, the muscles across his back stood out like hard-boiled eggs. I was livid. I was at boiling point. "What on earth were you doing to get a punishment like that?" I asked. 'I was talking to my friend' was the reply.

It reminded me of my own school days then. I had always been in trouble for talking. Was it such a major crime to talk? If it was, why not issue lines? I did millions of them 'I must not talk.......' Actually I have news for teachers. Nervous children, of which I was one and Jeremy was another, cannot help talking. In itself, it's a nervous habit. It's hardly naughty, is it? It's not like being rude or thieving or bunking off is it? Looking down at Jeremy, I thought of him suspended in the air. Supposing he'd fallen from where he was hanging. What sort of school was this after all? No wonder we produce so many thugs in this country, when children are treated with such disrespect and violence from adults. Doesn't it cross anyone's mind in this country that kids emulate adults? Off I went to the school again. If I could have got hold of this 'person', I won't call him a man, I could easily have hung him from the ceiling myself. I asked to see the games master, but he refused to see me. I looked all over the building, but he knew I was coming and I just couldn't find him. How cowardly, I thought, he didn't want to pick on an adult then. So I saw the headmaster instead. I told him all about it, and how disgusted I was that this master wouldn't face me. What could he say? Nothing. So I informed him that Jeremy would also be leaving, to go to Claverham College in Battle. How proud he must be of some of his staff. So Jeremy went off to school in Battle. This was becoming a habit! Fortunately, the experience didn't have any lasting psychological effects, and Jeremy settled into his new school, and he didn't have to see the school psychologist any more either.

I was still going to see Peter, and on one of my visits, I noticed on the bookshelf in the waiting room, books by someone called Ronald Beasley. They were all to do with spirituality and re-incarnation, and a college called White Lodge. Peter asked me if I was interested in going on a course and learning more about it, to which I replied that I was.

The course was to be held in a village just outside Worthing, called Steyning. I was extremely nervous at the thought of going to a strange place, with a lot of people that I didn't know, but I was going to go. I felt very strongly that this was something that I had to do. Peter suggested that I rang up a woman whose name was Pearl, who normally travelled up with him, and ask her if she would like to travel with me, I could at least get to know her on the journey, and then I'd know one more person apart from Peter. I rang her up and introduced myself, and explained to her what Peter had said, and asked if she would like to travel with me. But no, she didn't want to change her travel arrangements, as she enjoyed so much going with Peter. She sounded very nice, though, and we both said we looked forward to seeing each other on the course. I contacted Peter again and he found me someone else to go with. It was decided that I should ask Sylvia, who lived in Ashford, Kent, and so I rang her up. As it was a long journey from Ashford to Steyning, she was delighted to break her journey by staying with me overnight, then travelling to Steyning together. Good, I thought, someone to go with, I couldn't have got there on my own, and I looked forward to meeting her. I felt that if she belonged to White Lodge, she must be very nice. I had been told by Peter that White Lodge was a very friendly place, full of my type of people, upstairs people.

Sylvia came over as planned the night before we were due to go to Steyning, and we got on very well right from the start. When we got up the next morning it had snowed heavily. We debated whether to travel or not, because of the condition of the roads. I decided it would be alright to drive if I stuck to the main roads and was extra careful.

For breakfast Sylvia proceeded to eat what looked like ceiling tiles, and they smelt really weird. "What on earth are you eating?" I asked, "wouldn't you prefer some toast?" "I have an allergy to wheat," she said, "these are made from rice." Years later, I couldn't believe that I would also be told that I couldn't eat wheat, as I, too, had an allergy, and that I would actually enjoy eating ceiling tiles (I mean rice cakes).

We set off allowing ourselves plenty of time in case the roads were treacherous, so as to arrive in time for the course which began at 10.30 a.m. The roads were very slippery, but I was always reckoned to be a good driver, and I drove very carefully. Then a series of things happened that were uncanny. We were driving along a road at the back of Brighton, when suddenly, I slid into the snow covered grass verge. I assumed it was just the slippery road, and that I must be more careful. It was a fairly new car, so I got out and looked to see if I had damaged it, but it seemed alright, so I got back in. I apologised to Sylvia for what I thought was my driving, and we proceeded on our way. Then it happened again, but this time I felt the car was pushed, and I hit the verge with a bang. Sylvia felt the car was pushed as well, and we both felt very jittery. "What's happening?" said Sylvia, sounding very concerned. "I've no idea, I'll go more slowly," I replied, although not very confidently. We continued on our journey and a little way further down the road it happened again, but this time the car was pushed with such a force that I hit the kerbstone with a mighty bang. I was no longer confident, in fact I was terrified. We were both terrified. My car was slightly damaged this time, and I suddenly wanted to go home very quickly. Something very unpleasant did not want me to get to White Lodge. I say me because Sylvia had been before and had always arrived unscathed. "Why on earth would whatever it is not want you to get there?" Sylvia asked me, not quite knowing what she meant. I had no idea what it was, or why it didn't want me to go either, I just knew it was a dark feeling and very scary. I turned around and began to drive home fast. We both thought it was nevertheless a shame to miss the course. As I was driving homewards, I suddenly had a very strong feeling that I had to go to White Lodge. Was this the journey that I was told I had to go on, when Doug and I went to the Spiritualist Church? I had a strong feeling that I must not give in to whatever it was, but I must fight it. "I'm turning the car around," I said, to Sylvia's horror. I did turn round and with the bit between my teeth and great determination I drove, with both of us totally terrified. We were only a bit late for the start of the course, but Peter didn't seem at all surprised at what had happened. All in a days work it seemed! What had I let myself in for, I wondered? I was told to protect myself with white light at all times, because when you are a bright light, as I was told I was, the dark elements would be attracted to me. In other words, they would see me much more clearly, as I shone out. This I learned very quickly and I was to surround myself for evermore with white light before I went out, or if I was in a situation where I felt uncomfortable. In fact, I used to do it before I went anywhere where there were going to be a lot of people. If on certain occasions I forgot to do that exercise, I would get a very light headed feeling and sometimes my head would reel with dizziness, I knew then that I was out of my body and I would need to be put back in. It would be years before I learnt to control that side of my life.

I learnt all about auras, what they are and what they meant. An aura is like a rainbow around your head and your body. The aura is oval and consists of five colours plus a greyish white. The aura can tell your state of health and general well being, physically and mentally. And much more besides. It's a complete record of everything about you. I explain about human auras in a bit more detail later on, when I realised that I could actually see them. As I said earlier, I'd been aware of auras and seen them from a very early age around trees and plants. The glow had always fascinated me, and as a child I stood and stared mesmerised by the light. My mother would often say 'Come on dolly daydream, wake up'. I naturally thought that everyone saw them. Why wouldn't I? When I looked at the trees they glowed brightly like the Ready Brek advert, with a white light all around them.

I hadn't been on a residential course before, and I naturally thought I would be sharing a room with Sylvia. But no, to my shock and horror I was to share a room with a total stranger, and I was alarmed. I needn't have been though, because Wendy my roommate was a lovely, kind person. She very quickly put me at my ease, and I felt lucky to be with her. This course was also my first introduction to starvation. The course fee included lunch, which was a bit measly, but evening meals were down to us. We were supposed to go into Steyning and find a restaurant, and I was put in charge of the group. The blind leading the blind comes to mind. No one had researched this idea because eating places were either closed or very expensive. We ended up in a pub having an orange juice and crisps because that was all that was on offer. When I got back to my room I was starving. Courses and any type of intensive learning can make one very hungry. Bearing in mind that I had got up early, driven in thick snow and hair raising conditions, had a lettuce leaf and bowl of soup for my lunch, I was more than ready to eat anything. I went down to the kitchens and to my surprise found they were locked. My blood sugar level was dropping and I knew I would have to have something to eat. I began asking other students if they had anything at all that I could eat. One had a biscuit and another had an apple. Some of the others who were more clued up on the courses had the foresight to bring their own food, and had eaten it. I would know next time to bring essential supplies.

I ate as large a breakfast as I could muster next morning and wandered into the classroom ready to learn as much as I could. It was all so interesting, I listened to Peter explaining how we were miniature universes, living in a large universe. We learned how the body is a finely tuned machine quite capable of healing itself, but what with contaminated food, air and water, how difficult it is to stay healthy, even if one was very careful. On top of that, if one didn't care and over indulged in excesses of sex, drugs and alcohol, one could damage the astral body part of the aura. I liked the bit about how we were in the world but not of it, and you don't make friends, you just meet them again. Isn't that lovely? It means that when we come back for our next life we are with some of the same people again. What a reassuring thought that is. All the people doing the course believed in re-incarnation and healing, and the atmosphere was electric. The students included some osteopaths, naturopaths, and even a few doctors, who were interested in healing. There were simply masses of things to absorb. Some I will go into later in the book. At the end of the morning session, Peter was asking if anyone had any questions, and a middle aged woman asked a question about capital punishment. She seemed to be in favour of it. A shudder went through me. As I said previously, I am fiercely against this, and I must say that I thought this was a strange question to come up, as we were all supposed to be visionaries, and above revenge. I do not remember what the answer was. I was keen to get out of the room and away from that person. And I hadn't protected myself with light, I had thought myself safe in that environment!

It was lunch time and I was ready to eat a hearty meal. Then something very strange and horrible happened to me. I was aware suddenly, that I was beginning to shake, and I thought it was just me feeling nervous or something. I thought if I ate my lunch I would feel better. I collected my meal and sat down. Sylvia and her friend, plus three other people sat at the table with me. I could not control my hands at all, as they were shaking so much. I was getting very scared and was trying to attract Sylvia's attention but to no avail. The others were eating their lunch and discussing the morning lectures, not realising the torment I was feeling. The lady opposite asked me if I had lost my appetite, to which I replied that I seemed to have. I was very embarrassed and frightened at my dilemma, sitting there with my lunch untouched and the soup cold. I desperately wanted to eat and drink something, but I wouldn't have got the fork to my mouth with my shaking arms, and then my body began to shake as well, I thought it was some kind of fit. I tried to mime to Sylvia that I was in trouble, but Sylvia was oblivious to my dilemma, she smiled back at me and kept eating and talking. When the plates were cleared away mine was still full of food. I hadn't been able to eat anything and I knew I would be hungry later.

The others on my table moved away and left Sylvia and me behind. "I don't know what's wrong to me," I said, and by this time my body was shaking uncontrollably. She seemed to know at once what had happened, "I was afraid this might happen," she said. "When a person is dealing with this heavy spiritual stuff, they need to know how to handle it. It's dynamite." And she went on to say that perhaps, the new students should have been shown how to protect themselves before the lecture began. "It can be very dangerous." In fact, one of the things that we had discussed in the lecture was that mental homes were full of people who had woken up too quickly, in the spiritual sense, and how it must be done very gently. I was already a spiritually awake person, so that didn't apply to me, but what I didn't realise was that in that electrically charged environment I should have protected myself from people who maybe weren't as pure as they might have been. I should have surrounded myself with light, and maybe crossed my arms or legs, but I was still learning all about protection, and anyway in a place like that I wouldn't have thought it necessary to protect myself. Lesson number one learned! But perhaps that was part of my training, for me to see how dangerous it could be, and what could happen to me if I didn't protect myself fully. I was very alarmed by this time and my symptoms were just as I imagine a fit to be. I was out of control. Sylvia tried to talk me through it but it wasn't working. I felt I was in a dangerous state. 'I'm never coming again' was all I could say, and 'I wish I was at home.'

Just then, one of the senior members had come looking for us, as the afternoon lecture had begun. She quickly realised what had happened and told Sylvia to go back to the classroom, as she would look after me. I gathered that I was "out of my body". Shock probably had caused this. When a spiritual person is in a spiritual environment it's normal for that person to relax completely, like a rose unfolding its petals in the sun. We have chacras throughout our bodies and they are like flowers, but we must learn only to unfold their petals when it is safe to do so. My chacras must have been open when the lady talked about capital punishment and this was enough to send me spiralling into shock. I was put back together and had a walk around the garden with this lady. She insisted that I stand on the earth outside and get myself completely grounded. Then we went back into the classroom, and this time I was surrounded by light. Peter looked at me, smiled and said 'welcome back', as if he knew again what had happened to me.

I was to learn a lot about myself during the next few weeks, largely thanks to Sylvia. The course was over two weekends and I was naturally terrified about returning the next weekend, but I made myself go back nevertheless. It was still a bit snowy the next weekend but not as bad as last time, and I actually enjoyed the second weekend much more. I made friends with Pearl, she was so nice and friendly and held my hand when I felt insecure. Pearl was the deputy head teacher at a primary school and a much loved person. I also befriended Merlyn. What a wizard name! We only have to meet and we make each other laugh so much, like two naughty schoolchildren.

Sylvia came back to the house after the course, and we celebrated the end of the course with a Chinese meal. Back to real food again and lots of it. Sylvia suddenly said to me "You can see auras around people!" I replied that I didn't think so. She was very persistent, and offered to stand against the wall, asking me to look at the top of her head. "Stare at the top of my head," she said. "What can you see?" I looked and it was amazing. I could see a glowing light all around her head, and some colours, a pink and a green. "There," she said, "I knew you could see them." She was very pleased with herself. As I'd said earlier, I had always seen what I now know is called an aura around trees and bushes, but I hadn't thought to look above peoples' heads. After the Sylvia revelation I would walk about staring at the tops of peoples heads. Sometimes they would give me strange looks back, and I would have to quickly look away, only to look back again when they weren't looking. They must have wondered what on earth I was staring at. It was all so interesting, everything I looked at had a light around it, whether it was a person, a tree, a plant, my cat, especially my cat, an ornament or a book. I could even hold things and get a feeling about the person who'd either made it, owned it, or given it to me.

Everybody has an aura, and just like our finger prints, each persons differs, so none are alike. That is incredible when you think how many people there are on this planet! In our aura is stored all the information about ourselves. From the beginning of our life to the end. All is recorded in the six colours of our aura. Which again are, Whitish-Greyish in the history of our birth, Pinky-Red in our emotional record, Yellow-Gold in our mental capacity, Green - the astral body, Blue in our psycho sense, and Soft Mauve/Purple in our spiritual depth. Here is a more extensive description of each colour.

White. The first stage of the aura, in which is recorded the complete miracle of life, and how we came into being originally. We all have a magnetic field around us, which also acts like a thermal covering. This covering is a source of heat conservation and protection, and this is where what's left of our animal instincts and awareness of danger comes from. Any turbulence, disharmony, pain or discomfort in our lives will be recorded here. If we are healthy we shine clearly. If we are ill the white becomes dulled and turgid.

Red. This is the price we pay for being above the animals, the ability to suffer joy, pain and discomfort. This region in the aura is heart red. The blood and emotions are very interwoven making possible our participation in creation, so not only does this area show the emotional balance, but is the plane from which the family emerges. We have strong survival forces so the need to procreate is strong in us. The love of family, whether parent, child, brother, sister, or lover all have their roots in this sphere. Strangely enough, this is also the zone of love and hate. So closely are they related that it is sometimes difficult to tell them apart. Emotional disturbance is often the root of many illnesses.

Yellow. This is where we live and dwell. This is the thinking part of ourselves, and our personalities. Thought is the substance of creation, the invisible suit we wear at all times in our thinking life, and is the result of the existence of a higher consciousness - the permanent other self. It is not possible for a full conscious state to incarnate in a restricted mortal mind. So much of our wisdom, knowledge and mental capacity is held in reserve in the higher state and only in exceptional circumstances can full meditation and spiritual sensitivity be tuned into. We arrive with no memory of past lives, thus removing the possibility of ulterior motive. We must do things because we want to and not for any reward. Early formative thinking lives have to suffer much conditioning. One half of the mental life is spent collecting unsuitable material, the other half in getting rid of it. The mind is a long way behind its tremendous abilities, it's only on the fringe of its potential. We do not use our minds enough, we do not stretch ourselves enough, for we have come for spiritual development. The aura portents indicate the wonderful future awaiting the human and spiritual forces, once it can be freed from its primitive and destructive past.

These three colours are limited fields, instinctive, emotional and mental, and are what we refer to as our third dimensional selves. We have other fields of perception as well. The areas of intuition, mind creativeness, an awareness above the physical realm, the existence of another level of consciousness which has been referred to as the psychic or astral state, though neither word really describes this extra sensory extension of our higher or other self.

171

This is our fourth dimensional domain where our more permanent self resides, the invisible part of us, which can be seen only by those who possess this other awareness.

Green. The Astral Body, which is a psychic or astral state. This separates the two levels of man, the first three being limited to third-dimensional laws, the need for long hours of sleep. Sleep being the temporary separation of the levels of consciousness so that they may be recharged and re-instructed from the energy level to which they belong. Waking is the drawing together again of these levels. The physical body is, in a way, draped on the astral body very much like an earth suit on a model. Man being a two dimensional being. The lovely shade of green acts as a buffer between the higher and lower personality, and protects us from lower astral forces, when through wrong use, such as over use in sex, damage by prolonged drug taking, and the experimenting with drugs for kicks, also other drugs in uncontrolled conditions, cause the protective area to be weakened. This in turn opens the way to mental disturbances and in cases where astral protection is not strong, it is very unwise and dangerous, to expose oneself to psychic or astral phenomena conditions. Better to live a simple life of faith.

Blue. The Spiritual body, which is defined in the deepest of lovely blues. When it is radiant it is beautiful to behold; it seems to be a cradle holding all it's lesser but nevertheless important partners in its folds, holding together a celestial form of Divine origin. The soul form is that part of the spiritual structure which is able to project itself into space; the soul forms a sort of body attached to the spirit and acts as an intermediary between the other bodies. It is the link between mind and spirit. In sleep it uses the astral form as a means of travel and at the moment of death or re-birth, separates entirely from its physical attachment. The spirit is the true self, this is our eternal body.

Then we come to the Etheric Body This brings us to that part of the aura which is not always discernible in that it represents the light energy of the spirit and only in special circumstances can this be seen. This the Etheric Body is composed of pure light, but its wavelength to us shows as a soft mauve or purple. The etheric spirit form is composed of light atoms which make it possible to travel the great astral sphere as we know it. Where the astral body is able to travel the great astral sphere, the spirit body can soar the heavens in its pilgrimage towards the stars of its future home. This explains the apparent appearance and disappearance of these higher bodies because of the alteration of wavelengths. It also explains the fading in and out of our vision - by raising or lowering the vibrational rate, as our heavenly visitors come and go on their earthly missions - for each dimension merges into the other. We are surrounded by angel beings.

The human body itself is a beautiful complex co-ordinated mechanism, in health a delight to the artist - to the soul a vehicle to explore and learn of lovely things. In sleep using our astral form, can be united with familiar things and continue in touch with the home of our coming. The soul soars forth to places of learning, continuing its growth and upward path. The spirit on wings of etheric light has many mansions or dimensions to visit, learn and enjoy as it grows in stature and strength to become a light of the heaven, indeed Christ arisen in every one of us.

(Extracts taken from The Robe of Many Colours by R. P. Beesley. Now out of print, but incorporated into "The Robe of Spiritual Gifts", a White Lodge Publication).

After the experience with Sylvia and the discovery that I could see human auras, Jeremy and I were messing about one afternoon in the sitting room. He wanted to see auras as well, so I sat on the settee and told him to go across to the other side of the room and look at the top of my head. He went and stood by the television set, a good fifteen feet away from me. What happened next was nothing short of incredible. He became self-hypnotised, and looking over my head started to say in a strange voice, "Who are you?" I replied, "I'm Mum." Jeremy, still in his hypnotised state, said again, "No you're not, who are you? You have very dark skin, and there is a rainbow right across your head." I realised he was in a complete trance and told him again that I was his mother. He wasn't having any of it and continued, "There is someone standing behind you. It's an Angel. Who are you?" I sensed he was getting a little distressed now, and I told him not to worry, because what he was seeing was very good. He then went on to say that he could see a door opening behind me, and he could see a little girl go through the door. When I turned round to have a look myself, the picture behind me moved.

Julian had now come into the room and being a typical teenager and a bit of a cynic, made some remark to the effect of what the hell were we up to. He then said he would look at me from across the room to prove there was nothing there. He then let out a succession of expletives enough to frighten off anything Holy, which I couldn't repeat. "What can you see?" I was asking. "Oh, Christ," he said, "I'll never be able to tell anyone what I've just seen." "That's a shame," I remarked, "what have you seen?" "A face," was all he would say, "a face." And it really shocked him. I later took them both over to Peter's house where he showed Jeremy a picture of an Angel. "Is this what you saw?" he asked, to which Jeremy replied yes. "How wonderful," said Peter, "how absolutely marvellous." That was an incredible evening, but the sad thing was that we couldn't tell everybody about it, because they just wouldn't believe it. Julian was very busy studying for his A-levels at Bexhill College, and he wasn't really into all this spiritual stuff, as he called it. And it can be quite scary if it's not understood.

Life at Anglesea Terrace was many things, but never dull. I was extremely busy. I had my bed sits now, bringing in a regular income. I still had the special young couple I mentioned earlier, who were to stay with me for about a year altogether. The young woman, would like to sit with me during an evening if I wasn't busy. She'd had a tough life, with sexual abuse resulting in her having a child with learning difficulties. She very rarely left the room when they first lived with me, but gradually more and more she went out. I think love is the best medicine in the world, and time, giving people time. I became very fond of her.

I had converted the basement, with all that entailed, and then sold it. My sons both needed a lot of my time, and the three of us were very close. Any little problem they had I tried to sort it out. We talked about everything. Nothing was too insignificant to warrant a discussion. They were my life. Neighbours were in and out all the time. Our home was the hubbub of the Universe at times. Sally knew some very interesting people, and she would bring them round to meet me. One of them had been a Tiller girl, and in her seventies could still kick her legs right up in the air. We had a lot of laughter and occasionally a lot of tears.

I thought I might have another fight on my hands over Jeremy. His father had gone to the school insisting that I was a bad mother. I was called to the school, and ushered into a little room, where Mitch was in full flow telling a group of teachers, including the head of year, untruths about me. The things he said were unbelievable. One of the things was that Jeremy couldn't do his schoolwork because I made him vacuum our home at night! And lots of other things. I really thought that I was going to lose Jeremy. This was serious stuff being hurled at me. It was like a trial, but not a proper trial because I wasn't allowed to say anything in my defence. I don't know why they asked me to go, I never said a word. I left the room in a state of absolute shock, disbelief and total fear. I walked along the corridor towards the main door wondering what Mitch was up to now. Why would he want to harm Jeremy, because harm was what he would do to him. I thought that I would definitely lose Jeremy this time, when suddenly there was an arm on mine, and a strong but gentle voice saying, "How long has this been going on, I mean with your ex husband, I know the things he said are not true. Can't people see what's going on?" He continued, "Well, it's obvious to me, and I want you to know that I am here for you, Mrs F." How long had it all been going on? About twenty years, I thought to myself, then I repeated it out loud. "It's been going on for about twenty years, and no, no one has ever been able to help me fight him." "I'll help you, don't worry any more. I can see right through him." He was a very senior man at the school, and bearing in mind that Julian had gone to the school for five years, I guess this man would have known what sort of mother I was. I was so glad to have him on my side. At last someone in authority was on my side. Sally had gone with me and waited outside in the car park. When I appeared all hysterical and explained what had happened, she in her calm well-bred manner said quietly "You just wait and see my dear, all will be well. Things have a way of sorting themselves out." I didn't know how. I was worried sick again. This blasted man,

was there to be no peace ever? On returning home, I relayed the
story to Julian and asked if he would be willing to give evidence
for me if necessary if I had to fight for custody. He said he would.
What a thing for him to have dumped on him in the middle of 'A'
levels.

Within a couple of weeks Mitch suffered a heart attack whilst on
holiday in France. His brother rang up and told me to inform the
boys, as it was thought likely that Mitch might not survive. I was
then informed that it was my fault that his brother had suffered a
heart attack. What!!! I was very hurt and upset at that remark.
Mitch and I hadn't been married for years. I'd had very little
contact with him for ages. Even the business at the school had
been him saying things about me. I didn't even get the chance to
retaliate or defend myself, I had never ever been able to retaliate to
anything he did, but anyway that's not me to act like that. But
John needed someone to blame, and I was an easy target. That
was a hell of a lot to have dumped on me, and many times over the
following years I was to think about John's accusation. I knew in
my heart it was an unjust remark, but because all during my
marriage to Mitch I'd thought everything was my fault, even if it
rained it was my fault, part of my brain still carried on thinking it
must have been my fault. It was incredible really when I thought
about it. I hadn't seen Mitch to talk to since leaving Hedgerows. I
was even financially independent. The boys received
maintenance, but I didn't need it any more, I was well set up now.
I was told repeatedly by family and friends not to be so stupid any
more. I was not responsible for him. I remembered then that
Mitch had talked of dying young from when I first met him. He
was quite a gloomy guy. So was this a kind of self-fulfilling
prophecy that fortunately hadn't ended up with him dying. We
were all very relieved that he didn't die. It wasn't very nice of
John to say that to me, and anyway it's not really on is it, to blame
someone else? We all of us must reap the consequences of our
actions. I've done things in my life that I am not very proud of,
but I'm learning all the time. And I certainly wouldn't blame
anyone else but me for my mistakes. People are basically very
selfish aren't they? How often do you hear people say that
whatever it was, it wasn't their fault?

I had a good circle of friends, plus all those I had met at White Lodge. I felt that the romantic side of my life, or lack of it, was a waste of time. I couldn't meet anyone with whom I felt totally right, and I didn't think that I ever would, so one day whilst sitting by the fire I decided not to bother any more. I would settle for what I'd got. I'd got my sons, I had a nice home, an income and lots of friends and that was more than most, and I would be content with that. But fate was to take a hand, and all was to change.

I had to go to the accountant about company business, and whilst I was with him, he asked me how I was getting on with the bank, and did I have any problems? Well I did have a problem. I found the manager rude, offhand and generally creepy. He had even rung me at home, announcing himself as Chris, on the pretext of bank business. Keith suggested that I go to see the new manager at another bank in St. Leonards. I rang up and made an appointment to see the new manager, and I only had to wait a couple of days. Julian came with me, and we sat outside waiting to see the new manager, when all of a sudden this very tall and very lean youngish good-looking man rushed by us and disappeared into the manager's office. I didn't think anything of it at the time, and waited for my name to be called. I was very surprised to find out that this man was indeed the manager himself. He was not like any manager I had ever seen. They were usually over fifty, overweight, and balding. As I sat opposite him, we talked very easily as if we had known each other for years. I was very attracted to him, and I felt that he also liked me. His name was Mike, and he was getting divorced, he told me. It sounded better and better. I explained my difficulty with the manager at Barclays, and he told me that he would be only to happy to remove my account from there to his bank. As I had a very small overdraft with Barclays, Mike suggested he turned it into a mortgage, as I didn't already have a mortgage on my property. It sounded the obvious solution, what a brilliant idea. I would need to borrow to convert the rest of the flats, which I wouldn't even begin to do until Julian had taken his A-levels, then I could pay it all off when the flats sold. What a satisfactory meeting. He would have to come and look at the property to value it, so we arranged a suitable date.

When I next saw Sally I couldn't stop talking about my new Bank Manager, and she was to pull my leg about this every time we met. I mentioned earlier on when I was trying to sell Hedgerows about the retired Bank Manager who came and looked at the property, with a view to growing Christmas trees on the land. Little did I know then, in my sad moments, that his replacement was to play such a major role in my life.

Mike came round as planned to have a look at my property, and to value it for the bank. I knew I had done well in buying it. It was a five-floored Grade II Listed Decimus Burton house overlooking the park, a handsome house indeed. He was impressed with it and with what I had planned to do with it. A small mortgage he thought would be the ideal solution, as I more than had the income to sustain it, with my bed-sits, which were all let and bringing in a nice return. After coffee and a nice long chat, Mike left, and I sat wondering if anything might come of our meeting. I had a really good feeling about him.

A couple of months went by, and Christmas was coming. I thought I might have a party. I went and asked Keith the accountant if he might like to come and bring his girlfriend. To my surprise he told me to invite my new Bank Manager. I was not sure about this. After all I didn't really know him well enough to ask him to my party. Keith was adamant I should ask him, so very nervously I took an invitation round to the Bank and handed it in. To my surprise he said he would try and make it. He didn't know what other commitments he had on, but he would like to come if possible. Keith and Mike knew each other as they were both members of 'Mensa'.

I had been seeing a lot of Sylvia. We got on very well, and sometimes she would bring people from her group in Ashford to meet me. I told her about the party, and she said she would help me plan it. Unfortunately, Sylvia's idea of a party and mine were somewhat different. She thought loads of hot food would be a good idea. I only reckoned to do small bite sized things, nibbles and the such. I could no way afford to feed fifty people, it was

178

more of a drinks and nibbles do. This made her a bit disgruntled, saying things like 'Funny party. Party without food, whatever next?' I think it was very successful, nevertheless. There was plenty of alcohol. Jeremy was barman, which tickled everybody because of his knowledge of mixing drinks. He only looked about eight although he was thirteen. Mike did turn up, looking absolutely dishy, and perched on the Adam fireplace talking for quite a while to Keith my accountant. There were no expectations of lashings of food, and my nibbles did suffice, I think.

The guests gradually went home leaving just the few faithfuls, Sid and Wendy, Sylvia who was staying the night and Mike, which pleased me that he hadn't just turned up and then gone at the earliest opportunity. When he did eventually get up to go, I went to the front door with him, slightly nervous and awkward like you are with someone you like when you first meet them. To my delight he asked if I would go to a party with him after Christmas. I was over the moon with excitement. How on earth could I wait two weeks before I saw him again? I floated back into the sitting room. "I'm going to a party with him," I told Sylvia. "I thought you'd given up men," said Sylvia rather crossly. "So did I," I replied "but this is different, he's different." She was not happy with me, and she left very early in the morning with some excuse about having to meet someone. I didn't want to upset her, she was a good friend, but I knew that this man was different. I don't know how I got through Christmas. Mum came to stay, and Charles came on Boxing Day. It was all very pleasant, but I was wishing away the days until the 6th of January, the party. In fact, I didn't have to wait until the sixth to see him, he popped round over New Year with a Birthday card, and I knew he was just as anxious to see me as I was to see him.

I went with Mrs. Wallace to buy a dress for this special evening. She was just as excited as me, well not quite, but almost. Bless her heart, she gave me a fur coat, not real but a very good imitation made by a furrier. It looked like pale mink. I would be the bees knees. The party was in an oast house near Rye, and was the birthday party of a good friend of Mike's, a man called John. I very much enjoyed myself, and the evening was soon over. Mike asked me back to his flat for a coffee, and I agreed, glad he didn't just want to drop me off. As soon as we got into the flat he gathered me up in his arms and kissed me. I sensed his feelings for me and it was wonderful. I had a very good feeling about Mike. He was different to anybody else I had met. He was kind, considerate and so gentle. It was like coming home, I think I knew then that I had met my Soul Mate, and the man that the fortune teller had told me about, the one who was moving to Hastings.

We did so many things that I hadn't done for a long time. We went to a ball, to the theatre, we walked through Bluebell woods, we ate at lots of different restaurants. He belonged to Mensa and they organised quizzes and rambles, always ending up at the pub. It was all such fun, but I realised I wasn't spending enough time with my sons, and I was beginning to feel exhausted, so I suggested I spend a bit more time at home. To my surprise, Mike was quite happy to stay at home a bit more as well. He wasn't good with compliments. If I said he was lovely he would look at me and say 'No one has ever said that to me before'. I found it hard to believe that he wouldn't be showered with compliments, this very good-looking man.

Jeremy used to have transformers, which are toys that turned from robots into machines, and working Lego, and Mike and Jay would sit on the floor together for ages playing with these toys. Jay had tame rats, and Mike would let them walk all over him. His sons had never had any animals, due to the fact he said that his eldest son had asthma as a young child. I feel kids miss out if they don't have pets, as it teaches basic caring, when they have to look after the pets themselves. Sweeney and the two rats got on very well. They used to sit by the fire together. A lot of people encourage their animals to chase and be aggressive to other animals, but I never encouraged that. I used to tell Sweeney that we didn't do that kind of thing, and she didn't. I knew I had been with Sweeney in a past life. She was so beautiful, very Egyptian-looking and serene, hence I suppose her name, Serena. She was so affectionate and would sit and talk to me in her own way. She was lovely. I loved singing, and when I sang Sweeney would sit by my feet looking up at me and purring. I would sing 'I dreamt I dwelt in marble halls'. She loved that one.

I'd known that once Julian had taken his A-Levels we would have to move again in order to finish converting the other flats. I knew this was yet another upheaval for them, but there was no alternative, and before the exams even took place, I sounded out a suitable property to rent, back in Westfield, and signed the lease for six months. This was a great plus for Jay as most of his friends at school were his old friends from Westfield primary school.

I was worried then as to how my relationship would work out with Mike. At the moment he lived three minutes away, and it was all so convenient. I drove round to the flat to see him, and he was busy ironing as I relayed the details of what I'd had to arrange. He was very calm and collected. "Well it won't make any difference, darling," he said. "I can easily get to Westfield. Don't worry, nothing will change." I felt reassured. Anyway, I had no choice. I was doing the right thing.

Julian had opted to go to Hatfield Polytechnic (now The University of Hertfordshire), as the engineering course was ideal for him there, and I knew that as soon as we moved house Julian would be leaving us. Julian was glad that I had Mike around, if for no other reason than to operate the video player and the music centre! Cheek!

Going from an eight bedroomed house to a three bedroomed house meant getting rid of a lot of furniture, and Mike spent a lot of time going to and fro the dump for me. He was very helpful, and didn't mind what he did. He was so sweet. I had to rehouse the couple in the top flat who'd lived with me for a year. The Council gave them a flat, and we helped them move in and put curtains up. I wanted to make sure they would be alright. Rachael and Steve took quite a lot of things for their flat. They had got baby Shaun now who was about a year old. Everybody that came in was given armloads to take away with them. I had things like six metal teapot sets, six extra TVs, six fridges, all bed sit stuff. I was loading up everybody that came in with china, linen and goodness knows what. I just had to get rid of it all before moving day. Sally had a colour television set to replace her old black and white set. I was sad to leave her. She had been a superb neighbour.

It was yet another major upheaval for the boys, especially Jeremy, who had not long changed schools, back to Claverham College in Battle. Now he had to face another house move again. But at least he had friends in Westfield, so it wouldn't be quite so bad. We'd had such a lot of fun in this house, I thought, as I looked about me, with never ending people coming in and out. At least we'd laughed in this house, really laughed, which I hadn't done in previous years. Oh, happy memories. Memories that would last forever.

I said goodbye to Mrs Wallace, I would keep in touch I told her and I meant it.

Chapter 9 - Developments

It was great to be back in Westfield again, even if only for a short while. I hadn't a clue where I would eventually find a house to buy for the three of us. In that area I had hoped. We had a sweet old lady next door, who sometimes invited us in for tea. I'll always remember her because she was a great fan of Bob Geldorf, and was reading his autobiography. A more unlikely fan of Bob Geldorf you couldn't imagine. She used to giggle at some of the language, but it wouldn't be Bob Geldorf without the language. Most of us were totally overwhelmed at Live Aid, and how it brought the horrors of war and famine in Africa right into our sitting rooms. What a man. Nobody will accuse him of the road to Damascus. I digress.

Most of our furniture was in store again, but this time we were at least able to take quite a few more bits and pieces with us. Julian had taken a lot of his personal possessions with him to Hatfield, leaving all his other treasures in his room. I especially wanted my sons to have all their own belongings in their bedrooms, as we could be renting for up to a year. When the flats were finished and sold I could then look around for a suitable house to buy for us, and still have enough money left to buy another property for development purposes. This would enable us to have a nice home again, and for me to provide a good living for us all, with no more worries. I couldn't over the past few years ever envisage a life without worries, but at last my plans were now taking shape, and it was very exciting.

I entered into what was one of the most relaxed periods of my life so far. We were renting a sweet little house on an estate in the heart of the village. Although only ten years old, the houses had been designed and built with loads of character, and ours had been extended with great imagination. It also had a well thought-out paved courtyard garden with a few shrubs and a built in barbecue. The house in the village couldn't have been more different to Anglesea Terrace, my grand listed house, which I would always hold dear to my heart because of all the laughter and fun we'd shared there. I suppose the reasons I felt so relaxed now, were twofold. Firstly, I had Mike. My moving hadn't made any difference to us at all. He was still in and out as much as before. The second reason was that unlike the house in Anglesea Terrace, which had lots of to-ing and fro-ings going on all the time, now when I was at home I had a certain amount of peace. I could go home and shut the door, and that was worth its weight in gold. I would even sometimes have a nap in the afternoon, unheard of before. I felt at peace with the world. A nice young woman from the village called Pat came in and helped me with the housework. It was lovely to go home from the building site to a wonderfully clean and tidy house. What luxury. She was a clever young woman and a brilliant artist. She had a little girl to support and she needed the extra cash. There's such a lot of talent out there not really being used. Pat should have been teaching or running a gallery somewhere.

Mike had decided to do stage lighting at the Stables Theatre, the lovely small theatre in Hastings Old Town. Mike had so many interests he could hardly fit them all in. He had a check list of all the things he wanted to do, such as organisations he had to join, places he had to visit, restaurants we had to eat in. He was like a man who had been released from jail, a man who had felt life had almost passed him by, and had a lot of catching up to do. He exhausted me at times, and that takes some doing.

But there was another side to him, which I used to call his dark side. I had experienced it once or twice, and it was a little unnerving. His face would change, the shutters would come down in his mind, and he would go into a distant mode. He would then want to be all alone. He told me it was so that he could be sad on his own. I know we all need space, but this was different from that. This was a type of depression. He would say out of the blue, 'Leave me, I want to be alone'. And there was coldness with it. But the next day he would be all cuddly and sweet again and back to normal.

My agoraphobia completely disappeared in that house, it was incredible. It was as if I'd taken off a great big heavy overcoat, and the feeling of lightness was wonderful. Is that how other people feel every day of their lives? Wow! The freedom of being able to go out and about without that awful churning tight feeling was just fantastic. It shows what happens when the body is really happy and relaxed. And considering how busy I was with the flats conversion it was just amazing.

I had got together a brilliant team of sub-contractors. I couldn't use Ken any more, the builder who'd done the basement conversion for me. He had been very good, but I needed speed now. Speed was of the essence as I had a bank loan to think about. I had approached a couple of tradesmen whilst still at Anglesea Terrace, just before we moved out. One was the plumber who did the work on the flats I'd done previously with William. The other was a carpenter called Brian, recommended by the plumber. It is perfect when they recommend another tradesmen that they've worked with previously on a job, because you know they are going to work well together. Brian had come round and seen the job and found out exactly what was involved. Good tradesmen can pick and choose their work, so I hoped he would want the job. He took a set of plans away with him, in order to work out a quote for me, as I had to be able to afford whoever it was as well. Brian then came back with a quote that was acceptable, and when I enquired about other tradesmen he knew a plasterer whose name was John, and a bricklayer called Paul. One or other of them knew an electrician whose name was David, and somebody else knew some decorators called Jack and Mark. They all came round to see the job and collect a set of plans in order to work out quotes for me. The quotes were

185

accepted and so the team was formed. All I needed then was a roofer, a scaffolding company, the first of many skips, and an estimate for plastic windows.

A date was planned for starting the job, and I was very excited at the prospect. In fact it was an exciting time for the three of us. Julian was at University reading Engineering, Jeremy was back with his friends in Westfield, and learning to ride in his spare time, which he did very well, he was a natural. And I was just beginning the enormous task of doing my first major development on my own. I had been advised to form a limited company by my accountant, and this had already been set up in anticipation of this day. My company was called S.J. Developments Ltd. The S. J. was Stella Joan.

The scaffolding went up on the front and on the back of the property. The board levels had to be just right. They always ask you when you're ordering scaffolding what you need it for, so that they can get the levels right. For example, if they had a row of boards across the middle of a window you wouldn't be able to replace the windows, or mend them or paint them. And it had to be high enough for the roofer to put on a new roof. The first of many skips arrived, and work commenced. Everything had to be stripped out in readiness for the new flats to take shape. I felt so confident about this development and life in general at last.

The speed at which the flats took shape was amazing. Walls were coming down, there were tons of rubble, and dust flying everywhere. Stud walls were starting to go up to form all the different rooms. Each unit was to have two bedrooms, a sizeable lounge, with the usual kitchen and bathroom. First fixing for electricity and plumbing would be placed into position when the walls were up. Outside, the roof was being stripped off in readiness for re-roofing. Box gutters were to be relined with new lead. Any loose rendering on the outside of the building would be knocked out and re-rendered ready for the decorators. I was told by the planning department that I couldn't replace the windows as it was a Grade II listed building, so the sash windows were all to be repaired and where necessary have new cords. I did replace the windows on the top floor, however, when the time came. I thought that in case of fire windows that totally opened up would be quicker and easier to get out of, rather than trying to squeeze through a small sash window. And the windows would not be visible from the road, so I saw no harm in doing that. It all gave me such a buzz. I loved the smell of timber and new plaster. Strange woman me, I prefer it to perfume. My idea of a day out is to go and visit a building site. The contractors were terrific. I think I was a bit of a novelty at first, but when they discovered that I knew what I was talking about, they quickly told anyone new who came on site that they would be wise not to underestimate me. I never encouraged any familiarity either. I was always referred to as Mrs F. This made for a happy working environment.

I wanted to do the White Lodge course part two, which this time wasn't to be held over two weekends in Steyning. It was to take a full week, Monday to Friday, and was to be held this time at White Lodge itself in Speldhurst, Kent. Doing the course would have posed a problem for me, if Mike hadn't stepped in and helped me out. He would go to Anglesea Terrace everyday for me and get the list of materials for the sub-contractors that they needed for that day's work. I no way wanted the job to slow down just because I was away. I used to drive to the site every morning, collect their lists of timber, nails, plaster and sand, to name but a few of the many materials needed, and then drive around to the different builders merchants and either bring it back, or arrange delivery later that day. It was of the utmost importance not to slow down the work in progress. Mike told me that he would hold the fort whilst I was up at White Lodge, and go and see the men every morning for me. He would also be at my home when Jeremy came home from school. That was such a relief for me. He also, bless his heart, prepared and cooked the dinner, it was lovely to go home to a meal. What a gem he was.

I was driving with such freedom, it was like being reborn. On the morning of the course, I was up very early in the morning in order to drive over to Bexhill to Peter's house, where Pearl would already be, and we would travel up to Speldhurst together, in Peter's car. It was a wonderful week, and we were so lucky to have very warm weather as well. To be with my new found

friends at White Lodge again was bliss. I was reminded of the
saying 'You don't make new friends, you just meet them again'.
I knew it was true, I had known some of those people before, it
was like a coming home.

Course two was very interesting, and I hung on every word uttered
by the two tutors, Cicely and Peter. It was reassuring to be in the
company of like-minded people again. Students from all over the
world went to White Lodge, and without exception everyone I met
had an interesting tale to tell about their lives and how they had
discovered White Lodge. On that particular course there had been
a man from Malaysia, a girl from Canada and many from Holland,
and at meal times there were plenty of chances to have a good old
chin wag. At the end of the week, on the Friday evening, Mike's
cousins were having a family party in London, and he asked me if
I would like to go with him to meet them. I agreed. I wanted to
see what they were like. Friday was the last day of the course, and
we always ended a course with a meal together. It rounds it off
nicely. They had a nice conservatory come dining room at White
Lodge where we could all gather, eat, drink, chat, and exchange
phone numbers and addresses. Afterwards I bade farewell to the
lovely people I'd met on the course, and went off with Mike to
meet his family.

I didn't feel at all nervous at the thoughts of meeting yet more
people, after all, I'd just met lots of new people at White Lodge,
and I was on a bit of a high. I take people as they are and hope
that they'll do the same. I met Mike's mother, Kay, and his sister
and brother-in-law, and all the cousins. I had a sneaking feeling
that Mike wanted me to meet his family, as one day I might be
joining the family as a member. They all seemed very nice, much
like any other family really.

Back on the site the following Monday, I could hardly believe the
speed at which the conversion work was being carried out. Over
the following weeks it was magic to watch the little units taking
shape daily, and before long there were four separate flats, each
with wires hanging out of ceilings and walls where light switches
were going and pipes coming up through floors where radiators
were going to be hung. Because the fire regulations dictated that

we covered the ceilings with layers of gyproc, it meant that we lost a lot of the beautiful ceiling mouldings. John could re-create any of the mouldings. He was an artist with plaster.

Next, I had to go and choose the kitchens and bathrooms, in readiness for when they would be needed. I also needed to buy extra Victorian fireplaces to put back where previous ones had been removed. I had to choose wall tiles, paint colours and wallpapers. That was such fun, buying one kitchen or bathroom is great but four lots, five if you include the basement flat, this was retail therapy at its height. It was only three months after starting the conversion that the second flat (the first being the basement flat) was ready to go on the market. My estate agent friend, Sid, had all four of them on his books, although it would be a while before the other three were ready. I also gave them to a couple of other agents. The second flat sold straight away, and the feeling of elation was like a drug. As I mentioned earlier, I had a good architect, Basil, and between us we came up with some good ideas.

Meanwhile, on the home front problems loomed. I was told by the leasing agent that the owner of the house we were renting was unexpectedly returning to England and would need it. This was a bit of a blow, and rather a surprise, as I had not been told that when I had signed the lease, in fact, I was told the complete opposite. It was another move we didn't need. As it turned out, it was a ploy to get me out. It transpired that a neighbour had complained to the landlord's agents and told them she thought I was a person of ill repute because there were three cars parked outside, apart from mine, during the day and sometimes night. Other cars with men in sometimes visited the house at other times during the day. If it hadn't have been so stupid I could have been very hurt. I explained everything to the agent, who I might add, knew me very well, so didn't believe a word of it anyway. We had a bit of a laugh over it. Obviously someone had it in for me, she said. The agent had a list of the car numbers, and on reading them, I explained that two of them were Mike's, as he had changed his car from a red one to a brown one, and the other was my son Julian's, home from University. Other cars were owned by my sub-contractors, who would come round in the day time with their bills, to be paid. I had a vague idea who it was, and I thought what a strange and sad thing to do, to watch someone all the time logging car numbers. That person obviously had nothing much going on in their life, and probably couldn't even comprehend a woman with a building company, working in a totally male environment. I felt like a truly emancipated woman, I was finding out what my capabilities were, and who I was at last. It was all so exciting, and that in itself is quite threatening to some women.

During this period of my life, out of the blue Mike asked me to marry him. He got down on bended knee, the full works. I was ecstatic with happiness. Just one minor hiccup. He wasn't as yet divorced. Although he and his wife had separated, and bought separate homes a year before I'd met him, they hadn't actually started the divorce proceedings. They were far too busy, he with his first manager-ship in the bank, and she with her garden centre restaurant. The divorce was something that I wanted clarifying before I even went out with him, for my own sanity, I couldn't get involved in a situation which might hurt me again. Mike had constantly reassured me that it had been very much a mutual decision for he and his wife to get divorced, something they'd worked out way in advance to coincide with Mike's transfer with the bank, to Hastings. They were still good friends, however, and it was all quite civilised. They had even divided up their possessions, which Mike said would make the divorce easy. His sons were by now aged 16 and 21. He had hung on in that marriage until they were old enough to understand. Mike assured me that the divorce would not be a problem, and I hoped he was right. Although being the cynic that I am, I tend to think that when solicitors are involved they tend to want to make everything as unpleasant as they can, and string it out to get more money.

Meanwhile, I had to get on with the very urgent business of finding us somewhere else to live. When the local paper arrived I put it down and left it on the table. There was suddenly a very strong feeling that I had to read it, and not knowing why I flicked through the pages until I came to the page of property to let. There, on this page, was another house in Westfield with a phone number to ring. I didn't hesitate, and I was fortunate enough to arrange a viewing that evening. Mike by this time was living with us, as we couldn't see the point anymore of living in separate homes, so when he came home that evening, he was very surprised at the speed in which I'd acted, and very pleased, I might add.

It was imperative that I find a place for us to stay long enough for me to get some of the money from the flats to buy us a home of our own again, and put down some roots. Of the other three flats, two were nearing completion and one had quite a way to go before it to would be ready. All were on the market with Sid, two were already under offer, sold subject to contract, although not finished yet. Sid was also given Mike's flat to sell, which was lovely, and in a very good position, and Sid assured him it would also sell quickly.

We went to view the other house in the village, which was up for rent, and fortunately we met the criteria for the owners of the house, who had two dear little girls. They were going abroad for a least a year, so this would be better for us. It was a very old house with beams, 15th or 16th century, with a lovely inglenook fireplace, two sitting rooms and four bedrooms. Please God, could we stay here until we buy our own house?

We moved ourselves, with Lizzie and Derrick's help, and what we thought would just take the morning took the best part of the day. There was quite a lot to come from Mike's flat as well, including a nearly new double bed, which wouldn't go up the narrow staircase, so Mike took out a knife and cut it in half, much to Derrick's astonishment. We were totally whacked when the final boxes were put down on the kitchen floor. Lizzie and Derrick had kindly offered their services for the morning, and we honestly thought it would all be over by lunchtime. After all, we had a wedding to go to in the afternoon. Keith, my accountant, was marrying Sharon, and I had bought a new suit especially to wear. At three o'clock it was obvious that we weren't going anywhere, we were so tired and filthy. There was furniture and boxes everywhere, and still some of the contents of Mike's flat to collect, so going to a wedding was out of the question. By late afternoon we had just about finished, and we were just about finished. Mike lit the fire in the inglenook. It was such a cosy cottage. Jeremy went round to his friend's house, Mike and I had a hot bath, and after a good meal we sat back and surveyed the scene. Yes, yes yes! It was heavenly. We were so pleased with ourselves that we'd been so lucky and found something as nice as that. Our first home together, oh, what joy.

We were so happy in that house, and with what lay ahead of us it was great to have been given that year of bliss. The memories of our life together there, would carry me through many horrible years. Years when normality was something I would no longer know anything about.

We settled down for the winter. Christmas was wonderful. It was the first Christmas for eight years that I'd spent with a partner, and it was everything I'd dreamed it would be. Julian came home for the holidays, and was busy catching up with old friends from college. Jeremy had a remote control car, and some technical Lego for Christmas, the latter, which he spread out all over the floor. There were literally hundreds of pieces, but he was very good at anything like that. Mike wanted to have a go as well, so they ended up both of them sitting on the floor putting this elaborate technical Lego together. When New Year came and it was my birthday, we invited some of our friends round and to my surprise, Mike had had a cake made for me. I hadn't had a birthday cake made for me for twenty years. He was so thoughtful like that, and on every birthday afterwards I would receive a cake. Each one with a theme. That one had stars on it, as my name means star.

The flats were coming along nicely. One had sold in the October, two further sales went through in December, leaving the last one which was still being worked on. In the February, a friend of Jeremy's offered us a Jack Russell puppy, the last of the litter. Jeremy wanted us to have him, and so I went round and had a look. Fatal move that. When this little scrap crawled onto my lap and looked at me the way animals do, I was lost. He had been deserted by his mother. She'd lost interest in him, all the other pups had gone to their new homes, so I suppose she couldn't understand why he hadn't gone. So this puppy was being brought up by his Jack Russell grandmother. Wasn't that sweet? Mike came home, I told him about the puppy and we went straight round and got him. We called him Thomas. He was so sweet, and so tiny. Sweeney was not amused. The look on her face, what on earth were we up to, a dog ugggh!!! So she stayed upstairs for about a week, until one day Mike decided that she must come down and meet and make friends with Thomas, who was so small that he used to sit on the top of the video, underneath the television set. Mike brought Sweeney downstairs and holding firmly onto her collar introduced her to Thomas. She looked at him, arched her back and hissed a few times, then settled down in front of the fire glaring at him as if to say 'It's my home, so just watch it matey'. And he did just that. He wasn't daft this dog.

This was the second winter of deep snow and arctic conditions. It looked beautiful. All along the lanes it was like wonderland, the trees were heavily weighed down with it. I photographed Jay standing under a snowdrift that was three times his height. It was amazing. Snow makes everything look so pure. I love it, it covers up all the litter, and rubbish thrown out of cars. It covers up un-kempt gardens, in fact, it covers up everything and makes it beautiful. Why doesn't it snow more often?

I was still enjoying my freedom driving, and I amazed my mother when on one of her trips over to see us with her sister, Dot. I went to the station to collect them. I drove them back to the cottage where I had a delicious lamb and dumpling casserole cooking. The smell was so inviting as I opened the back door to the kitchen. Life was good, the flats were progressing well, the cottage was comfortable and I was happy. I spent a pleasant afternoon with my mother and Dot and then took them back to the station. It doesn't sound much to someone who has never had agoraphobia, but if you have suffered from it you will know what a major achievement that was.

I had an extraordinary visitation one day whilst sitting in one of the armchairs in the inner sitting room. I heard a voice, it said, 'You are going to have a child, and her name is to be Abigail Louise'. I was so amazed, I leapt out of the chair in a state of shock and exhilaration. I was excited. Could it be true? But I was worried then. Mike didn't want any more children, he'd made it perfectly clear when we were talking one day, and he'd made sure of it by having a vasectomy years earlier. I knew I couldn't tell him what I'd heard, he'd go mad. After a week had gone by, Mike suddenly said to me, "Alright darling, tell me what's on your mind, and don't say 'nothing', because I know you, you're very preoccupied with something." So I told him, and just what I said would happen, happened. He was not happy. "If you want children you're with the wrong guy, darling. You know my feelings on it, I made it quite clear when we met." I told him I couldn't help what I'd been told. But he thought it must be a mistake. So we forgot about it. A few weeks later whilst Mike was mowing the lawn, I took him out a cup of coffee and to my utmost surprise he turned to face me and said. "I think a baby would be lovely. My father always told me that if a woman wants a baby she should have one, and I want one too." Well, what a turnaround. It meant a reversal but that didn't bother him. He seemed very keen.

I continued going down to the flats every day, and collecting all the necessary materials from builders' merchants for the last remaining flat, and all the acres of hallways. I was still buying gallons of paint and acres of wallpaper, along with boxes and boxes of tiles. And the flats were all sold carpeted, so carpet fitters were hammering away. The last flat, the ground floor flat, was coming together fast, and looked great. It had a very large sitting room with an Adam fireplace, and there were a lot of possibilities for furnishing it. A chandelier would have looked lovely. It didn't sell as quickly as the others had done, which was surprising, so I put the price up, much to the surprise of my carpenter, who informed me that most people reduce the prices of things that don't sell. Not me, I thought the flat was too cheap at the previous price. Anyway, it worked and it sold straightaway, even though we were still finishing off all the hallways, and the outside of the building.

It was Spring, and I knew that I must look around for the next project, or I would have a gap in between projects, and a gap in my income, which I couldn't afford. There was a lot of property on the market but I wanted to buy a good one. I wanted an even larger property to do now. I'd converted the four and the five-floored properties, now I wanted to convert one with six floors. I had a taste for it. I scoured all the agents until I found the ideal property. And I found it, but I had to offer a closed bid for it. This I did and lo and behold I had acquired a six-floored block of disgusting flats on the sea front in St. Leonards.

The property was in a dreadful state of repair, and people had actually been living in those dreadful conditions. But no one could have lived in the top flat, the reason being that half the roof was missing. It reminded me of Hitchcock's film 'The Birds' because when I opened the door to the flat, seagulls would be sitting on their nests in there, with the sky for a roof. How quaint. It's amazing just how big some seagulls are. I felt quite wary of them. This building was to be a major structural job. I was very excited though, nothing seemed to daunt me. I revelled in it all.

There were sitting tenants in the basement flat, who were delightful. The only problem for them was that in order to transform and update these old fashioned flats into luxury apartments with all mod cons whilst retaining a lot of the period features, we had to install new drains. Not difficult to do usually, but there was a slight snag. We needed to take the drains right down the middle of the building through into the basement, digging up the hall of this couple's nice tidy flat. Well, they couldn't have been more agreeable when I told them. I did offer to move them out temporarily into a hotel, but they wouldn't hear of it. They wanted to stay. What a mess they had to put up with, and they were so helpful to my men. They understood that in order to develop this property it was a necessary evil. They still had the old servants staircase in their hallway, all blocked off, I said we would remove it. So apart from digging up the floor in their hall in order to create new drains, tons of earth excavated in front of their eyes, ripping out the staircase and putting in a damp-proof course they had a pretty good time! In return we completely re-decorated their flat. Well it was the least we could do.

The fabric of the building was in a terrible state, having deteriorated over many years. Most of the roof had gone, damp had penetrated big time through several floors, and it all stank. Lots of rogue landlords and weak local councils meant that a lot of people lived and still do live in that kind of squalor.

When the scaffolding was put up all the levels were wrong. I had explained at great length when I had ordered it what I needed it for, saying that I had to renew some of the lintels, rebuild some of the mullions where necessary and install new windows, and also to renew the roof. So when I arrived one morning and found scaffolding boards half way across the middle of the windows, I was not happy, and neither were the scaffolders when I told them to move it all. You have to be able to hold your own with men like that. What they were going to do with me was nobody's business. One of my men stepped forward to assist me, but I needed no help. It's not for the faint hearted, building sites, and as he hurled expletives at me, intimating that he would throw me of the roof, I hurled them back, much to his surprise. I stood my ground. I was paying and I would have what I was paying for or they could take it all down and not get a penny. Needless to say they did it again, with the right levels, so the window people could come and do their bit. Never a dull moment…

Life in Westfield was great. Jay got the school bus from the village with his friends from primary school that he had lost touch with when we had to live in St. Leonards. He was so much happier than he had been for years, thank goodness. Jay had always been animal mad, so he was delighted when Mike got Thomas for us. I was also pleased to have a dog as well, as he was such a dear little chap. I firmly believed that Thomas was meant for us. He was an adorable little dog. We also had a cockatiel that I acquired from a friend. When I visited her one day, she asked me to take the bird because her children wouldn't leave it alone. We called him Captain Beaky. So we ended up with a cat we had exchanged for a bicycle, a dog whose mother had abandoned him and left him to his grandmother to see to, two rats, no story there, and a cockatiel rescued from little boys. Quite a menagerie. So little Dr. Dolittle was happy. And mustn't forget to mention the stick insects......!!!

During the Easter holidays Julian had a car accident. He had gone out to visit some friends that he had been to college with. The telephone rang just after we had all gone to bed, "I'll answer it," said Mike. It appeared Julian had hit some black ice going round a corner and lost it completely. The car had slid across the road and hit a very high kerb, which did a lot of damage to the chassis. He told Mike that he was going to have to leave it there and walk home. We got back into bed, thinking that we would deal with it the next day. After a few minutes, Mike said that he couldn't let Julian walk all that way home, as it was several miles. He was going to get the car out and find him. So off he went into the night.

Meanwhile, the house, which I have omitted to say was haunted, got really active. I could hear footsteps along the landing, and cautiously I got out of bed and peered round the door. As usual there was nothing to see. I crept into Jay's room to see if he was awake, but he was fast asleep. I stood watching him like mothers do, and I noticed something sticking out from under his pillow. On closer examination, I discovered it was a large kitchen knife! What on earth did he want that for? I would have to wait until the morning to ask him, as there wasn't any point in waking him up. So I went nervously back to bed, hoping the footsteps would stop. I climbed back into bed and the most amazing thing happened. Suddenly right across our ceiling I could see a tree. It was nothing short of incredible. I could see all the branches so clearly. What did this mean?

I lay there for ages until I heard the back door opening and shutting downstairs. Mike ran up the stairs into our room. "I couldn't find Julian. I've been up and down all the roads, but he's obviously taken a different route home." I was worried now. Where was he? That car was the love of his life. We discussed the options, when we heard the door downstairs open and close. I shot out of bed and we both rushed downstairs to see if he was OK and to put the kettle on (my answer to everything). We all needed a cup of tea. Julian was distraught, and leaning up against the sink he relayed to me step by step how he had lost control of the car on black ice on a corner, and then about the state of his beloved car. "It's a write off," he said, wringing his hands in desperation. "Nothing goes right for me, nothing ever has. I might as well chuck myself off the pier," he said. "Don't be silly," I said, trying to reason with him. "Let's see the state of it before we jump to conclusions, it might be repairable." But there was no consoling

197

him. He was past consoling. It was true he'd had an awful lot to contend with over the years, what with all his illnesses, and his father leaving us, but I insisted that all would be well, and this car would be repaired and back on the road in no time. "I'm going back to University tomorrow, how am I going to get there?" he said angrily. "Let's sleep on it," I said, "there's another day tomorrow, I'll sort something out. Don't worry, Jules, it'll all be alright I promise." He looked at me so sadly. He loved that car, and when you're young things are so desperate.

We went to bed, and as soon as we got into bed I remembered what had been going on before Mike came back home. "Mike," I said. "Yes darling," he replied. "If I tell you something you won't think I'm mad will you?" I whispered. "No, of course not, what is it, my love?" he looked at me quizzically. "There's a tree all over our ceiling." 'I know," he replied, "I can see it quite clearly, isn't it amazing?" We lay there looking at this for some time, not knowing what it meant, then Mike put the lights out and we drifted off to sleep. In the morning the tree was forgotten. I had more urgent things to sort out.

Mike went off to the bank as usual, and when he'd gone and I'd had breakfast, I made a couple of phone calls. The first was to the garage to collect the car from the roadside and ascertain the damage. The second was to Lizzie. "Hi Lizzie, it's me. Have you still got your mini for sale?" I asked. "Hello, my little friend," she replied. "Yes, I have, why?" "I want to buy it. What time shall I come round?" I went round, taking Jules with me, and bought it. It was a nice little mini-clubman estate, and it would certainly do until the other one was sorted out. I taxed and insured it, and when Mike came home at five o'clock Jules was loading up all his gear for University.

"My word," said Mike, "you don't waste any time do you, darling? How can you buy a car, tax and insure it and be loading it up by the time I get back from work?" I smiled. "You should know me by now, Mike. I don't waste time."

Julian left the next morning, relieved that he had wheels again. "I'll ring you tonight, Mum," he shouted through the window.

"OK, Jules, take it easy, have a good journey," I replied, thankful that it had all been so easily sorted out. If Lizzie hadn't still got the car it would have been a little bit harder to sort, but she had. Thank you God. Another crisis sorted.

Now for the difficult bit! Why had Jay got a carving knife under his pillow? When I confronted him, he told me how afraid he was in his bedroom at night. He had a door to the attic stairs in the corner of his room, and he relayed to me the experiences that he had in that room. It appeared that someone walked about in the middle of the night, and on more than one occasion, walked right across the bed. He could feel it touching him as it went over him. "Why didn't you tell me, darling?" I asked, "and what did you think you could do to a ghost with a knife?" "I don't know," he replied, "but it made me feel a whole lot better." "Well, if you feel nervous again, you just come into our room," I said. "We'll make up a bed on the floor for you." "Thanks, Mum," he smiled at me. "Never a dull moment in this family, is there, Mum?"

We decided to go to Madeira for our summer holiday. I was, however, worried about flying. My panic attacks had returned with a vengeance. I had been to see a friend who had recently had a baby, and as I was driving back from her house in Hastings up a very busy main road, I had the most ghastly panic attack. I could feel it coming on, so had pulled over onto the grass verge. It was a bad attack and my confidence was very shaken. I managed to drive home after a while, but it was to damage my confidence considerably. Suppose flying brought on a panic attack? Perish the thought. But I had to do it. I was going to do it. I did not want this strange illness, or whatever you call it, to ruin my life. I would fly. I'd always loved flying, and I would continue to do it, come what may. It was just another hurdle to be climbed over! Julian couldn't come with us he informed me, as he had to work on something to do with Uni. I was very disappointed. I saw so little of him, but he was adamant that he couldn't spare the time. So Jeremy asked his friend Glyn to come, all expenses paid. He was delighted, and all was arranged for August.

Meanwhile, I continued going down to the Marina flats every day, taking Pat with me, I hadn't the confidence to drive on my own anymore. I was panicky at even the thought of being alone. I was always fine, however, when I got to my destination. I suddenly became a very confident person again. It was all so bizarre. This block of flats was so different to the last block. To start with it was much bigger, and this block required a lot of major structural work. The flats were archaic and needed re-designing, so walls were coming down in places and new walls were going up, in order to create bright new modern flats. It was my intention to produce some quite expensive flats, with as much of the original mouldings left as the fire regulations would allow, as we had to double gyproc the ceilings then plaster them. Each flat had a Victorian fireplace in the sitting room, replacement windows, gas central heating, German kitchens with built in appliances, and luxury bathrooms, some with bidets. I used to start my day by ringing around the builders' merchants and ordering lorry loads of timber, gyproc, nails, screws and plaster, along with blocks, bricks, sand and cement, and whatever else they asked for. I loved every minute of it all.

In the August we flew off to Madeira. What a beautiful Island that was. No wonder they call it the floating garden. Flowers grew everywhere in abundance, All along the roads grew Agapanthus, climbing over walls grew Bougainvillea. It was a lovely lazy fortnight. The hotel had a big swimming pool, and on one side of it was a refreshment area, which served the most delicious cakes I've ever tasted. Mike talked a lot about having a baby whilst we were there, and said he would book himself into the clinic for a vasectomy reversal as soon as we were back home. While we were in Madeira we also met a couple who were to become very good friends, Pat and Phil from Stockton-on-Tees.

When we came back home, Mike was trying to proceed with his divorce, which wasn't easy for him. Solicitors were involved! He was such a kind man, and wanted to do the right thing for his family. I knew he felt quite guilty about the fact that his marriage hadn't been more successful, and I admired him for that. I knew that he was the sort of person who'd always given his all. I do not think I would have wanted anyone who just walked out on a family. Families are too important.

We started to look around for a suitable home for us at last. I thought the day would never come! We placed enquiries with several agents to see what they could offer us, only to be told that there was a shortage of large houses for sale in our area. We found this rather surprising and somewhat disappointing, nevertheless, we were sent details of two properties that fitted our needs and that looked rather interesting, so we made appointments to view them. They were both nice.

The first one we viewed had all the accommodation necessary, but it was on a very busy main road, and although it had a swimming pool, and seemed a very attractive possibility, we decided on the other one which was in Battle, also on a main road but with a speed limit. When we saw the Battle house we fell in love with it. It was rather expensive though, but Mike assured me that we would be able to afford it with two incomes. Whilst we were viewing we were aware suddenly that the owner had become rather agitated, and turning to me he asked about my surname. "Unusual name," he said. "You weren't married to the accountant at a Hastings travel company, were you?" I was, I replied. Well this guy went mad. It appeared that he hated my ex and he hated my ex's wife as well, and we who were wanting to talk about the house etc had to listen to the mad ravings of this man. This continued non-stop for over an hour, all about what my ex had done to him at work and all about her. I'm not kidding, he was full to the brim with hatred. I did find it rather awkward, but at least Mike was hearing from someone else's lips a little of what my ex was capable of. Well the upshot of that was that although he accepted our offer on the house, when we came back from our lovely holiday in Madeira and contacted him to see when exchange of contracts was, he calmly informed us that he had decided not to sell the house after all. A bit later on we heard he had sold it to someone else. I thought my past was never to go away. Was my ex to keep popping up and spoiling things, not only for me, but his sons? I thought it rather sad that this guy couldn't see that we were also victims, and that he with his actions were keeping us as victims.

That was the Year of the 'Great Storm'. I went to bed as normal that night. I didn't get to sleep straightaway. I tossed and turned a bit, then sat listening to the wind, and noises coming from outside. What on earth was going on? I got up, feeling that this wind was somewhat abnormal. Looking out of the window across the garden I could clearly see trees bent double, and what was so interesting were all the colours I saw dancing in the wind, and I knew then that it was a hurricane. I woke Mike up. "Mike, wake up, it's a hurricane, listen to all the noise." His reply was very to the point. "We don't have hurricanes in this country, it's just a storm, it'll be over soon." After my insisting just long enough to hear chimney pots crashing to the ground and greenhouses smashing, he then jumped out of bed. What a night. I imagine it was rather like going through an air raid, and as by now the power had gone off, we tuned into a battery radio for news of what was happening, and it was as we now know a major disaster. How anybody slept through it I can't imagine.

In the morning when it got light, the true horror of it all struck me. It was like a knife through me. I am a person who loves order, cleanliness, no litter on the verges, lawns mowed. It was total chaos. I remembered feeling very angry. It's bad enough when humans destroy things, but you don't expect nature to do it, although of course it goes on all the time in other countries. But this is England, and we have been very spoiled. Was this our first taste of things to come? Was this the start of Global warming?

The flats were my first priority. Phone lines were down so we had to make our way down to the town, zig zagging our way along the roads because so many trees were lying across the main roads. Two of my properties had rain pouring through huge holes in their roofs. We needed tarpaulins quickly, and so did everybody else. We drove to the builders' merchants as fast as we could, only to find that they'd sold out of them, as everybody needed them. What a situation to be in. I didn't know what we'd do. We went to look at the properties, assessing the damage, and it could have been worse. When we got to the marina, Brian was already there assessing the damage. He was standing on the parapet six floors up on the sea front in the aftermath of the hurricane, with the rain coming down like stair-rods. We had lost a bit of our new roof. This house was destined to not have a roof, and we had nothing to cover the hole with. The rainwater was spoiling the newly decorated flat. On our journey back home wondering what to do next in the absence of tarpaulins, I noticed a van with a roofer's name on it that I knew. I saw his van parked outside a house that had real problems, much worse than mine. I hurried across and asked if he could help me, and to my relief he said he could. He would put my properties on his list and go round with the necessary tarpaulins. Meanwhile I contacted the Insurance companies.

We got back home, relieved and very tired, looking at the mess in our own village. I don't know how long we were without power, but with a blazing log fire and mugs of soup one soon feels human again. I went and bought a chain saw, and we were able to help clear the churchyard of fallen trees. Jeremy was a dab hand with this machine, fearless Fred! I made him wear all the protective clothing, shoes, trousers, jacket, and goggles. He just seemed very at home sawing up this enormous tree.

We continued with our house hunting and found another potentially suitable house in Beauport Gardens, St. Leonards, and I made an appointment for us to view it. It was a lovely big house, with everything we needed. But when we went to view it, Mike seemed totally disinterested in all of it. He even admitted later on that evening that he had not been even the slightest bit interested in the house. Well, that suited me. I didn't particularly want to live there either, not because of the house, which was lovely, but because The Ridge hangs with fog all the winter. So I naturally assumed from his reaction that we would keep looking for a house that we both liked.   I know Mike was disappointed about the house in Battle, so was I, and maybe he thought that we might be let down again, so far better not to get excited about a house again. The houses in Beauport Gardens were very large and rather American in their design. I had watched them being built when I had lived in Moat Lane, and I remembered how expensive the houses were when they were built. So what with Mike's disinterest and me having strongly expressed my desire not to live there, I was somewhat surprised when Mike out of the blue rang the agent and made an offer on the house on behalf of both of us, regardless, and the offer was accepted. I did at that precise moment have another panic attack. Was that an omen?

Chapter 10 - Collapse

We moved house in the November of 1987. It was a very exciting moment for me, and my sons, to have our own home again after three years. Mike and I had viewed the house again after our offer was accepted, and it was a strange situation to be in, with Mike making an offer on behalf of both of us, for a house that he was indifferent to, and I didn't want either. But the second time Mike saw it he was suddenly very enthusiastic about it. It was as if he hadn't seen it the first time round. I even got caught up in his enthusiasm, and I too became quite excited about it. I couldn't think then why I'd had a panic attack. Perhaps I had picked up some of Mike's negativity. Anyway, that was all forgotten now, we were going to make a new home for the four of us. It had been three years since my sons and I had left Hedgerows, our last family home. Anglesea had been a purely business decision, and we had all known when we moved there that it was only a temporary home (albeit the greatest fun home we'd ever known to date), until the business was up and running, and I, or as it now was we, Mike and I, could buy another family home.

I wanted to alter some things in the house that we both weren't keen on before we laid new carpets. I was in the fortunate position of being able to take some men off the site to do the work quickly for us. The work involved blocking up a large archway between the open plan sitting room and dining room, then plastering and decorating it. Then I wanted a doorway put through from the hallway to the dining room thus making a completely separate room. It was all done and decorated in time to have a Christmas Party seven days after we moved, and you would never have known the house had been altered.

The house was very large, on a small development of twelve houses, some with swimming pools and most with basements, very American indeed. The houses stood on a hill overlooking Hastings, and at night it was lovely to go to the upstairs sitting room and look out of the window, and see all the twinkling lights of the town. It was all quite magical. Christmas was great, we were in our own home at last and we'd bought the biggest tree we could get in the room, one that went right up to the sitting room ceiling. Mike's mother Kay came and stayed with us for Christmas, which made it a little tense, because although Mike was naturally very fond of his mother, he had always found it very difficult to talk to her. She didn't like unpleasantness, and she didn't want to know anything at all about her son's divorce. I think she really found the whole thing disagreeable simply because it meant that she would not have the same friendship with Mike's ex-wife's mother again. I could understand that, as they had known each other for a very long time. But I also thought that Kay's loyalties were a bit misguided.

During that Christmas a row blew up. Mike's sons were coming down on Boxing Day for the day, and were being brought down by their mother to a half way spot, a pub in Hawkhurst where it was convenient to hand them over. The upshot was that Kay wanted to have coffee with Beverley at the pub, but Mike didn't want to linger any longer than was necessary, he just wanted to pick up their sons and bring them home. Kay wouldn't listen to Mike and dismissed him out of hand. She was going to do what she wanted, and she wanted coffee. I was in the kitchen all through this, trying to keep well out of it, until Mike came to find me. "I can't talk to her. She doesn't take any notice of me. She doesn't understand why I don't want to have coffee with Beverley. Will you talk to her, she'll listen to you?" he said. I was horrified at being dragged into it. "I don't want to talk to her Mike, she's your mother, make her listen to you, you do have a valid point after all," I explained. But he insisted that she would not listen, so I gave in. "Alright then, I'll see what I can do." And I seized the moment and walked nervously into the sitting room. "Look at your son, Kay, look how tense he is. He can't even talk to you, he's asked me to do it." My heart was racing, and she looked angry. I carried on. "Mike does have reasons for not wishing to see her. She wasn't very reasonable over the divorce settlement." I was getting very breathless, and hyperventilating. "I don't wish to know the ins and outs of anything," Kay insisted. "I don't want to be involved." By this time I was exasperated. "I'm having a panic attack in my own house," I said, trying to breathe. "This is your son, Kay, your only son, and you've judged him and you have judged him wrongly. Look at the state of him. He's a wreck. If one of my sons had gone through what Mike's gone through and I'd turned my back on him, I'd be ashamed of myself." She then said that she had never realised there had been any problem. How was she to know there had been any problems, she asked. "Well," I said, "I can tell from the flicker of an eyelid if something is wrong with one of my sons, I wouldn't need to ask." It was an unpleasant moment. She looked hard at me, not knowing quite what to do. It was obvious that she didn't really like me. I know she thought that I had married Mike for his money, but the truth of the matter was that he had very little capital when I met him. He did have a reasonable salary, but he'd come out of his marriage quite badly, with very little money and a mortgage on his flat. Beverley had come out of it very well with a property bought outright from the sale of the matrimonial home. Money which had been lent her out of Mike's share of the matrimonial property to help her set up her business, was money which she later decided to keep as terms of the divorce!!! Mike couldn't have fought her any more, we were living at Chapel Cottage at the time the divorce settlement was being worked out, and I well remember how exasperated he'd been with it all. He told me he'd had years of not winning with her, and he certainly wouldn't have won in that situation. So being the perfect gentleman he gave in.

When Mike sold his flat after carrying out substantial renovations to it, he had, however, made a nice profit on it. I continued talking to Kay. "I don't know who you think bought this house," I said, "but the majority of the money was mine. Your son came out of his marriage with very little." Kay looked shocked. She really hadn't thought it through at all. I found it hard to comprehend that a mother wouldn't take the side of her own child. But we left it at that, and they went off to collect Mike's sons, just collect, and I got on with preparing lunch. Oh, happy days, I don't think!

The last day of Kay's stay coincided with an invitation to Janet's house for a drinks party. Janet and Francis now lived in Tunbridge Wells, and it was decided that we would all go. We would take two cars, so that afterwards Mike could run Kay home to Surrey and I could stay a little longer with my friends and then come home under my own steam. I knew straight away that Kay was very impressed with my friends. They were a terrific couple, and they had a wonderfully large house, which included a suite of rooms for Janet's parents. Janet had been a debutante in the fifties, and there was a lovely portrait of her on the wall. Marjorie, Janet's mother, had always been very fond of me and had always made such a fuss of me. This was an eye opener for Kay, to see me in a situation like that. After that day, Kay's attitude towards me changed. She even asked Mike's Aunt Eve about me after Christmas, and Eve replied, "Stella's magic. Can't you feel the magic in the air when Michael and Stella are together?" So that sealed it, and Kay accepted me. After that she would often ring and we would chat away. I just wanted to be friends, that's all. No more, no less. I never wanted to replace her first daughter-in-law, I just wanted to make Mike happy. After Christmas Mike kept his word, and he went into the private clinic for his vasectomy reversal.

In the New Year, we started to plan our wedding for June, in five months time. It was going to be a lot to organise, what with the flat conversion which was well and truly under way and more than a full time job for me, Mike's job at the bank, and having not long moved house. But we would manage somehow. The flats were taking shape nicely, and how splendid they looked. I had pushed the boat out a bit and spent a lot on the conversion of that property. My 'piece de resistance' I called it. Two flats were under offer quickly. The basement flat had my sitting tenants in it, so that left three to sell, the third and fourth floors, and the ground floor flat, which was lovely.

Then something absolutely catastrophic happened, that was to change our lives completely. There was a landslide at the rear of a property near to the one I was converting. The first I heard of it was when my tenant, Mrs. Morris, rang me one morning to tell me that a huge piece of the cliff, which hadn't moved in two hundred years, had fallen down, and landed mainly into buildings up to three houses down the road, and that it was a major disaster, which I ought to go and look at quickly. Mike and I went down straightaway and we couldn't believe our eyes at what we saw. Hundreds of tons of earth and trees had come down. What an atrocious mess it was. As I said it had affected several houses, but fortunately, it had missed mine. I was nevertheless very worried, it was far too close for comfort. To make matters worse, it was then in the newspapers and on national television. Oh, dear God, what a dreadful thing to happen! How would this affect me financially? Would I now be able to sell the other flats? Of course I would, I said to myself praying hard. The remaining flats were nearing completion, of course they would sell. But I knew deep down that the publicity was not going to do me any good. This was a major disaster, whichever way you looked at it.

When I went down a few days later to survey the damage again, the painters Jack and Mark were in the ground floor flat painting away. The flat looked wonderful, with lovely large rooms. I could have lived there myself. I naturally chatted to them about it all and how worried I was, but they were very optimistic, "Oh, you'll sell them, Mrs F.," one said to me. But I was not convinced. I was very, very worried indeed. Why did nothing go quite right?

With the wedding planned for June I had to put the problems of the landslide out of my mind temporarily. Worrying wasn't going to make it better, and I had a wedding to organise. Mike and I had always said that our wedding would be a small affair, and we'd always fancied eloping, but certain of our friends thought that was selfish, they didn't want to be done out of a wedding. So then we decided to have a registry office wedding, but after visiting the registry office in Hastings to discuss possible dates, it just didn't feel right, it didn't sit right with me at all. So somehow the wedding got larger and larger until it was to be quite a grand affair. The minister of Battle Baptist Church said he would marry us, and that pleased me because of my going to the Baptist church as a child. So we ended up with planning a church wedding, with top hats and tails and me in a full length straight white lace dress, with a matching three quarter length coat, and a pretty little bridesmaid, also in white, trimmed with peach. The reception was to be at Netherfield Place in Battle. We had very kindly, been offered the use of a cream Jaguar special sports car by Bill Slack, the engineer, who had designed and built it.

Then very sadly and totally unexpectedly, Kay died the week before our wedding. She had tragically suffered a fall at her home, which unfortunately led to complications. It all happened so quickly, one minute she was there, cracking jokes, then she was gone. We thought in the circumstances, that the best thing we could do, would be to cancel our wedding, but Mike's sister said no, we should go ahead as their mother would have wanted us to. Mike was naturally very sad, but he didn't want to cancel it either. In fact, Kay had been really looking forward to it. The last time that we had seen her, which was in the hospital, recovering we'd thought, from her nasty fall, she said she'd come to our wedding in an ambulance if necessary. So that was very sad indeed for Mike, his sister and the whole family. And me.

When our wedding day arrived it was sunny, thank goodness. Sylvia, the wife of Scott, who were good friends of Mike's, had offered to help me get ready, and it was their grand-daughter Kerry who was to be our bridesmaid. What a glorious day we had, surrounded by our loved ones, both family and friends. My mother looked very glamorous, with a large straw hat with a flower on it. Even the Mayor of Hastings was there!!! As a friend I might add. Mike's friend Sandie, was Mayor of Hastings, she and Robin, her husband, were a thoroughly nice couple. Plus the president of the Chamber of Commerce and his wife were there. It was a bit like a page out of 'Who's who'. I had a chuckle to myself when I overheard a wife of one of one of my sub-contractors' say, 'Blimey it's like a day out of Dallas!' It was a bit like that, especially in those surroundings. Netherfield Place is a Georgian mansion set in acres of beautiful gardens. Inside the

209

hotel, pine panelling graced the walls of the dining room. I'd chosen peach and white flowers and displays were on all the tables, it was truly lovely. Derrick was Mike's best man and he gave a hilarious speech, which included the story of the new bed, which Mike cut in half. Everybody roared with laughter, he made it sound so funny. It was a lovely day, marred only by the fact that Kay wasn't there. But I suspect that she was there, watching, happy that Mike and I were at last married. After the reception we continued partying at our home well into the night. Eventually we had to throw Sid and Wendy out into the night, as we were falling asleep on our feet. It had been one of the happiest days of our lives.

The next day we left for our honeymoon in the Lake District and Scotland, where we spent a very romantic week touring. After visiting Keswick and the lakes, we drove on to Edinburgh, then worked our way across to Ben Nevis. We stopped en route at a loch, got out of the car and stood there, marvelling at the peace and beauty of it all. I thought it must be Heaven on earth. Suddenly several R.A.F. jet planes screamed just over our heads without warning. My ears were ringing from the dreadful noise. It seems sometimes that there is nowhere to escape noise in this country. When we got to Fort William I stood looking at Ben Nevis. I was reminded of my earlier visit to Scotland when I was just eleven years old, when I had been youth hostelling with the guides. The colours and the beauty affected me just as much as they did all those years before. There's something very spiritual about mountains, they lure you. We spent a magical romantic week in Scotland, but like all good things it had to come to an end, and we had to go home.

Our last night in Scotland was spent on the shores of Loch Lomond, in a bed and breakfast establishment. Nothing wrong with that, Loch Lomond is beautiful, but the bungalow had got a drains problem, and have I got a nose for drains? It hit me the moment I walked through the door, and I spent the entire night wandering about inspecting the bathroom and sniffing. How could my new husband have slept through that dreadful smell? And there was a lump in the mattress, so what with the drains and the mattress I was awake all night long. I sometimes wish that I wasn't so sensitive. Mike always laughs at me, and next morning was no exception, he laughingly said, "Why don't you just go to sleep like other people." If only!

On our journey back home, we had arranged to stop off and stay with Pat and Phil, the couple that we had met whilst on holiday in Madeira. Their house was in Stockton-on-Tees, a part of the country that we were to get to know very well over the years. We were very pleased to see each other again, and we spent a delightful evening reminiscing about Madeira, and all the interesting things we had seen on the island. I was glad when it was bedtime, however, as I'd got a dreadful headache, the result of being awake all of the previous night. I sank into the lovely comfortable bed and drifted off straightaway. In the morning I awoke refreshed and ready for the long drive home. Pat and Phil were to become very good friends of ours, and to have met in Madeira was incredible. I'm going to say it again 'You don't make friends, you just meet them again'. I felt that was so true of them.

When we came back from our honeymoon I knew there was going to be a lot to sort out with the flats and the landslide, and I was right. I came right down to earth with a bump when I realised that I might have a real problem selling them, as a result of all the adverse publicity. The estate agents assured me that the flats would sell, it was just a question of time, and if necessary they said, I could always send them to auction. But that was jumping the gun a bit, as the remaining three were only just being finished off. The last lick of paint was literally just going on, so I was trying to be hopeful.

Meanwhile, my social life was very busy, with lots of engagements such as the Institute of Bankers dinner at the Grand Hotel in Eastbourne, at which I was a guest of the bank, in my customer status. We also attended the Mayor's Ball, as guests of Sandie and her husband Robin. And we went to the Chamber of Commerce Ball, of which Mike was the treasurer. I wore some gorgeous gowns, it was all quite unbelievable to have a life like that, bearing in mind what I'd been through earlier. That part of my life was like a fairytale.

Meanwhile, I had to organise some more work to be done to our own house. One of the bedrooms which was extremely large, and been used as an upstairs sitting room, was to be made into two bedrooms, as we had plans for a nursery. Mike had had a vasectomy reversal and we were hoping to have a child. So life was very sweet. Then one evening whilst we were watching a film on television, I was suddenly aware that Kay was in the room. I could see her clearly, standing across the other side of the room, in a long blue dress. I was somewhat surprised, why had she come? She had come to see Mike. I always ask for a password when they visit, and I do this mentally. The word she gave me was 'Boggles'. I turned to Mike and asked him what Boggles meant to him, he replied "Watch the film?" I went back to Kay to verify the password, and it was right. I turned to Mike again and repeated, "Mike, could you tell me what Boggles means to you, it's important." He became quite irritated, "Why don't you want to watch the film, shall I turn it off?" I insisted again that it was very important that he answer the question. He answered straight away. "It was the nickname my mother gave our dog. Why are you asking?" I answered that I didn't want to alarm him but that his mother was standing across the other side of the room. Because I got the password right he knew that I wasn't joking. There was no way I had ever heard the name Boggles before, and Mike had never ever mentioned it to me. "What does she want?" he asked nervously. I replied, "Perhaps she just wants to see you. There's a bit of healing to be done because she is wearing blue, the colour of healing." Mike was very agitated. This was all new to him. I had grown up in two worlds so I was used to it. Kay stayed for about two hours. She was all over the house, Mike couldn't see her, he just kept asking me where she was all the time. Eventually, Mike told me to ask her to go. He was overwrought with the whole thing. I did ask her to go, but I questioned Mike about not wanting her there, although I fully understand that for most people it's difficult to understand these things. Kay must have had a good reason for coming, and I hoped that she got what she wanted, so that she could go on to where she was meant to be.

Then I had to sort out another strange phenomenon. I had

received several offers for the top flat, and then for no explicable reason (as it always passed the surveys), the sale always fell through. I felt there must be a presence up there. When I'd first bought the building I'd heard a story about an elderly man dying up there, but until now I hadn't thought anymore about it. I decided that I was going to exorcise the flat and the building. I had exorcised a building once before, in fact one of the blocks I'd converted with William, and it had worked then. I climbed up the staircase to the top flat with my bible in my hand and asked whoever it was to please leave the earthly realms and go on to where they should be. I worked my way down through all the levels, standing on each landing as I went down, repeating the words, until I reached the ground floor and out the door. Within days the flat had an offer on it and this time it sailed through and the sold board went up. That left only two to sell now.

After the Wedding excitement had died down it was time to get down to the reality of the horror of what had happened to the cliff. I rang Hastings Council to see if they owned the cliff. It appeared that no one owned it, so therefore, there was no urgency to clear the tons and tons of earth and trees that had fallen down. I soon heard that some of the blocks of flats along the Marina were blighted, and mine of course was one of them, as the landslide happened so close to mine. I was very aware also that there was a recession looming and time was not going to be on my side. I'd had no option but to finish the development and they did look splendid, even if I said it myself. I had spent a great deal of money on the fabric of the building, replacing lintels, in some cases rebuilding the complete windows where the mullions were broken through, putting in replacement UPVC windows. I put on a new roof, and they had new drains. I'd had the rear of the building Tyroleaned at some cost. I was trying to do the very best that I could for the people who would be buying them. Any dry rot was dealt with properly; every detail was restored where possible.

There is a funny story to tell about when I was in the timber merchants' one day with my list of timber requirements. I was asked why I wanted particular pieces of timber. "I'm replacing all the damaged and missing skirting boards, I want it all to be as original as possible," I replied. "You don't want to do that," was the reply, "nobody restores those skirtings anymore, everybody rips 'em off and replaces 'em with four inch these days." "I don't want to be part of these days," I replied. "I want to do a proper job, and restore them." "Oh, you'll learn," he sneeringly replied, "You'll learn." So will you, I thought. So many people want to do a shoddy job, and take the maximum money for it. I felt that pride in one's work was still the most important thing. A lot of new houses built today are built so shoddily. Roof trusses have been reduced to the minimum size that builders can get away with, plasterboard has replaced a lot of interior walls, floorboards have been replaced with sheets of chip board flooring. Not only are the houses not going to stand the test of time, but a lot seem to have problems right from the start. We shouldn't skimp on building work. Why can't we have pride again in our building industry and produce for example, houses like the Victorians built? And as there is such a shortage of land, why don't we build upwards, like the Victorians did, with three and four floored houses - the ground floor housing the cars with a hall a utility/laundry room, and a loo. The first floor having the kitchen, dining room, a sitting room and perhaps a study area, and then if it's three floored, the top floor could have three bedrooms and a bathroom. If it's four floored the top two floors could have four large bedrooms, two on each floor, with bathrooms. It all seems such sense to me. A lot of new houses are so small, people can't get away from each other. No wonder families get so stressed. Where are they supposed to do hobbies and the such? They always say that the biggest cost when building houses is the price of the land, so this would solve the problem, as the houses go upwards rather than outwards. Extra cost minimal!

Meanwhile, back to my flats, and I still had two flats left to sell, with no purchasers in sight. I did get the advice of an auctioneer as I felt time wasn't on my side, and I had a bank loan to pay off! He very kindly told me that in his opinion my work was too good for Hastings, adding that perhaps my next project might be Brighton or Eastbourne. I had used all the same sub-contractors that I'd used on the previous block, with the exception of the plumbers. I had John, the brilliant plasterer who's plastering was as smooth as silk, and who could copy just about any moulding, thus enabling us to repair any of the broken ones. I had Brian the carpenter, Paul the bricklayer, David the electrician, Rob and Noel the new plumbers, and Jack and Mark did all the decorating. They were a brilliant team. As a result of this development, I received my Master Builder certificate, and I had a very good reputation in the Building Control Department because I adhered to the building regulations. I felt my father would have been very proud of me. It took about a year longer than I'd planned to sell the remaining flats, and I didn't get the prices that I was told I would get, but at least they sold, and I am sure that this was because they were so well done. An Italian couple from Milan bought the first floor flat, and ended up buying the ground floor flat as well. They were an interesting couple. He printed the bank notes for Italy, and when they invited us to Milan for a weekend, (I had to take the contract out for them to sign for the ground floor flat), they drove Mike and I out to where one of the factories was. It was fascinating to think that this was where the bank notes were printed. We had lunch, then went for a little walk, and the primroses were out, and lo and behold, there was this very important man picking primroses for me! I was thrilled.

I had no option but to look for another property to convert quickly. Because although the flats at the marina had ultimately sold, any profit I would have made had been eroded away - firstly by having to reduce the prices, then the length of time it ultimately took to sell them, with a year of high interest rates and the expected recession, so all in all it had taken its toll. If the landslide had never happened, the flats would have sold straight away, I'd have been in a good situation when the recession started with all my money invested in other property, and rented out. So what should have been a handsome profit, making me very well off, had actually left me with a cash flow problem. My problems were due entirely to the landslide, and then not helped by the devastatingly high interest rates, due to a recession that the government refused to admit we were in! So I'd had no option but to re-mortgage our house in order to convert this next block very quickly and hope to get back to where I should have been financially. I wouldn't develop another property near a cliff, I might add!

I answered the phone one day, and a young woman asked me if I purchased property. I said that I did, and why was she asking? "Would you buy my mother's house in Godwin Road? It is in a dreadful state," she said, adding, "I've asked other builders and developers to buy it, but no one wants it. My mother doesn't want much for it. Just enough to buy a flat for us both." Yes, I was interested, and made an appointment to view. I went round and had a look at it, and could hardly believe my eyes. I had thought that the marina was in a dreadful state, but this was beyond a joke. Honestly I learnt such a lot about Hastings and the way so many people lived. It was enough to make me a devout socialist. Those poor women were living in a house that should have been condemned. There was so much wrong with it, major problems with damp and dry rot, and the back of the house was falling away into the garden, with floors that had come away from the walls. The poor couple were perched in the top flat, because as the building deteriorated, they had moved up another floor. I asked how much they wanted and we agreed a price. The deal was done, and two very relieved people moved into a nice warm flat. Why hadn't these folk been offered any help from the council? I had seen such a lot of squalor during the years that I had been developing property in Hastings. We've all heard politicians talk about what they would do for the unfortunates of our country if they were ever elected, but when I saw at first hand how so many people actually lived in my own town, it sickened me. I began to get quite interested in politics, and for the first time, I didn't feel very proud of my country.

Mike had become the manager of the bank's Battle branch during this period. Having built up the Silverhill branch from a first board branch bank to a second board branch in just two years his reward was to be moved out into a tiny branch in Battle. He was very hurt by that move.

The house in Godwin Road was truly the pits when I bought it. How well I remember the day when I took a friend round the house to show her how awful it was. I watched her face. She didn't believe anybody would take it on, let alone convert it into flats. There was not one bit of it that didn't need severe treatment. I know that she thought I was totally mad, perhaps I was at this point. I started developing this house with my head swimming. My anxiety level was very high, due to several reasons. Firstly, the effects of the landslide had left me in a precarious position with the bank, and with a large mortgage on our house, so I needed this block of flats to sell very quickly. Also the recession was now biting hard, businesses were starting to go to the wall. Secondly, Mike, who was forty-nine, had been told by the bank that he would have to take early retirement when he reached the age of fifty, which he didn't want. The bank were trimming 5,000 of it'staff at the time. Thirdly, there was the whisper of a major road scheme behind our house, which if true would inevitably make it difficult to sell. Lastly, I was told that I had to have a small operation. So all in all, I was out of my head with worry. We needed to work fast. My team of men tore into the building, starting by digging new drains in the floor of the basement. I love drains. They have always held such fascination for me. They are so important when you think of what goes down there. They were never designed to take what is put down them today, and I'm sure you don't want a graphic description from me.

We did just about everything to that house, completely re-building the back of the house from the new footings up. It had needed to be underpinned, and we had taken this down slightly deeper than necessary because that's what we were like. The 'belt and braces team'. Paul the bricklayer was rebuilding the back of the house, and when he reached a floor level it had to be tied in, something that it hadn't been for many years. The couple that had lived there had not been able to go to the back of the building and look out of the window because the floors had come away from the walls, leaving it very unsafe. As I said, when this problem occurred to each of the lower floors the couple had moved up another level until they were living on the top floor, like birds in a nest.

Basil the architect had done a great job designing the little flats, and as the row of houses was on a slight curve some of the rooms were like slices of cheese. The previous owners had left some furniture behind, including a baby grand piano. I rang up several different piano firms to come and offer me a price for it. One firm came and the young man promptly told me that the piano wasn't worth anything, but offered to take it away. Wasn't he a charitable young man, when you think what they weigh, and he was prepared to go through all the rigmarole of moving it, for a piano that was worthless? I wasn't born yesterday and I replied that if it wasn't worth anything we would put the chain saw through it. His face went very red, and he told me that I should let him have it as he had come such a long way. If this young man hadn't been so greedy and had offered me anything, even five pounds, I would have let him have it gladly, but because of his blatant lie I played him at his own game. "No," I repeated, "if it isn't worth anything we will just have to cut it up." I had no intention of doing that, it was the last thing I would have done. The man got really angry with me, but I kept to my story insisting that we would just have to cut it up. So he left. The piano was in the way of Brian the carpenter, who was by now sawing wood on it. I'd decided to take the piano home, so we got a lorry and some strong men, friends of Brian, and did just that. One of the men knew something about pianos and offered me a few hundred pounds for it. I declined his offer as I was by now getting quite fond of this piano and I wanted to know more about it. So it went into our garage for the time being.

As I mentioned earlier, I had to have a little operation. The problem had been discovered when I went for my 'well-woman' check, and as I had been experiencing pains and general discomfort for some time I was not surprised when I was examined to be told that I had a polyp, which would have to be removed. My doctor also did a smear test at the same time. I didn't think anything more about the smear test, which was done and sent off, as I had never had any problems before with my tests, and thought everything would be alright. My doctor asked me if I would like to see Mr. Pembrey the gynaecologist as he was a popular surgeon, but I asked if I could instead see Mr. Alaily. I had heard glowing reports about him when I had worked for Muriel, the doctor's wife. Off I duly went to see Mr. Alaily, and as I was a private patient I went to his house in Battle. He seemed quite nice and on the ball, and suggested that I went in the following week to have the polyp removed at a private clinic. I was nervous because of my panic attacks, but Mike reassured me that he would stay with me, so I felt re-assured. I had been assured by Mr. Alaily that I would not have to have a D&C. I was adamant that I did not want this procedure carried out on me, as we were trying to have a baby, and at my age it was hard enough to conceive.

I trustingly went along on the due day booked in, with Mike by my side. I spoke to the nurse and then the anaesthetist, and then I got undressed and got into bed. I was given my pre-med and I felt drowsy. The phone rang in my room and the next moment I was handed the telephone, it was put right by my ear. It was Mr. Alaily telling me to sign a form for a D&C with a paragraph underneath which said if necessary they would carry out a hysterectomy. I know these forms are general procedure, having signed one before when it was discovered that I still had some afterbirth inside me, so the form was fairly familiar to me. But firstly, I had been reassured that I would definitely not have to have a D&C, so that was naughty. But the thing that really worried me was that I was not given this form to sign until after I'd had my pre-med and was half asleep. I was in no fit state to argue the toss, so I signed it, and with absolute apprehension now of this surgeon I was wheeled out into the lift for the operating theatre. With my degree of sensitivity this was not good for me, and afterwards when I was back in my room, a nurse kept popping in every half an hour to check my blood pressure, I was told that it had dropped to a very worrying level. I know that shock did that to me.

They wanted me to stay in for at least one night but the room was unbearably hot. It was a very hot summer's day, and there was no air conditioning in my private room, and no en-suite bathroom. The room was also above something that was very noisy, probably the kitchens. Added to that was the sound coming from a lady in the opposite room wailing in distress, with no one obvious doing anything for her, which I found upsetting. Where was the service in this private clinic? I decided, therefore, that I would go home. I had not had very good experiences of hospitals so far, and I firmly believe that many more patients than we are told of, die from shock. Their operations might go well but, we are not just meat, we are mind body and soul, and until the glorious day arrives when this fact it is recognised, people will continue to die.

I went home to my lovely cool luxurious bedroom, and wondered why on earth anyone would pay good money for that lack of standard care. That was just the beginning of a long drawn out nightmare. I was told a few days later by my doctor, when he telephoned me at home, that my smear test had been abnormal, and that I had got pre-cancerous cells. He told me not to panic, but I immediately went into a panic. He carried on explaining to me that there could be several reasons why the cells were abnormal, and then sometimes the cells right themselves. He said I was to go every six months to Mr. Alaily for a check up. I could hardly wait to see Mr. Alaily, to ask him why he had performed a procedure on me that I had specifically asked him not to do. He denied in front of my husband doing the procedure, and then he must have had a lapse of memory because he billed my husband for just that particular procedure that he denied carrying out. I don't know why I continued with this surgeon, I suppose I was too traumatised to think clearly anymore. On the second or third check up I was informed that my cells had changed, not for the better and that I would have to have a biopsy. I went to the hospital and saw Mr. Alaily. Fear completely overwhelmed me, and I completely broke down. I was totally and utterly worn down with stress and I wanted to explain why I was so stressed. I tried to tell him about the landslide, the bank, Mike's forced retirement and the now threatened road-widening scheme behind our house. But no one listened or cared. Mr. Alaily explained that if the biopsy went a certain way, he would have to perform another operation to remove part of my cervix, under a general anaesthetic. I was aghast that having been a private patient under this man that he would over the twelve month period that I had been going to him, allow my cells to change to the point where I needed that kind of treatment. I wanted a second opinion, and more than that, I wanted to get away from that particular surgeon. I didn't trust him at all. Surely he could have carried out the removal of the abnormal cells when he carried out the D&C that I didn't want. It is my considered opinion that there might be a lot of money made in the private sector, from operations and procedures carried out on women that they might not need. What a frightening thought. Mike took over, I was too frightened to think anymore. If I get into the hands of gynaecologists and hospitals, I seem to get injured. I hadn't had a lot of luck with them so far. Mike rang Mr. Pembrey at home, the specialist who was originally recommended by my doctor, and made an appointment for me to see him. To my relief, I was told by Mr. Pembrey that I could have laser treatment for my abnormal cells in outpatients, instead of a full operation. I was so relieved. So why had Mr. Alaily wanted to carry out another operation on me under anaesthetic, and make me even more stressed out? I decided that the N.H.S. is a safer place to be for women. I changed over to the consultant gynaecologist Mr. Pembrey, and I never looked back. He was a super doctor, he put me at ease straight away, and most importantly I trusted him. The laser treatment was carried out in outpatients with the minimum of fuss, successfully. And then Mr. Pembrey put my mind completely at ease, he looked at me across the desk, and smiling, proceeded to tell me that my abnormal cells had nothing at all to do with cancer. Oh dear God, the sheer relief at hearing those words. How I'd worried myself into the ground over the last few months. I walked out of that hospital feeling positively light. Thank you Mr Pembrey.

During this period I was able to finish the patchwork quilt that I had started about ten years earlier. As I was putting it finally together, lining it, backing and edging it, I was aware that there was someone standing next to me, although all I could see was a full length rough woven brown woolen coat and sandals. The quilt took one and a half million hand stitches, and slightly affected my eyesight towards the end. I knew this had been a test to see if I had the perseverance needed for the job I had been chosen to do later on.

Both Mike and I were both showing signs of Battle weariness, but there was a long, long way to go yet.

Back to the flats, they were taking shape fast, and as forms my usual pattern the top one sold straightaway. Even though the recession was well and truly upon us, the government were still emphatically denying that we were in one. One thing I learnt was that if the government denied something you only had to wait and lo and behold the opposite was usually true. I knew we had to work faster. Meanwhile, we desperately needed a holiday and we decided to go to Portugal. We thought it might be our last family holiday together, as my sons were growing up so fast, and the young don't always want to go with parents after a certain age. We chose to go with the Portuguese National Holiday Company. It looked brilliant in the brochure; a large hotel on the Atlantic coast, with every kind of sports facility you could want. We all looked forward to it, me especially, as I felt I needed a holiday more than at any time of my life.

It turned out to be the worst holiday we'd ever had. When we arrived the hotel looked like an army barracks, very primitive and austere. It was greatly in need of renovating, and we learned that after that summer it was to close for renovating. It should never have been allowed to be open, there were holidaymakers moving rooms constantly to get away from leaking pipes, we had to walk around some areas where the floors were wet through. Our room was infested with ants, armies of them walking along the skirting boards. It was perfectly horrid. There were stinking drains just outside our window, and our clothing that was drying on the veranda was stolen. We had the noise of the refuse trucks very early every morning tipping huge containers of bottles into their carts. But worst of all, the brochure had stated that it was a sports complex. What a joke! The pitch and putt was in the woods! The tennis courts we were looking forward to playing on, hired out bent rackets. We purposely hadn't taken ours because it stated that we could hire them. I loved playing tennis and really looked forward to playing every day, but with bent rackets it was obviously hopeless. The swimming pool was not heated, and as this was the Atlantic coast with strong winds at times, the water was bitterly cold.

Julian went down with a kidney infection, and was in bed with a fever. We tried to get a taxi one Sunday to take us to the hospital, when we realised that he was not getting any better. We were told there were no taxis on a Sunday as everybody was in church. We were promised a lift by a member of staff, but we had to wait ages for him. He eventually turned up and took us to the hospital, promising faithfully he would return shortly to take us back to the hotel, but we waited and waited and he never turned up. After Julian saw the doctor in the hospital, which was all a bit barbaric, he was given a prescription to take to the pharmacy. In the absence of our lift arriving to drive us, we had to walk around the little town to find the pharmacy, with Julian feeling very ill, and then walk the two miles back to the hotel. I was feeling treacherous by this time. No wonder people flip their lids. By this time I'd had enough of dear Portugal. I asked at the desk if they could book us on the first plane out the next morning, only to be told that the air space was full of American bombers on their way to the Gulf war, which was raging at that time. We would have to wait maybe days to get out. That was my first experience of being stranded in a country that I didn't wish to be in. By this time I was in tears, and couldn't contain myself anymore. I told them I was disgusted with their treatment of us, making a sick person walk two miles when they had promised, faithfully a car would be sent. "But Madam," he replied, "everybody is in Church." "Yes!" I yelled, "and never did a country need to spend so much time in church. You're all there when it comes to taking money, overcharging for everything, supplying bent rackets and cold swimming pools." I was overcome with rage. When it comes to my sons, if anyone hurts or injures them I'm livid. "If you ever come to England I would be ashamed of my country if we treated you the way we have been treated." We filled in a complaints form, and the manager signed it, acknowledging the faults, and we left it at that.

We had to stay another week there and we made the best of it. There were table tennis tables, and Julian did play for his University, so he enjoyed taking on a few of the Portuguese staff when they were off duty. Poor Julian had been in bed for five days of the holiday, still, he did have the ants for company! We were all very glad to come back to England, I accept that we were unlucky with that hotel and tour company, but it has put us off going to that particular country again. Although we had a form listing eleven complaints against the hotel, signed by the manager and by the tour agent, when it came to claiming compensation from ABTA, the amount paid to us was miserly, and did not even cover the solicitor's costs.

When we got back from Portugal there was a letter waiting for me on the doormat, from the bank. To my shock and horror, the letter informed me that the bank had closed my business down, and sent my account to realisations. I hit the roof, it was ludicrous, as I was so close to finishing the project. I made an appointment to see the new manager at the bank, the man who had replaced Mike at Silverhill, to find out why they had done it without at least informing me beforehand of their decision. I didn't like this man at all. He was cold and totally disinterested in my business. All the decisions to do with my account had always been made at Regional Office, in case anybody thinks I might have had any preferential treatment with my husband in the bank. A bank manager's discretion is only enough to buy a car or to have an extension built, so most businesses of any size deal with Regional Office. Anyway, I'd made an appointment to see the manager, and what he told me was somewhat surprising, and staggered Mike. It appeared that my account had been sent to realisations, or the debt recovery department, and when that happens, the decision is usually final and the business is over. But my account had been sent back from debt recovery to the branch, because they considered it a viable business. Now, in all the years Mike had been in the bank, thirty odd years, he had never ever known that to happen!

I knew that upstairs had had a hand in this. The feeling was so strong, and gave me such confidence. It was just like dealing with an enemy dealing with the bank. Part of the trouble was that I had been regarded as staff when I married Mike, which was ludicrous, as I'd never worked in a bank. Wives of managers are treated as staff, and my account became a staff account and of course staff cannot go overdrawn. Mine was a business account and always had been. Mike said that the trouble was the bank didn't really know what to do with me, as I fell between two stools. No, I said, but I knew what I'd like to have done to them.

The project had run a little over budget, and I needed so little to finish. I was surprised that I had gone over budget because I am very good at costing my jobs out. It was thought that some of the materials left on site had disappeared. Could that have accounted for the shortfall? I'll never know. So, although my account was sent back to the branch because it was regarded as a viable business, the bank manager had no authority to let me have any more money, so the flats had to sit unfinished for what was nearly a year altogether, another wasted year. Is that good business practice? I hardly thought so. I had more than proved my track record of selling properties, having sold three previous blocks of flats and the first flat of this development, and the latter in a recession. This was in my opinion very bad business practice. Didn't they want their money back? Interesting concept that, and I will touch on it again later on. Meanwhile, it was stalemate. Mike's hands were tied, he couldn't help me, but he did have the Regional Director visiting his branch one particular day, and he was going to bring him home for lunch to meet me. Mike wanted this man to see for himself what sort of person I was, and I was able at last to see a face, and put my case forward, and he listened with interest. I explained to him why I had started the business in the beginning, to put a roof over my sons' heads and educate them; how I'd been trained by my father from a very early age, so I wasn't just someone who had decided to be a builder. I did have some inkling of what I was doing, unlike some of their customers I'd heard, who were milkmen one week and then builders the next week. I told him how much I had borrowed for each development, how my flats had always sold, even after a landslide and in a deep recession, and how I'd always paid the money back. I was a customer with a conscience, and I wanted to pay this money back to the bank. But it seemed to me that they didn't want me to do that. I asked him if it had made any sense for my flats to sit for what was almost a year, when I could finish them and then at least be getting some rents in. At least I could be coping with the interest on the loan. And quite a bit of the money would ultimately be mine in this block, money I'd earned with sweat and tears. He told me he would consider my case, and I thanked him for listening.

As a result of this meeting the bank agreed that I could complete the work and let the flats. By then property prices were so low that flats which would have sold a year earlier for £45,000 were now selling for between £8,000 and £15,000. The recession so strongly denied by the Tory government was biting hard, the economy had overheated to boiling point and burst. The dreadful effect of the Chancellor not keeping a tight lid on the country's finances was to send businesses to the wall every day. Some businesses had been in families for generations, but instead of banks nursing loyal customers through until things picked up, the banks were just pulling the rugs from under them, and anybody else who was experiencing any difficulty. This had a knock-on effect, because escalating unemployment meant people without income, and because nobody would wait for their money, homes were being re-possessed by building societies at a rate of over six thousand a month in 1991. The big boys were snapping property up at auctions for next to nothing. What was going on in this country was downright evil, and was to change the face of Britain forever. Loyalty went. There was to be no more loyalty to customers, in any institution. The customer was always wrong and easily disposed of. Bank accounts were made impossible for a huge amount of people who'd fallen by the wayside. Credit reference lists contained the names of anyone who had fallen on hard times, and they made sure that you stayed down. Quality went, with the lack of money in the average persons pocket, the introduction of cheap and cheerful shopping began, bargain basements sprang up, everything under a pound, and quality seconds.

But much worse than all that was the change we were all to experience in our family life, which had taken a hammering since the sixties. Now we were seeing the beginning of the end of the family in this country. The no loyalty at the top had spread right across the board and so loyalty to each other was also waning, with more and more people living together and more and more babies born out of wedlock. Anyway back to the banks. Banks and building societies were repossessing properties at such a rate, sending properties and businesses to auction and selling them off at ridiculously low prices, and then going back to the customers for them to make up the shortfall, but with what? Where was the common sense in all that? If you'd lost your business where were you going to make up the shortfall from?

The government was now forced to admit that there was a recession. Goodness me, they were bright, spotting that at last! It certainly wouldn't have benefited me at all, to sell my flats at the prices they were selling for at that precise moment. But at least I now had rents coming in, and the cost of my borrowing was being covered, so that was a much better scenario. All I had to do now was make sure my flats were always tenanted, and sit tight until the recession was over and property prices went up again! That was the end for many years of my developing programme. But I had learned such a lot along the way that I felt that that in itself had made it all worthwhile.

As I said earlier the bank decided to get rid of five thousand of their staff. Mike had already been informed when he was forty-nine that he would have to take voluntary early retirement at age fifty, another major blow, but when he asked what would happen if he decided he wanted to stay, they replied that this was not an option. If he refused to go, they would find some bad lending that he had done and in effect dismiss him for poor work. Mind you, he was forty-nine when they told him he was going to have to take early retirement, and then they kept him on for another year until he was fifty. Doesn't exactly smack of a manager producing bad work does it? They'd have got rid of him straight away if that was the case. As every bank manager knows, where you are in the business of lending money there are bound to be one or two cases over the years where it goes wrong. That was inevitable. So the bank had him over a barrel, and they knew it. This was a man who had been a true company man, who lived for his job and who had battled into work whatever the weather conditions, and however ill he felt. But loyalty was only one way, as I stated earlier, and he was just a number to them. Then they did something, which was a bit naughty. They coerced him into commuting a part of his modest pension, and use the funds to reduce my company's overdraft, because he was a director. Was nothing sacred, was there nothing they hadn't got the powers to do? Oh yes, there is one place that they will not be able to buy or push their way into.....!

Mike contacted the union, but they were powerless to help. Margaret Thatcher had dealt with the unions. They had gone from the sublime, and they did have too much power at one time, to the ridiculous, from powerful to useless. So Mike was to be another of the brainy men and women of this country thrown on the scrap heap of life in their forties and fifties. This was the example set by government and institutions, a non-caring society to whom people were a throwaway commodity.

Then came the final awful hideous blow. We had known when we'd bought the house that there were plans to widen the road behind, but the close had been screened by a little wood, so we hadn't really worried too much about it. We'd heard rumours for a while of a possible road widening scheme, then suddenly out of the blue there was talk in the road of a massive interchange to be built at the back of our houses, with the possibility of also knocking a couple of our neighbours houses down. Suddenly our house was worth a third of its original value, and because nobody would want to live near a massive interchange, it became un-saleable, so therefore worthless. We were well and truly cornered, with no visible way out, and were out of our minds with worry. To think that I had owned over a million pounds worth of property during a five year period, twenty two properties in all. I'd even had my own insurance agency. But because of the series of events, and because of Mike's enforced early retirement and then the road scheme, it had all being eroded piece, by piece, by piece. But somewhere inside myself, I knew there was a good reason behind all of it. I felt that there was a definite reason as to why I had been able to have a good look into so many aspects of life, which I wouldn't have been able to do if I hadn't had my business. What was upstairs leading me to do?

I then had a dream that was to give me tremendous hope. The dream was of me standing in our garden at Beauport Gardens talking to my two sisters over the fence. We were all young girls in this dream, and then I left them standing in the garden, and I started to run. I was running up the road which was uphill, through a series of fire doors, quite a lot of fire doors, until I got to the top of the road where there was a car park. In the car park, standing there with her two daughters, one in her arms and one standing holding onto her hand, was Janet. I realised the significance of this. The uphill bit was to be the struggle, my constant uphill struggle with life. The fire doors were dangerous obstacles to be got through or over, and the car park was somewhere flat, where you leave your vehicle or in this case, problems, and Janet represented familiar ground, and happier times. I was always having dreams, which are information from the Spirit World, and the dreams guided me through all my trials and tribulations. It was to be many years, I might add, before I got to the car park, but at least I was given the knowledge that I would eventually get there.

I felt utterly wrung out, like a rag. Breathing wasn't something I took for granted, panic attacks make you feel like that. I knew that I was being tested to the n'th degree, but I didn't know at that time what the reason was. In the early days of knowing Peter, he had told me that I was in training, and I had replied 'What for, third world war?' I was in need of some earthly help and reassurance, just to confirm that what I felt was going on in my life was on track, and that I hadn't got off the spiritual track which is so important to me. I went up to White Lodge to talk to the senior tutor there. I liked Cicely, and had a lot of respect for her. I explained to her what was happening in my life, and I wanted to know if I was dealing with it properly. First of all she gave me some desperately needed healing, and the top of my head was cold which Cicely said was due to my being out of my body. I did try so hard to control that side of myself, by surrounding myself with light and meditating. But at times because I was so pre-occupied with the stress of daily life, I forgot, and as a result I would come out of my body, fortunately nothing like the first time at White Lodge. I was learning gradually to control myself.

With regard to the advice I needed, Cicely felt it was best if upstairs talked to me direct, and she gave me a mental exercise to do, which would show me how to communicate with them. "Don't do the exercise in the bath," she said, "in case you fall asleep." She added that it might not work for me the first time, but to try it anyway. I couldn't wait to do it, and that evening made sure I was all by myself and that I wouldn't be disturbed. The exercise was this. I had to meditate, and then in my mind I had to find a cave. The cave could be anywhere I liked, in the country or by the sea, in a wood or in a city, wherever I felt the most comfortable. The cave could be furnished to my liking, as it was my home. I was to enter the cave, walk down a long dark corridor where I would come to a door on the left. I was to go through the door into a room. The room was filled with light. I had to go through the light and then I would find a room. That was as much as I was told. This is what happened to me. I chose my cave by the sea. There were many steps up to my cave and the view out to sea was of the tide out and miles of lovely sand. My cave had a door, which I went through into a small room or hallway, where there were people standing around, who were familiar to me. Then there was the long dark passageway, which I went down, and at the end of the passageway on the left was the door, which I went through into a room. The room was filled with light, and I went into and through the light. I then saw another doorway on the right, which I went through, into a room where people were sitting around a table. It worked first time for me and I spoke to the people sitting around the table. I refer to them as the Elders, the heavenly councillors, and I could ask them about anything at all that I wanted to know.

But something else happened to me after I had spoken to the elders. I was invited through into the halls of learning, which is a massive library. It would have to be massive because that is where the books of our lives are stored. I was shown to a shelf where there were a lot of very large books, all different colours. I was told that the white one was mine, and when I picked it up it was the book of my lives. It was so amazing, and I was told that I could open it if I wanted to. I did open the first page, and I saw my first life. I didn't wish to read any further than the first page, as something inside me told me that it wasn't necessary. Suffice it to say I was a very ancient soul. I think it could have hindered my incarnation to have read any more. I might have dwelt on it too much and not got on with the job I've come to do. So I closed it and put it back on the shelf. In order to come out of the cave, I had to reverse it all. Walking through the doorway of the library back into the room where the elders were sitting, through that doorway and back into the room filled with light, through the light again and back through the door leading to the dark passageway, making sure I closed the door properly behind me. I had to walk back up the dark passageway to the entrance hall and out the front door. I was to make this journey nearly every day whilst life was tough and decisions had to be made, asking the elders for advice. I realised how lucky I was to have that kind of ability at my fingertips. Gradually over the years the journey changed, through nothing that I did consciously. I found many more rooms and staircases leading to different levels. It was wonderful beyond words.

Because the bank had made me wait a year to complete my project, I had missed the opportunity to sell the flats at reasonable prices, which I know I would have done. I had lost out by having money tied up in flats that had gone from being worth £200,000 down to £40,000 and then having to be rented out. With the money I would have got back, I would have cleared the second charge on our house, thus enabling the mortgage to be much, much smaller. Then I would have invested in another property, probably one already converted into flats, and that way I could have used the rents as my income. I had now to find another form of income. And fast. We had a house we had tried to sell but couldn't, and I had a husband thrown on the scrap-heap like thousands of other brainy men and women in their forties and fifties, and on a reduced bank pension at fifty. I felt then that something very wrong was going on in my country. Businesses were still going to the wall every day, good businesses that had been in families for generations, and for every business going to the wall, there was unemployment. Unemployment equals no money, equals no mortgage payments, equals eviction. Two hundred and fifty thousand homes were re-possessed during the period of 1989 to 1993, and for every house re-possessed there was the possibility of a family getting divorced because of the economic strain, with the added possibility of illness for the parents, again because of the strain. Heart attacks, strokes, cancers, nervous breakdowns etc were inevitable for many, and the effects on the children of those families are now coming to light. Years later we can see with our own eyes, the result of a lot of those actions. Because of the incompetence of the government's management of the economy, and the blinkered ideological dogma of a government who had put owner-occupation at the top of every list at the expense of affordable rented housing, we now have a nation of very insecure people. And I might add, very aggressive people, many of who are still being hounded because of negative equity when their houses were sold off too cheaply. Job security is a thing of the past, divorce is commonplace, many are now afraid to risk marriage in the first place. As a result we now have a nation with many youngsters totally out of control. Well done government! It was like a war, but a war that no one had experienced before, because it felt like the enemy was our own people. I felt if I could just hang on, and many is the time I didn't know how I would, I would somehow get through it. I had to trust my faith. It hadn't let me down before. Things went from bad to worse until one day.....

In late October 1991, I discovered that I was pregnant (that was the exciting bit). It was only a couple of months since I'd had my laser treatment for my abnormal cells. Mr. Pembrey couldn't understand why I'd had such a bad reaction to the treatment. Well no one could have guessed that I was pregnant, not even me, because I was having normal periods at the time. When I discovered I was pregnant, Mike and I were ecstatic. We thought I must have been about three and a half months pregnant. I only enjoyed it for literally a moment, because not long afterwards I started to get pains in my abdomen and frightening palpitations. I knew I was having a miscarriage. Oh, why did that have to happen to me? Mike rushed home from the bank and rang Mr. Pembrey, who came straight round to the house. I was to go to the hospital straightaway for a scan, just to make sure that it wasn't an ectopic pregnancy. As it was bonfire night Mr. Pembrey wanted to go home and let the fireworks off with his children, he said he'd meet us at the hospital about an hour later. I had a scan, it wasn't an ectopic pregnancy, I'd had a miscarriage. He advised a D&C for me but I declined. Was my nightmare never to end? I wanted, this time, to be in control of my precious body, I wanted to see Nick Sofroniou my homeopathic doctor. I told Mr. Pembrey of my decision and he was somewhat surprised. What could a homeopathic doctor do that a surgeon couldn't? I was adamant in my decision, so I was given three days, on the third day I was to return to the hospital for a scan to see if everything had cleared. If it hadn't cleared we all know what he was going to suggest. Yes a D&C. I went to see Nick, a man I'd consulted lots of times before, and a truly brilliant naturopathic doctor. I was told to boil up a concoction of red wine and cloves and drink it, it tasted lovely. But more than that it worked, everything came away, and when I went back for my scan, it was clear. Mr. Pembrey was totally amazed, and because of that incident and my dedication to alternative medicine I was able to tell Mr. Pembrey about my dream of orthodox medicine and alternative medicine one day working together in the same building. He was very interested and he asked me if I would be able to help at the Hastings Cancer Help Centre, which was a registered charity set up to bridge the gap between orthodox medicine and alternative medicine, with advice to patients on the various treatments available to them. I readily agreed.

When I was in bed recovering from my miscarriage, I heard my child speak to me. I heard her voice so clearly as she said 'I'll be back, Mum, don't worry'. That relieved me, and although I was sad, I coped much better with it. Then I heard my mother talking to a visitor downstairs, then I heard footsteps and the door opened, it was Janet. She had just popped in to see me on the off chance, on one of her trips to Hastings. She looked at me worriedly, "Are you really ill Stella?" she enquired. "I've just lost my baby, Janet," I replied and burst into tears. She hugged me.

That dreadful experience had a frightening effect on me. My stress level was dangerously high, I was traumatised by everything going on around me. What would happen to me next? When Mike left the house for the bank and Jeremy left for college, I found myself standing on the same spot in the hall for up to three hours until they returned. Sometimes I would look longingly up the stairs, wondering how anybody got up there. I was unable to move. Fortunately, this condition did not last for more than a few weeks. I thought I was going mad.

There had been a time when I was thinking of developing two large derelict hotels. I had a lender interested in backing me for development purposes, but I was turned down, because it was Hastings, because of the huge amount of drug addicts, unmarried mothers and high unemployment. I had always wanted to do really well for Hastings, a town that I had become so fond of, a town where I'd had my business and met my husband. And a town that at one time in the eighties looked as if it might well and truly get on the map. It's a town that had been done a great injustice by successive councils, by bringing in maybe too many of the overspill council house dwellers from London, and then too many of the mentally ill, when mental homes were closed down. I'm afraid Hastings had a reputation for being a dumping ground.

233

It's good to help people, it's essential to help people, but the people must also be given the means to help themselves once they've arrived, with jobs and proper healthcare. In order to get well paid jobs investment was badly needed for the infrastructure i.e. roads and rail links. Hastings was left behind with no main roads. Who would invest in a town like that? The result was poorly paid jobs keeping a lot of people on the breadline.

With the mentally ill, I felt that it wasn't so much a case of it's much better for the mentally ill to be in the community, (for some it was), but rather that the government was washing its hands of a whole group of people, some of whom desperately needed help and care. Care was a word that was fast being eroded from the English dictionary. I was to look at several properties for development that housed the mentally ill who had been re-located from mental hospitals when Thatcher decided we no longer needed to look after them. I agree that there were many people who should never have been there in the first place, but there are also many, who should for their own sakes never have been put into the community. The squalor that these wretched people lived in the community was unbelievable, with urine soaked beds, disgusting toilet facilities, and kitchens so filthy that I would be afraid my dogs would catch something. I often used to ring Social Services and inform them of what I'd seen, but what could they do? I also met a lot of young people sleeping rough in derelict hotels. What a sad indictment for this country to have so many homeless people. In the twentieth century when man had the technology to land on the moon, I find it unacceptable that there are any homeless people in our country. Every town should have enough hostel accommodation for them. Some of the youngsters were drug addicts, and I had to be very careful where I walked because of used needles. I wondered how many of the kids were from children's homes, and had to leave when they were sixteen. Stupid law, that, just when they are at an age when they really need guidance there isn't any, and so many of the girls end up pregnant in order to get a home. And some could be from homes where there was a stepparent who they couldn't get along with. For a country, who is always sending aid to other countries I found it all much too hard to take on board, I became more and more political as time went by, and the more I found out about what was really going on the more disturbed I was becoming.

When Mike was in the bank we had received an invitation to visit the House of Commons as guests of Janet Fookes M.P. She was a customer of Mike's at the bank, and a lovely person. What a wonderful day that was. Everybody was there that I had wanted to see; Ted Heath, Margaret Thatcher, Neil Kinnock and many more. It was Prime Minister's question time, and we watched from the gallery. Afterwards we had lunch on the terrace in a large marquee. In the corner of the marquee was all the food laid out for one to help oneself. Janet's mother was busy tipping several sundae dishes of raspberries into one bowl for me. It was one of those wonderful moments you never forget. I had been brought up in the Labour Party and had only moved over to the Tory Party when Margaret Thatcher was their leader. In many ways she was a very brilliant lady and was not afraid to go out on a limb. But in other ways she didn't understand the psychological side of life, everybody owning their own home was ideology and not realistic as we are all on different levels of capability. When the economy overheated and the recession bit hard, it became the party of very little compassion for the ordinary man and woman in the street. I was gradually returning to my socialist beliefs but when election time came round, the Tories were returned, much to my horror..

Meanwhile, we were in a dreadful financial predicament. I had lost my income and I had commitments like anybody else. We were suddenly living on Mike's bank pension, with Mike applying for any kind of job that came along, anything from fitting blinds to being a maintenance man. He was shell shocked, and couldn't believe that after thirty-one loyal years service there was not any loyalty back. He couldn't have been more of a company man if he'd tried. Mike had lived for his job. It was a country of no loyalty anymore. If you were loyal you were thought to be nuts. 'Look after number one' everybody said.

When clever men and women have to take early retirement between forty-five and fifty-five, an enormous amount of talent is flushed down the lavatory. What price do you put on experience? Actually, it's priceless! I felt more and more convinced that something far more serious was going on in my country, and I really felt that respectable, middle aged, hard working married people who'd given the best years of their lives to their companies and country were no longer required. Insensitivity was the order of the day. Banks, building societies and credit card companies were employing youngsters who were little more than robots, all working to a formula. If you fell behind with any payments you were automatically put on a credit register, where you could stay for up to six years. I hardly knew anybody who wasn't on a register. I used to write to Margaret Thatcher and ask if she was aware of what was going on. Because what was going on was wrong. I always had a reply from Margaret Thatcher. That's one thing I admired about her, the lengths she went to answer my letters. Meanwhile, I tried to think of all the different ways I could earn some money. Should we let part of our house, have students, or run a catering company from home, dinner parties and such? I was a good cook. Then one day...

A chance remark about buying and selling fridges to make a few pounds got me started on what was to be our salvation. We had invited one of our neighbours, Ray, over for coffee one morning. Ray had been made redundant from a very good job, and he was only in his forties. He had needed to make some extra money, and so he started buying and selling fridges. I knew a little about auctions, from my days with William when I'd had to furnish our flats for letting. I listened to what Ray told me about prices, what certain items could be bought for, and what he was selling them for, and then I went along to a few salesrooms to have a look for myself. I very soon got the knack of buying and selling. I started with five fridges and freezers in the garage and ended up with a garage filled to the brim, not only with fridges but with furniture as well. I had quite a shop in the garage, at one time Mike told me he'd counted fifty-two items for sale. I bought cheaply and sold for a nice profit, and the money from the profit was an absolute lifesaver. And yes, I paid tax on it all!

The recession had affected many of the families in the road. One day, my mother came over to stay, and she remarked about the number of cars parked outside the houses in the middle of the day. I replied that at least half of the husbands were at home, through either early retirement, redundancy or they'd lost their businesses.

It was shocking, and I was even more shocked when the Chancellor said that 'unemployment was a price worth paying' for getting the economy going again. It was a far more serious situation than the government had ever acknowledged, and there was quite a wartime spirit in the close. All of us in the close were in negotiation with the Department of Transport about our homes, homes that were all blighted because of the enormous interchange that was to be built behind us. Eventually the D.o.T. sent a man to see us, who after careful consideration made us all offers. We accepted our offer straightaway. Mike had by this time got a job as a Fund Manager with the NHS at a surgery in Rye, so we thought it would be nice to have a fresh start in Winchelsea, near Rye. The D.o.T. took its time paying out, but we didn't expect that it would ultimately take a year! We couldn't wait for a fresh start, so we were the first to leave the close. It was a sad day in many ways, but we needed to turn our backs on all that horror and have a fresh start.

I had found a lovely house to rent in Winchelsea town, the smallest town in England, where we could collect our thoughts. I had taken over a shop in St. Leonards, and moved all the furniture from the garage into it. Jeremy was going to live in the flat over the shop, and run the shop until he decided what he wanted to do with his life.

On the day of moving, two large removal vans came, as we had an enormous amount of furniture, some of it very valuable. They packed it all for us and then unpacked it all at the new house. That was the best way to move, and they were such cheerful men as well. Eventually when we were installed in our new home we sat back and smiled at each other, and we hadn't done that for a long time. This was the beginning of a new chapter, a chapter in which a lot more was to happen to us, but at least we were able to get our breath, even if it was only temporarily. Julian graduated for the second time, with honours in Engineering, and was grabbed straight away by the Ford motor company. His childhood dream had come true.

Chapter 11 - Recycling

I felt much better in myself than I had done for years. Even my eyesight seemed much improved. I'd always been very fortunate with my eyesight, and I hadn't started wearing glasses until my late forties, but I think all the hand stitching in the patchwork quilt eventually weakened my eyesight, enough to wear glasses. It's also amazing the bad effect stress has on the eyes. But I was feeling total and utter relief that we were out of Beauport Gardens, and although we'd lived there for six years, and experienced lots of happy times in the house, the last two years had been so dreadful, that both of us just wanted a fresh start. Pastures new often give you a fresh view on life, and we certainly reverted back to our old selves, if only for a short while. We knew that there would be a lot to sort out, but I am a great believer in one day at a time. We are only alive today. Yesterday has gone and tomorrow when it arrives is today. It works for me, and provided I have done everything for that day that was on my list. I didn't worry about tomorrow. I love lists!

We liked the area we had moved to very much. For a long time I had wanted to move over to that area. It slightly reminded me of parts of France as I looked across the Rother Valley. There were good walks for Thomas as well. It was all incredibly beautiful. We met Rosemary at a party, and she offered to come and help us in the house. She was a cheery soul, with always the right words for us. The house seemed massive. I had thought Beauport was large, but this was even larger, hence Rosemary was very needed.

I mentioned to Rosemary one day that the vicar hadn't called on us yet. I thought it a bit unusual in a place like Winchelsea where the church dominates the little town, and we were living right across the road from the church. She came back later in the week with a bit of useful information for us. "The vicar doesn't call on temporary people," she said. Well, you could have knocked me over with a feather. I had to laugh. "Aren't we all temporary people, or does he know something we should all know?" I couldn't get over that. Now I'd heard everything. Isn't that disgraceful, it wouldn't have happened years ago. The vicar would have called on all new people in his Parish, and we were in need of all the help we could get.

Meanwhile, I still had a business to run, there were several freeholds to look after and maintain, a block of four flats which I had to make sure was fully tenanted at all times with the rents going to the bank, and now a second hand furniture shop. I loved going to auctions, and to think, years ago when I first went I was so nervous I could hardly speak. Now I was positively bold. It's amazing what bargains can be bought from auctions. As I didn't have much of a cash flow when I first started going to auctions, I tended to buy all the furniture that no one else wanted. In fact I think I was relied upon to some extent to take all the unsold furniture away at the end of the sale, especially at one particular auction house. It was all rubbish in their eyes, but to me it was all wonderful, everything deserved to be loved. I loved making things feel proud again, I think everything has feelings, whether it's an old crumbling house or a tatty piece of furniture. When things are mended, cleaned, re-polished and in some cases re-upholstered they are transformed. I have such imagination. I'm sure I see differently to other people.

Mike was very busy with his two jobs, the surgery where he was the Fund Manager for the N.H.S. and the local Hospice, where he was the Business Co-ordinator. He felt much happier because at last he felt that he was helping people again, unlike the last few months at the bank where he wasn't allowed to help anyone! So there was a lot going on in our lives.

The property we were renting had originally been the coach house for the large house nearby. Upstairs it had five bedrooms, with the largest one turned into an upstairs sitting room, painted in a lovely duck egg blue, very elegant. Next to it was a kitchenette, very convenient, as it was quite a long way to walk downstairs if you wanted a cup of tea! Downstairs it had a large sitting room which we used as an office, a large dining room, the main kitchen, with a utility/dining area, and a downstairs bedroom with its own bathroom, which we had made into Julian's room, for when he came to stay. Outside there was a walled garden at the back, with a Victorian conservatory. To the front were high walls with high wrought iron gates and a paved courtyard area where you could park six cars. It was a lovely house, and our furniture fitted into it perfectly.

Life seemed fairly normal for us for a change. We even started going to the pub, something we'd never done, but it was right on our doorstep and they did lovely food. On Friday evenings we started going regularly to the cinema in Eastbourne, we even went to the occasional dance. We attended Julian's second graduation ceremony. Oh, how confident he looked as he walked onto the stage, stopping and chatting to the important guest speaker who was handing out the certificates. Was that my little lad, who all those years ago had wanted to die? The boy who'd thought life had dealt him the wrong cards! Oh I was so proud of him. How he deserved all that he had achieved.

Then after a couple of months, out of the blue one day, the phone rang. It was Julian. "I've been laid off," he said. I couldn't believe it. "Why, what's happened?" 'They've had to cut back on the workforce, so they have tried to keep as many married men on as they can, so it's a case of last in first out, and single men have got to go first. So I'll be home at the weekend, if that's OK." Of course it was alright. We were a family at war, and we would stick together come what may. I was sad for him and not a little worried. Ford had grabbed him when his results had come out, as I've mentioned before. Still, life was not the same for any of us anymore, and we had to keep going, come what may, with chins in the air at all times. Their loss was my gain. The house always seemed so empty without my sons. Julian could maybe help with all the shit shovelling that we were going to have to do, with regard to getting the D.o.T. to pay up, and dealing with other debts that had been incurred whilst trying to hang on with our fingertips. I got his room ready for him. It had been years since he had lived at home full time. I was nevertheless sad for him, but little did I know then what was in store for us, and how invaluable his help was going to be. Upstairs had a hand in this, although I didn't realise that for ages.

The shop in St. Leonards was doing very well. It was in a good position situated on a corner of a very busy cross roads. As cars were standing waiting to move across these busy roads they couldn't help but see into the large windows. I had to carry out a lot of improvements to the building before we opened. The building was owned by the Council and in return for me carrying out some improvements, they gave me a rent holiday in return. The building was damp, riddled with dry rot, and of course filthy! I expect to find filth now, we are fast becoming a truly dirty nation. Jeremy had a hand in doing the flat up, it was all good practice for him, and he made a nice cosy home for himself above the shop. He hadn't wanted to come to Winchelsea with me and Mike, and it seemed an ideal time for a bit of independence for him, so he could live there, and run the shop until he found something he wanted to do for a living. As it turned out he went back to college to do his A-Levels. He had tried earlier to go on to sixth form college from school, but he found it all too much then. His phobia had been too much to overcome, and he'd spent most of the time sitting in the bicycle sheds smoking, probably trying to get up the courage to go into the building. So I was pleased that off his own back he had wanted another chance at college, and although I had to fund his living from the shop takings, I did give him the opportunity.

Keith, a friend of Jeremy's, offered to run the shop for me, until he found an opening in the job market working with computers, which he later did. The shop was to prove a useful stopgap for many of the people who worked there.

Having got Julian back home I decided that we needed to open a shop in Rye. We needed more income, and as I had Julian's help,

I would make the most of it. Rosemary had mentioned on more than one occasion that two young men had opened an estate agent in Rye. We both hoped that they would do well; it was a difficult time for all businesses. Little did I know that I knew one of them quite well. After looking around to find just the ideal shop for us, not too big, so not too expensive, I rang this particular local independent Estate Agent. "You have a shop to let in Market Road," I asked. "I recognise that voice," said the young man, "that's Mrs. Stickland." It turned out to be the young man who had shown me around one of the derelict hotels in Hastings that I had previously tried to buy. "Whatever's happened to you, looking at shops to rent?" Martin asked with utter disbelief. I wasn't the person I had been years earlier. I didn't even feel like her anymore, and I certainly didn't want to explain all my problems anymore. To keep going over it was exhausting, and people didn't really understand. I was, however, very pleased to hear a familiar voice, and there was a definite air of compassion in his voice. I had an ally in Rye, thank you God.

After viewing the little shop, I decided to go ahead with it. I called it 'Imagination', a logical name for me, as mine was rampant. I opened the shop with very little stock. All I had were a few pieces that we brought over from the St. Leonards shop. Rye was a very different market to St. Leonards, and I would have to build the business up again from scratch, something I'd got very used to doing. I had got Julian to help me now, which was a blessing. He was to stay with me for what was to be a year altogether, although we didn't know that at the time. The shop in Rye was different to any other shop in the town, in as much as it wasn't antique, or bric-a-brac, and it wasn't modern. We mixed it all up, a few antique pieces, mostly Victorian and Edwardian, up to modern day, with Art Deco, utility war time furniture, fifties sofas, alongside Parker Knoll and G Plan. And it worked. It became a very popular shop, and it wasn't long before you could hardly get in the door because there was so much stock in there. Julian proved to be an absolute slave driver, there was no slacking whist he was about. "What are you doing, Mother," he would say as I sloped off for a cup of coffee and a rest. "Have you polished all the new stock yet?" If I had polished everything, he would then suggest I did another job. Honestly, who's the boss? Don't answer that, I thought to myself. This was a family of all chiefs and no Indians. But to be fair Julian would spend days rubbing down a piece of furniture and re-polishing it. He was such a perfectionist in everything that he did. "If a job is worth doing, it's worth doing well, Mother," he would say. Well I'm glad that I was such a good teacher!!!

During this period, Mike was still working for the doctors' surgery and loving every minute of it. This was a man who had previously hated anything to do with illness, and certainly wouldn't have discussed illness, and now was really interested in it all, learning all the different names of diseases. Patients would come up to him in the streets and thank him for their new knees or new hips. It was lovely for him to be helping people again.

One day whilst visiting friends, who had sadly been one of the countless thousands who'd lost their business and subsequently had their home re-possessed, I was asked if I was interested in marketing a new product, which was an ingenious radiator valve. They themselves were unable to do it as it was going to be a costly affair. I replied that I was very interested, and it turned out to be an isolating valve for radiators, that when fitted you no longer had to drain down a system when decorating. You just turned this screw in the valve at each end of the radiator, and lifted the radiator off the wall. Well it seemed like a good idea, well a smashing idea actually. And this is where Julian's knowledge of engineering drawing came in so useful and my business acumen. We even got a Grant from the DTI to help us get started. We patented it, although you can't really effectively patent something like that, as someone else only has to tweak the design slightly to make it their own. Anyway we did a lot of work on this valve, Julian on the technical side and me on the marketing side. It was so interesting, we learnt a lot about an area we'd previously known nothing about. We even got an interview at B &Q's head office to see the senior plumbing buyer, I say even because it is very difficult to speak to anybody at those places. B & Q were very keen, and gave us a preliminary order for when we were ready to market it. The buyer told us to ring him when we were in a position to go forward. We left that building on cloud nine, wow, and our first order and with one of the biggest DIY outlets.

We visited several large companies after that and got them interested in our valve. We were very pleased with ourselves. As I said it is hard enough even to get through the doors of those places, so we had done extremely well.

Julian during this time was asked to go back to Ford, and to my amazement he said no. I was sitting opposite him in the office at home. It was early closing day in Rye, and we took the opportunity on those days to market the valve and deal with apportioning the money we'd made in the shops to the various creditors. When his phone rang, and I quickly realised who he was talking to I was shocked. "What are you doing saying no?" I demanded. "I'm not ready to go back yet," he replied, "I can't leave you with all this unfinished business." I was so concerned that he had given up a golden opportunity, and with a company like Ford, as well. But he argued that he knew what he was talking about, so that was that. I couldn't argue with Julian. So we continued with the valve. I was trying to get a manufacturer to make it for a price that was sensible, and I rang a company in Israel and one in Italy. We also continued running the two shops, going to several auctions a week, then restoring and cleaning all the furniture before it was sold in the shops. And of course not forgetting the flats and their tenants in Godwin Road. He was such a support for me, such a worker. Such a slave driver! I was not allowed to slope off even for a moment!

Mike and I still hadn't had a pay out from the Department of Transport. They owed us one hundred and fifty four thousand pounds, which we in turn owed to the building society. We both thought that having accepted their offer, which was very much on their terms, take it or leave it, the matter would be settled quickly. We never dreamt that it would take a year, during which time the mortgage still had to be paid. It was ridiculous, we were paying rent as well during that period. We contacted various solicitors to see if they could help us deal with the Department of Transport, but we found that finding a good solicitor was to be the most difficult job. Many solicitors had jumped on the bandwagon in the eighties, threatening letters, repossessions and court cases were easy money for them and they changed just like the banks had, from gentlemen's clubs to the opposite!!! The firm I had used for years in Hastings had always been brilliant, but the solicitor I had used for the company in the early days had left, and gone to work in commerce. It was a big blow at the time, I knew he would be hard to replace. I was handed over to another solicitor in the firm, he was nice but we just didn't gel. He wasn't quick minded enough for me. I needed a quick-minded person. The lady legal assistant, Barbara, was brilliant, and had been excellent with my conveyancing. But I needed a tough solicitor now, someone who could fight for us.

I'm a person who hates change for the sake of it, but I had no choice but to find another solicitor quickly. I spoke to a barrister friend and he recommended a man in Lewes, with whom I quickly made an appointment. After a lengthy meeting with this solicitor, and after he'd promised swift action and compensation from the D.o.T. not only because of the time they'd taken to pay us, but also for the thousands of pounds worth of items they'd insisted we'd left behind, which he thought was a cheek. For reasons unknown to us, he totally lost interest in our case. So I had no option but to find yet another solicitor, which I did. I suggested to Mike that we use the firm I had worked for in Worthing, and he agreed. I made an appointment to see the son of one of the solicitors who'd been a partner when I'd worked there back in the sixties. He seemed very nice on the phone, and on the ball. I hoped that this time all would be resolved, but when this latest solicitor needed the deeds to my properties transferred to him, we discovered that the Lewes solicitor had lost some of the deeds of my properties. Well, maybe I should have waited to see what the Lewes solicitor was like first before transferring all my deeds to him but judging by what he said, I thought, at the time, that I might as well transfer all the company business over to him, and that included the deeds of four blocks of flats. Anyway he'd lost several of them, it was great fun, I don't think! However I did think that I had made a good decision to go back to Worthing, as the solicitor was much better. At least he looked fairly interested, which was a start!

I had been trying to get a price from different manufacturing companies abroad for manufacturing the isolating valve, and after speaking to various companies, I ended up contacting one in

England, who seemed very interested. After several phone calls, they sent someone down to see us. Julian and I thought it was to talk over quantities and prices, but to our utter surprise and horror, this spokesman for the valve company stood in our office and told us that they were going to pinch the valve, and what was worse, he said that he was on his way to a firm of solicitors to make sure that they got it. "You can't play with the big boys," he told me. We have plenty of money to make the valve, and you will not be able to afford to fight us. Well what could we do? This was my first insight into big business and what goes on. I never cease to be amazed at the fact that so many people have no conscience at all, and no fear of any consequences for their actions at the end of the day. I know they are not bothered about that, they just live for the moment, and their God is money. We were totally horrified, after all the hard work we had put into it, to lose all that was beyond belief. It was another major setback, and another experience to go into my database of life.

After licking our wounds we went back to the shops and back to dealing with ordinary folk, the salt of the earth type people, wondering again what all that work on the valve was about, all the hard work that we'd put into it, and the cost of it all. I reckoned that the work had cost us about ten thousand pounds altogether, and now it seemed all wasted. Still I was never one to sit crying or worrying for long. We had two busy shops to deal with.

And then it happened. Julian had another phone call from Ford. Who could believe it. A major motor company like that, who could have anyone they liked. I thought he had cooked his goose with them after he had said 'No' to them the last time, but there they were again, on the telephone. This time things on the financial front were sorting themselves out, the D.o.T. had paid up, after a year, which was a fairly disgusting amount of time to make anybody wait. There had been a hell of a lot to sort out financially, one way and another, and between us we'd managed to do it, we'd managed to pay off a lot of creditors, thanks to the shops which were running well. I thanked Julian for all his hard work and commitment to our family and welfare. Incidentally, you may be thinking what a waste all that valve work was, but on the contrary, Ford were so impressed with Julian's drawings, his patenting and marketing skills they were even keener to have him back on the team. So as you see nothing in life is a waste of time. You might not be shown the complete picture at the time, but later on most things slot into place. Thank you God for lending me Julian.

I continued with the two shops. I had to take on some part time help in the Rye shop, because without Julian it was too much for me on my own, particularly as shops have to be open nearly all the time now. I must add that I am not happy with shops opening on Sundays, but at Easter, Christmas and Bank Holidays, if all the other shops are open one is obliged to follow, especially in a town like Rye, with its thousands of tourists. When Sunday opening was first introduced we were told by the government of the day that it would be optional for shop workers as to whether they worked or not. It hasn't worked out like that and many staff working in large organisations are obliged to work, or look elsewhere for a job. Which I don't think is terribly optional. It's another example of doing away with values, treating Sunday as any other day. It's the day that I always refer to as family day, and whether you go to church or not, it can still be a day dedicated to family values. I put an advertisement in the window and along came Rose, a cheery soul and a very hard worker. I could at least have a couple of days at home now. My dogs must have wondered who I was at times. Yes, I said dogs. We had acquired another little Jack Russell terrier, an adorable four months old female who Mike called Mattie after Jerry Rafferty's song Mattie's Rag. Sweeney took to her straight away, another girl! So did Thomas, and they all got on very well.

As I stated earlier, I had been asked to help at the H.C.H.C. by Michael Pembrey. This was my first real chance to show my healing gift to a member of the medical profession. I had been waiting for this opportunity for years. This was what I most wanted to spend all my days and time doing. Everything else was of secondary importance to me. Michael had, along with a cancer patient Jane, set up The Hastings Cancer Help Centre, a charity which aimed to offer advice and support for cancer sufferers. They'd both felt that there was a great need for more information for sufferers. Patients were being diagnosed with the illness and being put forward for treatments without being given all the information they needed and which is readily available today. There are all sorts of alternative treatments, and complementary therapies which could maybe work alongside the orthodox treatment, or instead of.

Michael was interested in my dream of orthodox medicine and alternative or complementary medicine one day being used together, with patients not having to choose one or the other, but both working in hospitals side by side, which was why he'd asked me if I would work in the centre. What we have between the two forms of medicine is suspicion, orthodox medicine is suspicious of alternative medicine, although it is changing slightly now. Suspicion belongs to the dark ages when they used to burn witches at the stake. There is a need for both sorts of medicine, therefore we should have both if we want to, and we shouldn't need to choose. I would like to think that one day, soon, everybody will wake up, believe in a God, live in peace with their fellow man, not worship money, and most importantly, look after their bodies. Perhaps not stick lighted objects into their mouths that they have known for years causes cancer and respiratory diseases. And not consume junk food and drink too much alcohol.

I had already demonstrated to Michael that natural medicine, as I prefer to call it, worked for me, as it had saved me from having another operation after my miscarriage. Nick's way had worked for me, and believe me I wouldn't have taken any risks with my health. I knew only too well from my previous history, after I had given birth to Julian, of the dangers of leaving the afterbirth behind. Nick was then and is still a brilliant natural doctor. Several years ago, when I'd contracted yet another chest infection, Nick came to the house and performed acupuncture on me, putting what seemed at the time like dozens of needles into my chest. He was suspicious of the fact that I kept having chest infections, so he carried out some allergy tests on me, there and then. It appeared that I was allergic to so many foods, and after he'd told me all the foods I couldn't eat anymore, it seemed that there was nothing left for me to eat, but actually I just needed re-educating. I was mostly allergic to wheat and dairy produce, and Nick was adamant that eating the wrong foods was the reason for my chest infections.

The reason being, he told me, that my allergy to certain foods had caused me to have six hundred times the mucus level of a normal person, adding that he was surprised I could walk about and work at all. The needles worked, and the next day I was in Battle Town doing my shopping. And I felt great.

I changed the way I ate, eating only Rye bread, Ryvita and rice cakes, and drinking Earl Grey tea with no milk in it. I noticed an enormous difference quite quickly. I also had to give up red meats, ordinary tea, coffee, chocolate and sugar generally, but I could eat Belgian chocolate because it is made from different ingredients to British chocolate. I was not to drink any alcohol, which was not a problem for me, as I am teetotal. Also most tinned food, excessive salt, and highly refined foods were out. I'd wondered why if I ate a rich tea biscuit I almost passed out, and why coffee gave me dreadful headaches. Our ready-made food so plentiful on supermarket shelves is inexpensive, because that's what people want, they want cheap food. BUT that same cheap food is making a lot of people very ill, which ends up being VERY expensive for the N.H.S. It is full of preservatives, colourings and E numbers. It's making children hyperactive to the point where they are sometimes out of their minds, and gets them into deep trouble. Very costly for social services and the police force.

The N.H.S. is beginning to use some of the alternative treatments now, which is great, because not only is a lot of it much better for the patient, because it's natural, it could also save the N.H.S. millions of pounds a year in unnecessary costly procedures and operations. Doctors have been trained in a certain way, to give drugs, and if the drugs don't work, then to send the patient to the hospital for costly tests and operations. Some of it belongs to the Dark Ages. But to be fair, some doctors are becoming worried themselves, because not only are a lot of the regular treatments simply not working anymore due to the misuse of antibiotics, but patients are expecting more and more of the services. Some doctors are becoming ill with stress and many are leaving the profession. Years ago you didn't go to the doctor for simple ailments, you went to the chemist and sorted yourself out. The N.H.S. is in crisis, of that there is no doubt. But that could be just what we need. A door has to shut before another opens. We need a completely different attitude to health. We, the population of this country, need to be much more responsible for ourselves, starting with what we eat and drink, then looking at how we conduct our lives. Are we happy, because if you're not happy you will not be healthy. Do we lead fulfilling lives, as we need self-esteem for a healthy life? Do we get enough sleep? It's endless the list, these are just a few suggestions.

Of course there is a lot of brilliant work going on all the time in our hospitals, with fantastic medical breakthroughs all the time, with truly dedicated doctors and nurses, and we couldn't do without them. But natural medicine seems like common sense to me. The sooner the two are married, the better. I find it such a fast asleep planet. 'zzzzzzzzz!'

At the A.G.M. of the Hastings Cancer Health Centre, I went along with Mike and I was voted in as a trustee of the charity. I never expected that to happen. What a surprise that was, I was delighted. I started going to the monthly meetings and I really enjoyed being involved with it all. I felt it bridged the gap between diagnosis and treatment. Many cancer sufferers needed more than just drugs and treatments, they also needed a place to go where they could meet other sufferers, so they didn't feel so alone. Illness is a very isolating experience. You feel it's just you, so it's very helpful to talk to others in the same boat as yourself. And at our centre they could also see what complementary therapies were available as well. Anything that made them feel a bit better was very worth while. We ran regular monthly meetings, and we set up a help line. I offered to have the help line in the back of the shop at St. Leonards, which was agreed. Every month more and more people came to the meetings, and eventually after several years, it was taken over by the local Hospital Trust and they had a help desk in the foyer of the new Conquest Hospital in Hastings.

As a result of getting to know Michael he asked me one day if I would see a patient of his. She did not have cancer I must add, but she was nevertheless very poorly. This girl had had eight or nine exploratory operations, each time they couldn't find anything really wrong with her. I agreed to see her and I drove round to

250

her flat one morning. I was horrified to find a young woman in her early twenties, sitting in the semi dark, all screwed up in a chair and in a lot of pain. Her colour was putty-like and she was very clammy. After a while she became more relaxed with me and came and sat next to me on the settee. She proceeded to get out numerous photographs of her family and her boyfriend. The meeting went well and I felt she trusted me. I suggested that she came with me to see Nick, and she said she would. I meanwhile managed to find out quite a lot about this poor girl and the life she had led from an early age, and learnt that she'd had a very tough time. Nick put her on massive doses of vitamins to boost her organs, none of which he said worked properly. I continued to see her weekly, and speak to her on the phone. Then one day she rang me up at the office. "I must see you Stella," she said, "I have something to tell you." I couldn't wait to know what it was. "Go on, tell me now," I urged, "I can't wait until the weekend." "I'm pregnant," she said gleefully. "Really, that's wonderful, are you pleased?" She was very pleased. Well I was so surprised, but that wasn't all of it. She continued, "My doctor wants to know who you are," she said, "only they said I could never have any kids." She had actually been on a fertility pill for a long time, and they'd only given her those to show willing. And after having had so much unsuccessful treatment, and operations, there she was pregnant. What a shock, but a nice one. She had been in a long-term relationship for many years, so I naturally felt happy for her. I wanted more than anything to be doing healing all the time. It's so satisfying.

Later at one of the HCHC meetings Michael announced to everybody that I had made somebody pregnant! Well everybody laughed, me most of all. I've been accused of some things in my life, but never making anybody pregnant.

Some years later this young woman, who gave birth to a son, had a problem with him and I was called on again to help by Michael. The problem with her little boy, who was only three years old, was that he had an addiction to chocolate, which was very serious. He wouldn't eat anything other than chocolate. This resulted in him being very underweight, his teeth were badly affected and discoloured, his hair was falling out and his skin was very pale.

251

He could have developed diabetes. When I was asked to intervene he was in a very bad way. Lack of proper food for so long had obviously made him a very ill little boy, his throat had all but closed up, and so swallowing had become very difficult. I was only too happy to help. I was asked to go to a meeting where I would meet other people working on his case. There were about five different people involved with this particular case, and each person had different advice to offer, which resulted in the mother getting more confused than helped. I always prefer to work alone, and I knew I wouldn't be able to work with the team, as we thought so differently. I told the psychologist, and it was agreed that I could take him over for a month, to see what I could do, reporting back to the psychologist every few days. I gained the confidence of this little lad, and gradually he began to eat. The worst thing with eating disorders is to make a song and dance about food. Make it all very unimportant, make it a game, but most of all don't sit over them and make them eat. It's a strange illness that has nothing whatever to do with food. It's about control. That particular case had a lot to do with the mother's problems, and I got quite involved with the family. The mother changed beyond belief and as a result so did the child.

Then we had to move house again. It was becoming such a joke with our friends. They would say that they had run out of space in their address books, ha, ha. The house we were renting unfortunately had to go up for sale. The owner had good reasons for wanting it sold, and offered it to us first. This was very unfortunate, as we weren't quite ready to buy yet. It's funny really. Years earlier we could have bought the house just like that, but now things were so different. So we started thinking yet again about moving house. Martin, the estate agent with whom I had various dealings, stepped in and helped me once again. There was another house in the town, he told me, which would shortly be up for rental when all the work on it was finished. It had actually been a house that we had once thought about trying to buy. We'd noticed it on one of our many walks around the town, but it was going to auction and it needed a lot of money spending on it. So we were naturally intrigued to have a look at this house all done up, and certainly interested in renting it. The couple who owned it ran Lamb House in Rye, a National Trust property, and had

252

bought the house for their retirement, which wasn't happening for a few years yet. The agent told them about us and they wanted to interview us, so off we went to Lamb House in Rye to meet them. We got on immediately, and after a short chat all was agreed. A viewing was arranged and oh my, it was charming, all Laura Ashley wallpapers, and cream carpets. It was even larger than the one we were already in. Oh what fun we would have setting that house up. I could hardly wait.

Meanwhile, it was Rachael and Steve's wedding, and as Rachael's aunt and godmother I naturally wanted her to have a nice wedding. I wanted to buy her wedding dress and pay for some of the other expenses, so that it would be a day to remember. I planned to meet her at a wedding shop near to where she lived, and together we chose a beautiful ivory silk dress. There was a lot of fun and giggles when she tried some of the dresses on. She was so excited at the prospect of being married, and I was thrilled at the thoughts of her at last getting married!!!. Their two sons, Shaun and Ashley, were to be page boys and Steve's little niece Zoe was to be bridesmaid. My friend Lizzie was making and icing the cake, and when it came to icing cakes, Lizzie was an artist with icing sugar. I have never seen flowers as delicate and perfect as the ones she makes. On the day of the wedding, Mike and I were to transport the cake. I was terrified in case it got damaged, along with all the table linen which I had hired, and some of the food for the evening buffet, deposit it all at the community hall and then go on to Rachael's home and help her get ready. I felt more like mother of the bride than aunt, and I enjoyed very much helping her into the magnificent dress which we had so carefully chosen. Rachael looked radiant.

Mike gave her away, and it was everything I wanted her day to be. They got married in the Methodist Church in Burgess Hill, and had the reception in the community hall, which had just been completely redecorated. They must have known Rachael was getting married. There was a sit down wedding breakfast, and in the evening a buffet was laid out for the evening disco. There was a huge amount of food at this wedding, and then they partied until midnight, at least I was told they did.!!! Mike and I were so tired, and we had a long drive home, so we bade them farewell with the party in full swing. They were a popular couple, judging by the amount of friends that turned up for the evening party, the hall was packed. Rachael looked so beautiful dancing the night away with her girl friends. They seemed to know all the actions to all the songs. It was like watching a cabaret act. I was so pleased for Rachael that she had the wedding of her dreams at last.

We moved into The Little House a week later. To call it the Little House was, I think, a joke, as it was actually a massive house. It was glorious. The sitting room had the nickname of the ballroom because it was about forty feet by twenty feet. There was a dining room twenty-five feet long, with two windows, each with full-length pale green velvet curtains, with pelmets, a pine fitted kitchen, a conservatory, a laundry room come cloakroom and a large entrance hall. There were five bedrooms and two bathrooms. And a ghost! The owners were so kind to us, and went to great lengths to make sure that we had everything we needed. They restored our faith in human nature for a while.

I joined the labour party at this time. I was watching a political programme on television one afternoon, and during this particular programme I learned that the New Labour Party under the leadership of Tony Blair wanted more women in the party, so I rang up. I was immediately welcomed into the local Labour party by Bill the chairman of Rye and District, and put up immediately as the Labour candidate for Winchelsea in the forthcoming local elections. I was a bit taken aback at the speed of it all. I thought I would need a bit of training. Didn't I need to know a bit about New Labour's policies? Wasn't there a lot I should know about national and local issues? Bill said not to worry, I wouldn't win the seat anyway, as it was a very Tory area, but that it was good to have a candidate for the seat anyway. I was quite excited at the thoughts of it.

Bill was right, he knew what he was talking about, and I didn't win the seat, but not for the lack of trying. I didn't just sit back and say. "Oh I won't win that seat so there's no need to try." I gave it my best shot. It wasn't long before I became the Chairman of the local Labour Party, which I never dreamt I'd ever be. That experience gave me a confidence that I never thought I'd ever have, the confidence of speaking to an audience, albeit only a small audience. I had the opportunity to attend a meeting at which Tony Blair would be giving a pre-election speech. Entry was ticket holders only, and there were not many tickets available, so I was very excited at the prospect of going and meeting him. There was no doubt in my mind when he arrived that this man had an enormous presence, and when he spoke he was extremely articulate, and straight to the point. He said things that I had wanted to hear for years, and used words like caring, and compassion, words that had been totally erased from our vocabulary over the years. I liked him, and was thrilled to have shaken his hand at the end of the meeting. The general election was coming up and I for one was desperate to get the Tory party out before they did any more harm to my country.

I wonder just how many people really think about their political persuasion, or just how many vote the same as their parents', without really thinking for themselves. I had been brought up in the Labour party. My parents had both voted labour, but when Harold Wilson started going over to Russia and the party moved more and more towards the left, and as my father started to do well and became a manager, they had both felt happier voting elsewhere. The first time I was allowed to vote, I voted labour, and continued to do so until I was totally fed up with the constant strikes. The unions had the country in a stranglehold. Then during the early to middle Thatcher years I was very impressed with her, and I suppose I was also delighted with having a woman at the helm. She seemed like a breath of fresh air to the country, and seemed unafraid of anything. She sorted out the unions, who had needed sorting out. They'd had far too much power. The strikes of the seventies had done much to harm our manufacturing base, the three day week in 1974 was dreadful, I well remember the rubbish piling up everywhere, such a health hazard. But we do nevertheless need a voice for the working man. One minute the unions had all the power, the next minute they had no power at all. Why not a happy medium? All in all it made it less viable to make, mine or build anything much here in Britain. Thatcher sorted out the civil service. We had far too many Civil Servants, and she trimmed it all down. But all was not well.

Then Thatcher changed, and seem to get power mad, de-regulating, re-organising, telling everyone what they would do or else. What is the saying 'Power corrupts, absolute power corrupts absolutely' The selling off of council houses seemed wrong, especially as they sold them off so cheaply and then announced that they were going to have to build more to replace them. With the price of land, that seemed ridiculous. The selling off of the utilities also seemed wrong. Foreign investment was rife. As a nation we were not going to own anything anymore. Plus everybody wanted shares in everything, money was keymost in people's minds, I hated it. We had lost a lot of our identity. No one seemed proud to be British any more. Why don't we celebrate St. George's Day? The Scottish, the Welsh and the Irish all celebrate their Saints Days, why not us?

Meanwhile, there was a new trainee GP at the surgery where Mike worked, and according to Mike, this young man needed somewhere to live for six months. So that was when Andrew came to live with us. Because of my experiences with some doctors in the past, my confidence in them was a little shaky, so this was going to be very interesting for me. I had been on the 'Alternative Medicine' route for thirty years, but I always been sensible about it. One should always go to the GP for check ups, like well woman check ups, or well men check-ups, and be sensible about your health. If you have are pregnant or need urgent treatment you must go to your GP, but then the choice of treatment should always be yours.

Andrew was very nervous when he first came to stay, and we were all very polite to each other. But after a while we were like any other family with a son at home, and I would talk to him in the same way that I'd talk to one of my own sons. Andrew had a car that was to say the least, problematic, and one day after he'd tried to fix yet something else on it, he asked me what I thought he should do about his beloved car. I couldn't resist the opportunity to tell him, I loathe old troublesome cars, and I'd had so many problems with old cars in my first marriage that just the mention of them gave me the creeps. I laughed and replied, "Dump it, it's a liability. If you are on call and get called out to an emergency, and it lets you down, you could get into trouble." I tried to say it in a jokey way, so as not to offend him, but I was deadly serious, he took it quite well, and laughed. He was also covered in grease, and I said bossily, "You're not going to the surgery looking like that. You'll have to change." I became very fond of him, and was quite sorry when he left to take up his own practice. I learned a lot about doctors. I was surprised at how many really trivial call outs he had in the evenings and in the night, things that could easily have waited till the surgery next day. He was called out for things like splinters and period pains. No wonder they get so irritated.

Meanwhile, the lease on my shop in Market Road was coming to an end, and I had to make a decision as to whether to continue in that little shop or go for something a bit bigger. I decided to look around for another shop. There had been a major setback in the second hand furniture trade during my time at this shop, which sent a lot of second hand furniture dealers to the wall. The Tory government had made it illegal to sell upholstery with foam that wasn't fire resistant. This was nearly all the upholstered furniture made during the sixties and seventies, up to the mid eighties, and included good names like Ercol, G Plan and Parker Knoll. Bearing in mind that these items were perfectly legal when they were made, it was odd to say the least that they were suddenly pronounced illegal. Most of the items of stock I sold came under that heading, things like three piece suites, easy chairs, beds, dining chairs, (the seats were illegal), and even upholstered dressing table stools. In fact most of the furniture I had been selling. Now on the face of it that sounds sensible, all furniture should contain only fire resistant materials. Ah! but this was a ridiculous law, because it was only illegal for traders to sell them, it didn't prevent ordinary people from owning or selling them. If my neighbour or friend wanted to sell their three-piece suite, or bed etc with the illegal foam in it, they could sell theirs. So this was a law of double standards. I state again that these were items, many of which cost a lot of money when they were new, and they were perfectly legal when they were made, but were suddenly declared illegal. I am a sensible person, a person who when I was converting flats adhered strictly to the fire regulations, a person with a huge conscience, who wanted as much as the next person to save lives in house fires. But did it make sense to bring in that law, when all the government had to do to help save lives in fires

in homes was surely to make it law for every home to have smoke
alarms? And if the government was so worried about
inflammatory materials, why do they still to this day allow
children's clothing to be made out of inflammable materials? It
didn't make any sense at all. A lot of shops went out of business
because of that law. Good furniture was dumped. If you were
caught with any of the goods in your shop the fine was
horrendous.

I did have a couple of warnings when inspectors came round.
Even if I thought my shop didn't contain any of the illegal
upholstery, there was always some piece I'd overlooked, and for a
while I thought I'd lose my business again. The worry I've had to
cope with over the years is quite ridiculous. The government
seemed hell bent on doing away with small businesses in this
country. I was lucky, very lucky, because I have a very agile
mind, and I got around this law by changing what I sold. I went
over to French beds and much earlier upholstery which had
horsehair in it, in the Rye shop. And in my St. Leonards shop I
had to sell white goods mainly, that's fridges, washing machines
and the like. I also sold wardrobes, chest of drawers, tables and
anything wooden. But for a while my business teetered on the
brink again. The bank was giving me a very hard time, and did not
seem to want to understand the needs of small businesses.
Businesses were having an atrocious time generally. I had to hang
on, and keep my wits about me all the time. Against the greatest
of odds, I did have an enjoyable time with my little shops, and I
had some super customers. There was definitely a need for shops
like mine, and I valued all my customers, especially the little old
ladies who couldn't get out to get that certain piece of furniture,
which I would find for them. I started to work from orders, so I
was able to make my business myself. My clientele in Rye
included Rod Hull, and several Lords and Ladies. Rod Hull came
into my shop one day and asked me if I would exchange some
chairs he had for a wardrobe in my shop that he wanted. I made
an appointment to go to his home. I was rather excited at the
prospect of meeting and talking to him, and I was not
disappointed. He was a very nice man, not at all like the madman
on the television, he was a rather quiet, serious man, I liked him
very much. The chairs that he wanted to exchange were like

thrones and I knew that they were worth a lot of money, and although the wardrobe was also a very beautiful Edwardian wardrobe inlaid with mother of pearl and brass I was worried that it was not a fair swap. I felt awkward about it and after his third phone call to me asking me to do the swap I agreed, in effect he gave me a great deal of money. Many people over the years have in effect thrust money at me, it was as if they all knew that I had to survive. Thanks Rod! Some of the furniture I sold in my shop was beautiful and I would have liked to have kept most of it. Then as I said the lease of the shop came up for renewal and as I didn't want to renew it, I started looking around for another bigger shop.

I found a shop up nearer the church, a shop which was on two floors. It was the most beautiful shop, with bow fronted windows rather Dickensian, and I fell in love with it. Things were definitely on the up for me at last, and provided that I kept the rents from the flats coming in for the bank I would be alright. My main objective all along was to make sure that the bank was kept happy. I knew that they were capable of making my life hell again, and I purposely hadn't wanted us to buy a home until I felt the bank was happy with me. Then one day on a routine visit from my business manager, who actually came out to the house to see me, told me that the bank was very happy with me and I had no reason to assume that there would be any more problems. I'd proved to be reliable and diligent in my business affairs. For the second time!

So we could look around and find a house to buy at last. We had come through a war, a personal war, and to have the bank say what they did to me was terrific news. I must say though that I'd worked myself almost into the ground doing it. Most times I would find it very difficult to be alone, but of course I had to be, I had to run a business. My chest always felt so tight, and the old panicky feeling was ever present. I do not know what I'd have done without my faith. I had nothing else to rely on. In fact Mike had said to me on more than one occasion, whilst wringing his hands in desperation, "What else do you work on apart from faith?" To which I replied, "I have nothing else to rely on, it's all I need, thank you." He couldn't decry it. He had seen me at first

259

hand walk through the most ghastly situations which most people would not have been able to cope with. But I knew I wasn't alone. I had my silent army working out which way I should go next, and I listened to my conscience to hear what to do. And I had my dreams, which always occurred just before something difficult and dangerous came up, then I acted on it. Mike also used to say that the bank didn't like people like me because they worked on scare tactics which usually worked with folk, but I played them at their own game, always saying 'Take me to court, I'd like the country to know what you did to us'. They of course, are not in favour of adverse publicity, and I hadn't done anything wrong. I was just trying to run by business.

The flats had gone up in value quite a bit, and were proving to be a very good investment once again. On top of that I had retained a few freeholds, one of which was very valuable. Plus I was renting two shops. So I felt quite pleased with myself.

Then on a routine trip down to the supermarket on the beach one Saturday evening to buy a lottery ticket (in the pouring rain I might add) Mike overshot the turning onto the supermarket forecourt. He had such a job to see where he was going as it was raining so hard. We then had no option but to drive on for a bit in order to find a turning area. Suddenly we found ourselves outside a sadly neglected house. It was almost derelict, and had a for sale board outside. "Oh stop, Mike, stop. Look at that house, we must have a look at it." I was very excited at what I'd seen. "What, in this rain? You can't be serious. It's coming down like stair rods, darling. Let's come back tomorrow," he urged. But there was no stopping me. "No, Mike stop, I must get out and look at it. You can stay in the car if you want to." With that, we both got out of the car, and in the pouring rain we ran around the outside of the house, just pausing briefly to look in the windows. I just knew this house was to be ours, and funnily enough it was the one house out of fifty house details sent us by all the agents, that I'd thrown away!!! Three months later we would move in.

The house was in a disgusting state. Yet again! It never ceases to amaze me the squalor people live in. Neighbours told me that it had been let go because it had had tenants in it. What tenants would want to live in that filth? My own tenants had everything, and it was funny really, because on my various visits to my flats, perhaps a minor repair was needed, I would often remark to a tenant 'You should see where we live. Our house needs everything doing to it'. I know they never believed me. They always thought I was Rachman. On one occasion I was called a 'Fucking capitalist pig' by a tenant's boyfriend. How charming, how eloquent some people are!!! This particular young man was black, and when I'd first seen him I thought how nice for this young white girl to have a black boyfriend. I referred to them as ebony and ivory. Well, I quickly changed my mind about him, as he constantly hurled expletives at me, in person, and on my answerphone. And then one day when my tenant was moving out and I had to go and inspect the flat, return the deposit, and collect the keys, this young man was there. I told him in no uncertain terms that it would be wise for him to get rid of the chip (or was it log) that he had on his shoulder. I told him that I had never been racist, and all the animosity had come from him, not me. He surprised me then, because he said that he would not leave the flat until I'd shaken hands with him. This I did happily and he smiled at me.

On the day that we left the Little House, a strange thing had happened to me. I thought I was seeing things, mainly because I wasn't feeling very well, and moving is always very traumatic isn't it, especially when it's your third move in four years! We were to-ing and fro-ing, driving back and forth from one house to the other, with never ending boxes filled to the brim. Where does it all come from? We'd used some guys from the auction rooms to help this time, to move what was left of our furniture, (we'd sold a lot of the valuable pieces to help pay for the new house). And there we were trying to cram what were still masses of things into quite a small house! I couldn't think where was it all going. How do you get a quart into a pint pot? Hey, I've been here before!

A strange thing happened whenever I looked at the removal men, wherever they were, and whatever they were doing, because there in the midst of them was this black figure, a man in a black cape. I mentioned it at the time to Mike, and I know he didn't take me at all seriously. "A man in black, whatever next?" he replied.

261

I put it down to the fact that I wasn't feeling well. I thought no more of it until much later in the day. After the removal men had finally departed, Mike and I were left to pack up all the small items, and you never think it's going to take long to finish the last bit do you? You'd think we'd learn as we get older that it takes forever to collect the last bits and pieces. There were all the kitchen things that we had been using all day, bits left in the larder, house plants, plants from the garden, the dogs beds and then our coats. Oh it goes on and on. On the next to last of the trips to the Little House, to collect another car load, I told Mike that I felt too ill to continue, and asked if he could continue on his own. I think he wondered why I couldn't hang on, as we were so nearly finished, but ran me back anyway to our new home on the beach, where Mum was trying to find the kitchen under piles of boxes. After dropping me off Mike went back to get the last load, put some Jif round the basins, and of course collect the birdbath!

He wasn't gone long, when he came back his hair was almost standing on end. "I was cleaning one of the upstairs washbasins," he said, "and it felt as though someone walked straight through me. I felt as cold as ice. I'm not going back there. Whatever is left there now can jolly well stay there." "I hadn't imagined it then?" I asked. "No, you hadn't," he continued, "and I felt as if there was someone watching me all the time." I then repeated my story about seeing the man in black. This time Mike believed me, oh how he believed me. He was no way going back there. He had removed nearly everything that was ours, and what was left Mike said we could live without. He's a big man, my husband, and not easily scared, but whatever, whoever it was, had scared Mike. Fortunately I had vacuumed right through the house before I'd left. We always leave everything ship shape, the way I'd love to find a house that I buy! Whoever was haunting that house did not want us to go. I felt he was angry that we were going, as he'd obviously got used to us.

I'd had to go to bed then. I felt dreadfully ill. Not a good omen. My mother was staying with us, helping us move again, and she came upstairs to see if I was alright. I had my overcoat on in bed plus the electric blanket was full on, and I was still freezing cold. It turned out that my temperature was 104. No wonder I felt ill.

Mike called the doctor, who confirmed what I had thought, the drinking water in the house had been dirty. I should have run the tap for a good while before drinking it, but I didn't think, even though I had seen things floating in it, I still drank it. What a fool I was, but I was thirsty from heaving boxes and suchlike.

Mike had employed some people to clean the house before we'd actually moved in. I couldn't have faced the sheer amount of cleaning that was needed. It was dreadful, no kidding, the house was filthy. I vowed that if anybody else remarked about the French being dirty they obviously hadn't been in many English homes, because I can vouch for the fact that in my experience a lot of the English are thoroughly filthy, as demonstrated by the houses I bought through the business and homes bought for ourselves. We were always going to the council dump with our own rubbish, So why can't other people do the same? So yet again we spent £400 paying for a lorry to clear the rubbish from this house, a house that I was to refer to as our beach hut for many years.

I had taken on the lease of my new shop in Rye, which had involved a large amount of expense. The shop was on two floors, and there had been a certain amount of decorating to be done. A room upstairs at the back of the building was made into my office, and it looked very smart with my rosewood office furniture on a dark blue carpet. A shop that size had taken a lot of stocking, so in order to raise some of the necessary money, I had arranged to sell the lease on one of the properties to help pay for it all. The sale of the freehold was I thought progressing well, alongside the contract for the lease of the shop, until one day I realised the leaseholders weren't going to sign the contract, they were disputing the price, which I thought had been agreed. Mike took care of most of the financial aspects of the freeholds and I had no reason to assume that the leaseholders wouldn't be pleased to buy their freehold, and therefore be able to make their own decisions with regard to the property. The dispute dragged on and on, and in the end I couldn't wait for them to sign any longer, as the owner of the shop I was to lease was anxious for me to sign. And there was the real danger that I could have lost the shop, so I signed the lease. I had no choice but to sign the contract for the shop and of course this put me in an unfortunate position with not having as much capital as I should have had. In fact it was quite a blow for me, and I started off financially behind again.

We opened as planned. Mike asked the Mayor of Rye, who was a labour member, to open it for me, which I thought was a bit over the top, but Mike liked to make everything nice for me, he was so sweet. The press came and took a few photographs, and then we had a few drinks with friends who'd come to see the opening. It was all very exciting, and the shop looked beautiful. I'd had it freshly painted outside, and sign written with 'Imagination'. There was a swinging wooden sign which had S.J. Developments Ltd on it, I thought it was all very smart. The windows were well set out with the best furniture and china pieces, and I'd had a beautiful silk and parchment flower arrangement made by a florist which set the windows off perfectly. It was an unusual shop, because no one else sold the mix of furniture that I did. You either had an antique shop or a second hand furniture shop, which usually was a bit tatty. Most people's houses are a mix of both old and new furniture. I based my shop on the 'Period Living' magazine, in fact I used the magazine as a decoration, placing it on pieces of furniture that were similar in the book. For example if I had a 'lit en bateau', I would strategically place a magazine with a picture of a similar bed on the piece of furniture. I wanted people to use their imaginations much more than I thought they already did. Hence the name.

Back at home we had little money to do anything much to the house. It didn't bother me unduly. I was so relieved and pleased that we'd got another home, and we were in the house so little time anyway, that when we were there, we just chilled out. It seemed that every penny I earned from my shops was used on one or other of my properties, and our home came last. So nothing much got done. As I said I called it our beach hut. I had a dream about this time which was quite daunting. It was of me sitting on a chair, tied up in chains, and I was told that I would remain shackled, as they referred to it, until I had written this book. But when was I to have the time to write a book? I asked Upstairs. I had become very used to calling them Upstairs, but they were adamant I had to find the time. I had started writing this book years earlier whilst still in Beauport Gardens, at Mike's suggestion, I might add. He must have had a premonition because he obviously thought it was the right thing for me to do even then, and on his suggestion I had started writing, what I thought was just an autobiography. On reflection if I hadn't started writing the book all those years ago, a lot of things would have been harder to remember. I started by writing down all the bits that were the most interesting to me, like the night that the space ship came, the standing in the garden by the sumach bush and receiving the Holy Spirit, and all the goings on at Anglesea Terrace. A lot would have been difficult to remember, especially about my early life. Now the book was for real, it was to be a serious book based on my life and experiences, about a society on course for disaster if not righted. I did the odd five hundred words every now and then on my word processor, but I couldn't put any serious time into it as I was always at work, and my mind was so filled with survival. But I knew I had to try harder to fit it all in.

Living in the beach hut was quite a culture shock for us both, considering the houses we'd lived in before. It needed everything doing to it, and I mean everything. I got a bit paranoid about it, especially after a remark from a neighbour one day, who clearly thought we didn't look as if we could afford Laura Ashley wallpaper. I felt that we'd reached rock bottom then. How the mighty falleth comes to mind. Was I really the person who only a few years earlier had been told that I'd got everything? It was strange to be thought of like this, and I must say that I didn't like it. But I used to feel quite differently about the house when I was in the shop, in fact my feelings were the complete opposite, especially on a hot airless day when other shop owners had to live in flats over their shops with little and sometimes no garden. I felt great then, swanning back to my house on the beach. We had done a few vital things to the house, like re-wiring and some re-plumbing. We had also decorated a bedroom and laid a cheap carpet. It never ceases to amaze me how quickly a room is transformed.

Christmas was great. My assistant sales woman, Anita, had created a lovely display in the three windows. She was very artistic, and liked fiddling about with baubles, tinsel and snow. I can't do things like that, no matter how hard I try. I do not have the patience. Our first Christmas in the new shop we did very well, and the takings were better than I'd hoped they would be.

And then it was New Year. This was the big Birthday for me, my fiftieth, gosh, getting old now! I'd been fighting one thing or another for eight years now, it had been eight years since the landslide, and it just didn't seem possible. Mike had arranged a small afternoon party for me with a few friends. Anita's husband Geoff played 'Happy Birthday' outside our front door on his trumpet. He had his own jazz band, and in the good old days, he'd played with Terry Lightfoot, it was a good fun afternoon.

We were progressing well with everything, the business and the house, when another major catastrophe hit us. Julian, who had just bought his first house in Essex, was expecting Mike and I to arrive one particular Saturday with a lorry load of furniture. Furniture which I had been collecting for him over a period of time, and had stored in the back of my shop in St. Leonards. So on this particular Saturday we just had to make our way to the shop, load up all the furniture I'd stored, and start out on the long journey to Julian's. We were merrily driving along the road in the lorry, when we came around the corner at the Green, St. Leonards. I saw the shop up ahead, and I couldn't quite make out what was going on outside it. It looked like an enormous pile of rubbish outside on the pavement. What was it, I wondered. As we drew closer and I realised what it was, I completely lost it. The whole area was cordoned off with Police tape, saying keep away. The pile of rubbish was burnt furniture thrown there by the fireman, and the windows were all broken and blackened. The flat over the shop was burnt out!

The fire wasn't my immediate concern at that moment. Words cannot describe how I felt. Where was Jeremy? Oh God, where was Jeremy? He'd lived in the flat above the shop, and it was now burnt out. Where oh where was Jeremy? I went totally frantic, I couldn't breathe. It was as if someone had put my chest in a vice. Mike wanted to go into the premises, but I had to get away. I couldn't bear the sight of it. It was obvious that no one could live there anymore and besides I wanted to know where Jeremy was. Was he in hospital, dead or what? I hardly dared to think. We

266

went to the police station and enquired as to any relevant details, but they were totally unhelpful. By this time I had truly lost it. I was totally overcome by desperation and grief. I didn't want to do a tour of the hospitals with Mike, I couldn't get my breath, so Mike decided that he would take me to Pat and Gavin's, and then go and find out all that he could.

Pat sat me down and put the kettle on. What would we do without the kettle? Mike and Gavin went off together to see what they could find out. I had to sit for what seemed ages, until they discovered that Jeremy was at his friend's house. He had been taken there in the early hours of the morning, suffering from acute shock. I was to learn afterwards that a passing motorist had noticed smoke coming out of an upstairs window at two o'clock in the morning, and had raised the alarm, kicked the door down, and got Jeremy out. I would probably have lost my son if it hadn't have been for him. I never found out who he was but whoever you are, my eternal thanks. I later learned that the road had been cordoned off and three fire engines had fought the blaze. No one thought to call me. Can you believe it?

Nobody had thought to tell me, not the police, not the fire brigade, no one. I had to find out by going to the shop. This was the final straw for me. I didn't want to continue any more. I had felt continuously let down by just about everything, especially the legal system. There had been several times when the shop windows in St. Leonards had been smashed by gangs of youths in cars, with air guns and catapults with ball bearings. So often we'd had to board up the windows, and this had obviously stopped us from selling anything until they were repaired. But wages still had to be paid. Jeremy's car which had stood outside the shop had also been vandalised several times, and went from being a top of the range Montego Ghia, to a wreck at the breakers yard. The police had always been powerless to do anything. When you have been a victim of crime the anger is beyond belief. The anger that I had felt over the two-year period of crime culminated, and I felt such anger towards the police. They say that they just don't have the powers they used to have, but they have plenty of power if you park in the wrong place or if you speed in the car. I wrote a letter to the local paper setting out my complaints about the police, and when the letter came out all my wording had been altered. Why?

I didn't see how I could carry on with the business and to be honest I no longer wanted to carry on, for the first time I felt like a complete alien in this country of many unscrupulous, immoral people. There were no lengths the powers that be wouldn't go to make the inhabitants of this Island ill with stress and utterly demoralised. So I decided to wind the company up. I had needed the income from both shops anyway, so I couldn't see how I was going to satisfy the bank now. After all my efforts, and fighting to stay in business over a nine year period, I didn't want to continue any more. I was tired of fighting. I was tired of not being able to breathe properly. I had even felt at times that I didn't want to live anymore. I would often go to bed, and say to Mike that I didn't want to wake up any more, and the look on his face was one of horror. I'd gone through the horror of my divorce, and the unfairness of that. I had picked myself up and started a business to support my sons, after having been told that I was unemployable, and that I didn't qualify for any benefits either. (If I'd been irresponsible and been an unmarried mother with six kids, I'd have qualified for benefits). We'd paid for an operation that the surgeon insisted he hadn't carried out, then admitted he had. I'd lost my baby, the baby the doctor told me I wasn't expecting. I'd suffered the landslide behind the block of flats, the cliff that according to the council no one owned. Mike had been got rid of by the bank along with thousands of others, so he was pensioned at fifty. We had been made to wait a year to be paid out for our house by the D.o.T. I had been subjected to nine lots of crime whilst having the shops, four lots of smashed windows, three break-ins to my son's car, which I'd bought for him and was parked on the shop forecourt, and then it was taken by joy riders, and finally wrecked. On one occasion a policeman told me that if I caught the little thug and wanted to take him behind the shop and give him what for, he'd turn a blind eye. WHAT!!! Why couldn't he do his own job? I wouldn't dream of doing anything of the kind. I'd had a gun incident in the Rye shop, when two youngsters came into the shop, locked the door, put the lights out and held a toy gun at us. We didn't know immediately that it was a toy gun. I'd had counterfeit money taken off me at the bank in Rye, when I was paying in the day's takings. Money that I'd had no idea was counterfeit, money that was taken to the local police station, and weeks later when I'd heard nothing from the local police, I enquired about it, only to find there was no entry in their books, and no knowledge of it either. Lovely country, isn't it? Doesn't it make you feel proud to be British? No wonder so many decent folk are going to live abroad! Not only is it a country not fit for heroes, it's not a country fit for honest and respectable folk anymore either.

Mike rang the accountant and told him about my decision to close down the company. He was sorry to hear about all the problems, but said that if I was sure of my decision, then I had to contact a Company Administrator in Eastbourne. Mike asked me if I was sure. I was sure, so Mike on my behalf rang and made an appointment. That was a horrible day, listening to that man talking about my company. It wasn't personal, he said. Why do people say that? Of course it's bloody personal, but as he said he had to let me know the procedure for winding up a limited company.

When he'd had a chance to go over the figures he informed me that he wouldn't wind my company up. He said it was a good company with assets and possibilities. What would have made it difficult to operate properly with a reduced income, would have been the possibility of the bank breathing down my neck again. So he said we could take out an Administration Order, and that if we went straight down to the court in Eastbourne we could do it there and then. This would mean that I could continue to trade, and my creditors couldn't touch me, as I had the protection of the court. I had to do a complete mental turn around then. Did I want to continue? I didn't really know anymore what I wanted. But I would give it a go. No one could call me a quitter. No one wants to be forced to give up their company. When I eventually had to quit I would like it to be my decision.

I had to tell the staff in the shop, that we were continuing under an administration order for the time being. They knew it was going to be difficult. With not having the other shop I needed to come up with another idea to replace the income that the other shop had produced. So I had the idea of doing property management and starting a letting agency. There wasn't much I didn't know about letting. I'd noticed on my way into work for months that any letting boards in the area seemed to belong to a Battle firm. So we turned the top floor into an office, and it looked very smart, with matching desks and blue chairs, lovely swags and drapes. Even getting the office furniture was strange. A lady had come into the shop one day and asked me to go round to her house to look at some furniture she needed to get rid of. When I went round to her house to my amazement she had desks and office chairs, in just the right colour for our new set-up. She also had some beautiful Chinese furniture, and a three-piece suite, all from Harrods. This lady was amazing. This furniture would have fetched good prices from the auction rooms, but she wanted me to have it, and I didn't have to pay her until it was all sold. Isn't that incredible? Was she my fairy godmother or what? I had such a lot of help from people like her. It was as if they all knew that I had to survive, and they were sent to help me. With the new desks we started the letting agency. To all the customers who helped me survive I thank you all.

There was definitely an opening for this kind of business in the town. Mike resigned from his job at the surgery and together we proceeded to build up the business over the next two years. Unfortunately, I had to let Anita go, that was a horrible day as she had been a valued member of staff and popular with the customers. I just couldn't warrant paying wages any more, but I nevertheless felt like I'd let her down. That's the down side of being an employer. Mike and I worked for very little financial reward, but at least we both felt that we had at last overcome our problems, and that we could now get back on track generally. Little did we know what was in store for us again...

A year went by, a quite good year all in all. I was concentrating on the furniture side of things and Mike was building up the letting side of the business. We had decided to decorate the shop, that's how optimistic we were feeling, and we were painting the walls of the shop a lovely deep pink. Mike had gone upstairs to put the kettle on for a cup of tea, and as we hadn't been in the shop all morning, Lin our part-time assistant had been in on her own, the post had lain there for us to open when we got there. I was happily painting away, when I heard Mikes voice calling me to go upstairs. I didn't go straight away as I had a wet brush, so he called me again, only this time his voice was different. "I have something very important to show you," he said, "please come now." I put down my paintbrush and hurried upstairs, where Mike was sitting at his desk holding out a letter for me to read. I was a bit mystified at the look on Mike's face, but took the letter and proceeded to read it. I couldn't believe what it said. It was from the administrator, and it said that he had closed my business down as from two days earlier. He gave the reason as 'Pressure from the bank' and all the bank accounts were frozen as from that date. I felt incredibly sick, and very afraid. We probably had about five pounds between us. "Can he do this, Mike? We are doing so well. We have money in the bank. Why didn't he ring me? Why didn't he do it face to face? Oh God why?" I felt dead. My world came crashing down round my ears. What a dreadful, ghastly way to end my business. It felt so sick. My business had been like a child to me. In effect I'd given birth to it. I had started it up on my own, seen it through the recession, the fire and the last year. Now my child was no more, and the administrator didn't even have the decency to tell me. Why couldn't he have done it to my face?

I rang his office on the off chance that there had been a mistake, only to be told that he had gone away. Gone away? Is that the man who'd hugged me on that dreadful day a year ago, and told me my worries were over? There was nothing else I could do now. It was finally over, and we sat helplessly looking at each other, and at everything we had tried to build up, and thought we'd succeeded. We had no option but to pack up our desks and leave. We both felt numb and sick. We locked up in an absolute daze. We were totally and utterly gutted. We went across the road to our friend Clive, the bookseller, and told him what had happened, and that we were going. He was a genuine man, and he was very upset for us. We didn't feel we had to sneak off like criminals although that is how we felt. He said the usual things people say. "If there's anything I can do, don't hesitate." Nice man Clive. I did have one last delivery to do, a lady had rung up at the last moment about a pair of Staffordshire dogs that she'd seen in the window, and could I deliver them. That ninety-five pounds was to be the only money we had for a while. I was being looked after again.

I thought it was a terribly cowardly act not to have a meeting and discuss the situation face to face. Not to look at the books and see the much-improved situation, and see how much property there was on our books. I felt it was very un-business like. This wasn't a game, it was our living. I didn't know how we would manage to pay the mortgage, or pay anything. I was so afraid. I also knew that the administrator had lied to me about it being the bank's decision. The bank was quite happy with me now, so why should he lie to me!!!

Back at home we sat staring at the walls like zombies. By this time we'd had enough of everything. We had been pushed about for years, but this was the last straw. This was intolerable. We had really had it this time, but something always seemed to lift me, a feeling would come over me, and I always heard the words 'Everything will be alright Stella'. And I always knew inside that it would be. I had a dream, in fact I'd had a couple of dreams about my company in difficulties. The first dream was of me pushing my pram with a child in it, along the sand on the beach. Suddenly the tide had started to come in very quickly, I managed to get off of the sand but the wheels of my pram got stuck in the shingle. I ran for help and a man came and helped me drag it off the beach. The pram represented the vehicle, i.e. my business, which carried the child, the child was my project, my destiny. The man who helped me was the administrator. He got me on to safe ground if only for a while.

The second dream was of me pushing my pram through what seemed like a market, where people were selling things. I parked my pram outside a white building in a car parking space. (Remember one of the earlier dreams said I would get to a car park). I parked it very neatly by the kerb. Which meant it was intended to be finally left there. My child or the project no longer needed the business as a vehicle to carry it, I could carry it myself. I went inside the white building, which was a sanctuary for me, the business was over, I needed a rest, and I also needed to get on with what I'd come to do. The dreams were very reassuring on one level, but on a human level I was totally and utterly distraught.

I rang my sister Liz and asked if we could go and stay with them for a week to get away from all the horror. She readily agreed. We were to go in two days time. Meanwhile, I needed to pack, and arrange for our dear dogs to go to Alan and Margaret's. I did feel that I had fallen from a great height. It's a strange feeling that comes over you at times like that. The body shuts down with shock, and has the same effect on the body as a bereavement. It's a wonderful safety valve, you shut right down, quite sub-consciously. And things flow over you for a while. I call it mental hibernation.

We could hardly wait to get to Devon. We needed time to think, and collect our thoughts, without the phone constantly ringing, with people and friends wanting to know how we were. People meant well, but no one could really understand the severity of the situation. We'd lost our livelihood, how on earth were we going to manage financially? I'd lost everything that I'd fought so hard to keep, the flats, the freeholds, the shop and the letting agency, as well as my income, in fact our incomes. I knew that I would have to deal with the bank now, no flats meant no rents coming in, that in turn meant there was a loan to be repaid, but how? With what? The effect on my health from all the fighting over the years was the reason I had constant panic attacks. I had been told on more than one occasion by Nick, that if I didn't give up my fight, I risked a heart attack, because the stress was too much for my body. I couldn't give up, I was meant to do this thing.

On our way to Devon, we delivered the Staffordshire dogs and collected ninety-five pounds that represented the total amount of money we'd got between us. We hadn't been given any opportunity to draw money out of the bank, because the administrator had closed the accounts two days before his letter arrived at my office. As far as he was concerned we could have starved. I knew that the money made from selling the dogs, would have to last us until Mike's modest pension was paid, a couple of weeks away.

We arrived at my sister's house, in an ancient Ford Fiesta, that I'd paid five hundred pounds for only weeks earlier, when we'd decided to return our car to the garage. It had been on one of those lease/purchase schemes, and when the time had come for the last payment we decided to give it back and look around for something else to buy instead. I meanwhile purchased an old banger. No way did I think that car was to be our main car for months to come. On arrival at Liz's the first thing David said was, that we'd all go out for a meal that evening at the local pub, where they did the most fabulous food. It sounded just the job, but after Mike and I had eaten all the food we could eat, the bill arrived, and to my horror, David then said to us, "We'll go Dutch, shall we." We were horrified. It was twenty-five pounds out of our last remaining money until goodness knows when. If we'd known we were going Dutch we'd have had an omelette and a cup of tea each. They didn't realise the dreadful extent of our situation, they even asked us to a farmers dance on the last night we were with them. "The tickets are only ten pounds," announced my sister. I declined, of course, making the excuse that I had nothing to wear. How were we to pay another twenty pounds out of our remaining seventy pounds. So they went without us! We stayed in and watched television. The next day we headed homewards, although neither of us wanted to come back home, and certainly not to another house that we didn't know whether we were going to keep. But when we got back home, there was a lovely surprise awaiting us on the doorstep. There was a small wooden trough containing the most beautiful polyanthus plants in full bloom, with a note. 'Thinking about you. If you need anything, ring me. Love Shirley.' It lifted us so much. Thank goodness that God put flowers on the earth, wouldn't it be a miserable place without them. Shirley was one of those rare thoughtful souls that didn't just think about herself. She was the Practice Manager at the surgery where Mike had worked as Fund Manager.

The next few months were a real trial. I don't know how we got through it. If it hadn't have been for my dreams I don't know what would have kept me going. I would keep being informed of the next stage, and I can't tell you what a relief that was. Mike came to understand my dreams, sometimes interpreting them quicker than me. I was still being told in certain dreams to continue writing the book. I knew on one level that everything would be alright. But as a human being I still worried about the day to day surviving.

It was a very depressing time for us. We usually sat around just talking or watching television. Our favourite programme at that time was 'The Village'. We found that we just could not miss this sweet programme about a village in Hampshire, near to where Mike had lived as a young man. It was about real life with real dramas. We felt we knew all the people in that village, and our life for a while revolved around this programme. It was pure escapism.

We discovered that we were able to have our mortgage paid, as we had paid in for redundancy and unemployment insurance to the Building Society, so that was the single biggest hurdle dealt with, apart from the bank! They, the bank, informed me that my flats would be sent to auction, and that my personal guarantee would be called upon. That was the moment I had been dreading all the years I had been fighting to stay afloat, now it was here. I did ultimately come to an agreement with them, which wasn't as bad as I'd expected although I was going to have to pay them so much a month for many years.

I was going to counselling every week, as Mike had mentioned to our doctor that I had difficulty going out alone. I felt that it was out of character for Mike to point the finger at me. It's true that during this period of my life I did have to have someone to accompany me when I went out, but when I got to my destination I was the one who did all the talking. I was the one who'd fought so hard to keep my business going. I was the one who'd taken on the bank, time after time. I was the one who refused to give in to all their bullying. Mike had wanted to run away from it all, many times he had said 'Call it a day darling, let's change our names and live in Spain'. I was such a strange mixture, on the one hand I'm not very worldly, I do not enjoy being in crowds of people, and when I'm out of the house I feel very vulnerable, exposed. When I have someone with me, I feel protected, and safe. I can't explain why I'm like it. But as I said when I get to where I'm going I do not need any help. My brain works overtime, I'm a quick thinker and if I think I'm right I'll go for the jugular. I've even represented people in court who couldn't afford a solicitor. That doesn't smack of a nervous person does it? I do no way think of myself as nervous. I am a highly sensitive and spiritual person and that is something quite different. As I said in Chapter 6 I vibrate at a different rate to other people and that is quite a difficult thing to deal with at times. But as I'm getting older I'm getting more and more able to deal with it. The doctor seemed irritated with me and I felt he thought I was the main reason for Mike's depression. I felt angry at the insinuation because I had been the one with all the get up and go, the one who always knew which way to go and how to sort things out. Mike did say many times later on, that he thought if it hadn't have been for me and the way I'd fought through, we would definitely have lost everything But I went to counselling to keep the peace, and I loved it. The counsellor was just like a favourite uncle, and it fast became the highlight of my week. After three sessions he told me that there was no need for me to go anymore, as most people in his opinion would like a mind and a sense of humour like mine. I was horrified. I looked forward to going. I begged him to give me some more sessions, and after a bit of cajoling, he did. Then one afternoon he asked me to repeat something I'd said about Mike, and I did so. The counsellor then said, "Do you think Mike would go to the surgery and make an appointment?" He had realised which one of us was really ill. I didn't know how Mike would react, but I needn't have worried. He was only too keen to get down to the surgery, as he also knew he wasn't well. Mike was diagnosed with a form of Depression, and as a result of that diagnosis he was told he qualified for disability pension. Every cloud had a silver lining, especially this cloud because the disability was backdated.

I suggested that we should do boot fairs, as we needed every penny we could earn to survive. I couldn't believe what we were doing. Was this really us? Had we really sunk that low? Well it certainly felt like it. But pride doesn't pay the bills, and I put on a brave face and tried to overcome any feelings of worthlessness that I had. Mike and I would load up the car on the Saturday night, ready for Sunday morning, with all sorts of things, even plastic flower pots. I didn't throw anything away anymore, everything had a value to me. We had a friend Margaret who did house clearances. She had a little charity shop which she ran from her garage, in aid of the Crohn's and Colitis Association. Margaret had raised an enormous amount of money for the charity. I couldn't believe that I would rescue items from her dustbin, but I did. The things that Margaret threw away from her house clearances were items that were actually worth quite a bit of money, such as musty old carpets and ancient curtains. I gathered it all up so proudly and put it in the boot of the car, with Margaret and Mike looking on in total and utter disbelief. Mike and I would then get up at four o'clock on a Sunday morning and drive to Polegate, set up our stall and be all ready for the customers, and it would still be dark. It was such hard work. Sometimes we were freezing, and we would take it in turns to sit in the car to try to get warm. The loos provided were filthy, but if you were desperate you had no choice. We discovered a whole culture of people out there in all weathers, trying to earn a crust. I can hear you now muttering 'Oh yes, the tax dodgers', and some of them probably were. Yes, there were those who turned up in their four-wheeled drive vehicles, and put up massive awnings. But there were also a lot of people who lived at a very low level. The illiterate, unshaven, unwashed, overweight and just very poor people with very under privileged children. I really believe that I had to experience many things in order to gather the information necessary to write this book. I had no idea that I would come across all the poverty that I had. No one expects it in England, with the welfare state, but it's there, I've seen it for myself, and I believe it's getting worse.

The class thing still survives, except now there is an even wider divide, the very well off versus the very poor. It used to be upper, middle and lower class. Not any more. I often wonder, when I'm watching a programme on television on the third world, whether people in this country really know the poverty level so many live at here in good old England. I don't think so, and I don't think many of them care.

We continued to do our house up, bit by bit, and it was beginning to look interesting at last. I was totally into recycling, everything about recycling and restoration fascinates me, whether it's turning big old houses into flats, mending, cleaning, and polishing old pieces of furniture, or selling unwanted clothes and discarded flower pots at boot fairs, it's all wonderful. Everything could be used and loved again.

Meanwhile, we needed to turn our integral garage into another room. We needed an office, as Mike had decided to set himself up as a website designer. He'd always been a genius with computers. But in order to convert our existing garage we needed another garage to replace it. The garage had become my shop by now, as I had started going back to the auction rooms and selling furniture again. We couldn't afford to have a garage built, so when I spotted a sectional garage for sale in the local paper I told Mike about it. We went to have a look at it, and we bought it. It needed dismantling and then re-assembling next to our house, and Mike did just that with the help of our friendly van man and Mike's friend Alan. I also found a site hut that made a very large workshop/shed. I found used paving slabs and loads of other things besides, including a Belfast sink. We looked for a second hand bathroom suite on the internet. When we went to see it, it lay in a barn, covered in cobwebs and spiders. It had been one of Ideal Standard's most expensive suites in the eighties. Everything we used was good quality. My imagination went wild, and we ended up with a house that would definitely have made a good feature in the period living magazine. And the garden was gorgeous, it went from a wilderness to heaven on earth.

Meanwhile, my business was, I thought, being wound up, but after a year of waiting, of worrying and depression, no progress seemed to be being made. I couldn't get any sense out of the administrator, what was he up to? No creditors meeting had been held, and that is something, which is legally supposed to happen three months after closure. I decided to make an appointment to see my solicitor. He informed me that if I had gone to see him straight away after the business had been closed down we could have gone to the court and had the decision reversed. Well I didn't know that, did I? The administrator had been appointed by the court, and I thought he had total jurisdiction over my company. I could tell that the solicitor wasn't very interested in talking about anything else. He couldn't advise me as to my position with the bank. I could detect glazed eyes and boredom coming from him, so we left and went home. Mike wanted me to call it a day and just let everything take its time, but how much time was necessary to wind up a business of that size? I couldn't let it rest, the business was like my child and I wanted to have my child laid to rest.

Whilst on the phone one day to John, a long-standing friend of Mike's, I told him of my dilemma. He was still fighting a case over a repossession order that happened several years earlier, and he told me of a firm of solicitors in Tunbridge Wells, who, he said were brilliant. I rang them up the next day and made an appointment. "Let's see how brilliant they are," I said to Mike, who I could tell was thinking, Oh no, here she goes again!!!

Chapter 12 - Culmination

When I walked through the doors of the solicitors in Tunbridge Wells with Mike by my side, we found ourselves standing in a very smart building indeed. We were both naturally very sceptical, because of all the other solicitors we had approached over the years about the various problems, and basically felt very let down by. I had no reason to believe that I would receive any help here with regard to my business, but I just kept hoping. I had to. I knew that somewhere out there was someone willing to help me, and I would keep looking until I found him or her.

The first thing we were told on arrival was that the solicitor I had made an appointment to see when I telephoned the day before was not there. My heart sank. Here we go again, I thought. But then we were told we would be seeing another person, and would we mind waiting a while. I thought it was probably someone's secretary who would make a few notes, and them smile sweetly and tell us she would get someone to ring us. How wrong could I have been? We were shown into a very big room, with an enormous table, behind which sat not one but two solicitors to see us. It was a bit daunting really, and I wondered then if they would think that we were just small fry and a waste of time.

Mike had a thick wad of papers in his hands, all relating to different aspects of our demise. The main reason we were there as far as I was concerned was to get advice on how to wind my business up, but Mike said that as long as we were going to see a new solicitor we might as well get advice on everything that had happened. He had the bit between his teeth this time and he wanted to relay the story himself of our demise. He began at the very beginning, relaying the story of the landslide, not that anything could be done about that, and it was an act of nature. But it was relevant to our story. Mike went on about the Department of Transport's offer to buy our blighted house, but how it had taken a year for them to pay us out, and how they had instructed us to leave all the carpets, curtains, light fittings, the built in wardrobes and any built in kitchen appliances. The senior solicitor looked on with a real sense of interest. Mike continued with the bank, and how they had got rid of him. How they had told him that if he didn't behave himself and go quietly, they would find some bad lending he had done, and get rid of him, which would affect his pension. Mike explained how he'd gone to the bank union and how they said that their hands were tied. And then he told the solicitor how the bank had commuted part of his pension to pay off a part of my company overdraft, and there was nothing Mike could do about it. The solicitor looked quite disturbed at this, but Mike continued, telling how the bank had closed my company down twice, asking on both occasions for me to surrender all my cheque books and credit cards, and how on both occasions they had come back and apologised, saying it was a mistake, then opened my accounts up again. And finally how the bank had sent my accounts to realisations, and how realisations had sent the accounts back to the bank because it was a viable company.

Mike went on about the surgeon who performed the operation on me that I had specifically asked him not to do, that afterwards the surgeon denied carrying out the procedure, and then got caught out because he billed me for it. By now the solicitor was holding his head with both hands. Mike finally explained all about the closing down of my business, and how it had been operating under an administration order, because one of my shops burnt down. He described how I had been told by the administrator that I had a viable business which he would keep going, and then out of the blue how I had received a letter stating that it had been closed down two days earlier, and all the bank accounts had been frozen, and the accountant had gone away so that we could not contact him. "If that wasn't bad enough," said Mike, "that was a year ago, and he still hasn't held a creditors meeting, or shown any sign of winding the company up." "How can you both sit there smiling?" said the senior solicitor. "Most people under those circumstances would have had complete nervous breakdowns." "No point in that," I replied quickly. "They all hoped we would have done just that."

The solicitor went through everything then step by step, and to our astonishment explained that in every situation except the landslide we would have had a case for them to answer. No one had told us that before. We had always got the impression that we had no leg to stand on. It was like listening to a Beethoven Concerto hearing him speak. The Department of Transport had no right to keep us waiting so long to be paid out for our house. Almost a year was ridiculous, and he thought we should have had some compensation as well, not only for the length of time we'd waited, but for all the fixtures and fittings we'd been instructed to leave behind. And as I'm writing this book nine years later, the road scheme was never even started!!!! As for the bank, they had no right to do what they did, and as for blackmailing Mike as they did, that was outrageous. And making him commute part of his pension was apparently illegal. Pensions are sacrosanct.

I explained that the closing of my business and not being able to get it wound up was what we had really gone there for, as the administrator wouldn't answer my letters, or speak to me on the phone. "And when we went there on one occasion to collect some files he said he didn't know where they were," I said. They became very interested in this, as there are strict codes of practice to follow in this area, and maybe they weren't being followed. He told us how to go about dealing with this ourselves, as it was obvious we couldn't pay their expensive fees, which were one hundred and fifty pounds an hour!!! I was so pleased then that we had gone there, and that I hadn't just given up, which would have been so easy to do. It had really ground us both down over the years, the way it's ground a huge amount of other people down, but I always felt deep down inside myself that I had had to

282

experience those things so that I could uncover the cancer in our society, and expose it. As I walked out through the doors into the road, I felt as if I'd won the lottery. At last someone had said that what had happened was wrong. Oh thank you God for leading me here. Thank you, thank you, thank you.

The next day as suggested I sent a letter off to the Institute of Chartered Accountants setting out my case, with relevant dates etc, stating that after one year there still hadn't been a creditors meeting, and I waited. It wasn't long before I heard, and to cut a long story short the administrator was found guilty of several different things that should have been done, and he was fined. He also resigned. He was acting quite quickly now as the boot was on the other foot. His business was put into the hands of another firm of administrators. Was that justice? Well I was satisfied, mostly because he wouldn't be able to do to somebody else what he'd done to me.

I wanted to move on and get on with my life. What life? I'd felt less than a human being for so long, and that is not a nice way to feel. If it hadn't been for my unfailing belief in upstairs, and the support of my family and friends, I could not have done it, I really couldn't. I'd been up against it all, bureaucracy at its best. I'd felt like a person running before a tidal wave, running in case it came over my head. I remembered my recurring childhood dream of running all the time, and being chased upstairs, downstairs and along passageways, until I was exhausted. I believed that my dream was forewarning me of what was to going to happen to me.

But it was Mike I was most worried about now. He had been totally traumatised by the chain of events over the years, especially with what the bank did to him. He would ask over and over again how they could have treated him the way they did, when he had been such a loyal company man. 'I used to go in to work regardless of whether I was well or not, through deep snow, floods and more recently the hurricane,' he would say to me, adding, 'loyalty is only one way, it seems'. He was genuinely heartbroken over it. He really thought that he'd lived in an honourable land. I could only repeat the same thing to him over and over again, and that was that the bank had laid off thousands of workers, not just him. But I knew that it was the way in which they'd done it that had really hurt. Mike was such a gentleman, and some of the bank seniors were definitely not. I also reminded him, as he'd seemed to have forgotten, that towards the end of his time in the bank he hadn't enjoyed it at all. He had hated the way he had been made to treat customers, some of whom had been good loyal customers for many years. Just because they had fallen on lean times due to the recession, it seemed terribly wrong to repossess their businesses and homes and then sell them off at auction at ridiculously low prices, sometimes leaving the customer with no home or business, sometimes both, with the final blow of then being told by the bank that there was a deficit to pay off. What were they supposed to pay it off with? All that instead of nursing them through.

Once upon a time if you were a bank manager, you were treated with the same respect in the community as the vicar, but things had changed drastically and now banks had become institutions that weren't worthy of respect any more. The way they treated customers was insensitive and uncaring. Everyone now was just a figure on a balance sheet and a marketing opportunity, and yes loyalty was just one way, the bank's way. And Mike no longer wanted anybody to know that he used to be a bank manager.

Many's the time over the years I asked myself if it was worth me carrying on with my fight, whether it was with the bank or latterly the administrator. I definitely thought, "I've done nothing wrong" So in a way I now felt that there was enormous satisfaction of the job at last finished, although I still had to wait for the company to be wound up. I waited four years altogether to get my company finally wound up! The stress they caused me was ridiculous.

I never once regretted having started my business, because apart from the company having put a roof over the heads of my sons, and me, and provided us with a very good income, the knowledge which I had gained from it all was priceless. My sons hadn't missed out like so many children of divorced parents. They were educated, and that was my primary objective for doing any of it. I had achieved what I'd set out to do for them, and I felt that they'd achieved more than a lot of youngsters who'd had two parents. I have two successful sons. Julian's childhood dream of becoming a car design engineer has come true. He never once gave up his dream, and he has travelled all over the world with Ford, one of the largest car manufacturing companies in the world. What a success story. To complete his happiness he married Angela in 2002.

Jeremy married Sue, and they have two sons, Benjamin and Jack. Jeremy, after trying his hand at various jobs, went into garden design, following in the family market garden, nursery and building tradition. His artistic flair really came through, another success story.

Mike and I adopted Rachael, which meant so much to me after two failed attempts to get her, the first when she was born and the second when she was put into care, and although she was now an adult it still meant as much to her as to us. She cried when I eventually asked her if she would like to be a member of our family. But they were tears of relief and delight at having a mum and dad at last. It doesn't matter what age we are, we all need to belong. She, her husband Steve, and their three children, Shaun, Ashley and Bethany, are now members of our family, another dream I'd had for years, and another success story.

We continued doing the house up, and it no longer resembled the sadly neglected house we'd bought all those years earlier. It was totally transformed into a beautiful and exciting home for us, thanks in part to the Period Living magazine for the inspiration needed for some of it, plus my building knowledge, my love of furniture and plants and of course my love of re-cycling and Mike's willingness to roll up his sleeves and do a lot of the heavy work. The room we made out of the existing garage was converted into a big computer room, with Mike one end, designing web sites, which is his new venture. Working with computers was something he had wanted to do all his adult life, another dream realised. I was the other end of the room, ploughing through an Open University course. I chose Health and Social Welfare, which was a very good choice for me, although I didn't know at the time just how meant it was that I did that course. I learned such a lot about the social history of Britain pre-war, as well as post war, and it helped me to learn to write constructively. My tutor would say 'You ought to be a writer Stella, with your style and wit.' I know she was being a little sarcastic, as my writing wasn't very academic. I always elaborated to make it much more interesting. "I am writing a book," I told her one day. "It'll be a best seller," she said, smiling at me. I hoped so. I had started writing this book years earlier, but what with one thing and another it had always been put on hold. Now I was tapping it out to the tune of four thousand words a day.

I longed to get back to healing. From the first moment I realised I had healing hands, way back in my thirties, I had used my gift on anyone who'd asked me for help. But over the last few years I had been too exhausted to do it, I had needed all my energy for myself, and it would have been dangerous for me to have even tried doing any healing. But now I felt strong enough in myself to offer my services again, and I became very busy quite quickly. Healers are usually the last resort for people. How many times would I hear these words. 'We've seen eminent doctors/psychiatrists you know, and we've all but given up hope'. I liked especially working with young people, their minds are much more open to different ideas. During one period I was approached by three different youngsters who were all suffering from intense stress. The first one was a lovely young girl who had been mutilating herself with razor blades, because of bullying at school. The second one was a young man, a graduate who'd felt he'd let his family down, because he wasn't the sort of son his parents wanted. His mother had been very ambitious for him and he couldn't cope with it at all. He was a gentle soul, consequently he was suicidal. The third girl had no self-esteem at all. She was in an unhappy marriage with an unfaithful husband, resulting in her health deteriorating. Two of the three youngsters were suicidal. I had successful results from all three, but one girl in particular looked so healthy and happy on her third visit to me that I didn't recognise her. She rushed in one day and kissed me!

I also had good results from performing healing on a dog, who had been hit by a car. I had been told that his back was broken, but when the owners took him back to the vet for a check up the vet couldn't understand why the dog's back was not broken. It's a lovely feeling to help wherever I can, and I will carry on helping whenever and wherever I can, in between doing all the other things I have to do.

There is such a need for healing in the world today, mostly healing of the mind. People are so confused, to the point where many are not enjoying their lives as they should be. Life is such a wonderful gift. Hopefully my book will help people understand what life is all about. It's not about money and possessions. It's not about power and glory, it's about the journey of your soul. It's about passing the tests that are given to us all and sometimes thrown at us all, yes, at us all. I didn't try and escape any of my tests, I confronted them head on. That's not to say I wanted them or liked them, and at times I felt I couldn't take any more. But somewhere deep down inside me, the will to succeed was so strong. And looking back I would go through it all again, to come out as strong as I am now.

I can help other people now in a way that I wouldn't have been able to before. None of us escape the tests. People who appear to have everything do not have everything, you do not have to look very far in anyone's life to see problems and sadnesses of one kind or another. Money cannot buy good health and happiness. It cannot buy love. Which leads me on to Princess Diana. I wasn't going to mention her as so many people have told stories about her, but I think this is important. I had a visit from Diana from the spirit world, just over two years ago, in the winter of the very bad flu epidemic. I had flu very badly, and I had only just recovered two months earlier, from a serious chest infection. I'd felt dreadfully ill for the first few days, my temperature had been 104 degrees, and all I could do was lay in bed. At one point I'd seen Angels around my bed and I thought they'd come to collect me. Then I realised they had come to look after me. I don't remember how long it was after that I saw Diana, in the little blue suit that she used to wear. Diana stood in the doorway of my bedroom, and then came and sat on my bed. She told me to take some of the Arnica tablets that were sitting on the windowsill. I did what she told me to do. I had taken arnica for all sorts of things but never for anything like that. I felt well enough after a couple of days to get up and go for acupuncture at Nick's. Diana sat on my bed for a while and then went. The dreadful way she was hounded to her death by the crutch-sniffing press just emphasises the way our society has gone in another area. The need of the public to know everything about the royals and famous people's private lives is abhorrent, and in Diana's case, ultimately led to her death. Diana did, however, fulfil her destiny before going back to the spirit world. Home I call it. I believe Diana was the second Anne Boleyn. And just as Anne Boleyn was the reason we have the Church of England because of Henry VIII's falling out with the Church of Rome over his divorce from Queen Catherine, I believe through Diana's divorce from Charles, and her unhappy life in the royal family, that somehow the Church will be separated from the Monarchy, and go back to the Archbishop being the head of it. It's logical really that the Archbishop of Canterbury should be the head of the Church of England. It also means that Prince Charles is free to marry Camilla Parker Bowles. I think they should be our future King and Queen, they deserve to be happy, just the same as any other couple who've been through a divorce. I think Charles is a rare man, very humanitarian and very spiritual. And let's leave them in peace, by not buying any more cheap nasty tabloids.

We must all change the way we live. It is a new millennium, we've been to the moon and back and there is still poverty, and homelessness. If we don't change the way we live and work and behave and if we don't take stock soon it will be the end of our planet as we know it. The terrible greed has got to stop, and respect for our planet must take over, or we are on course for disaster. We are all beginning to feel the effects of a non-caring society, in the climate changes. We are living the results of non-humanitarian decisions made for short-term solutions. The world will grind to a halt if we don't take stock now, not tomorrow, but now. We could all start by making more humanitarian decisions about how we live our lives. What sort of cars do we drive, are they gas gulpers, could we walk a lot more? What sort of houses do we live in, are they well built? We should demand well built houses, built of quality materials where nearly everything doesn't need replacing every twenty years. And is your house totally energy efficient? Could it have solar energy? And perhaps some of the flowerbeds could go over to growing food, as nothing tastes like home grown food. And could we re-cycle all our tins, glass, paper, clothing, furniture, and household waste? Could we have dustcarts with separate compartments for re-cycling, for those people who do not live near re-cycling depots?

The intense farming methods used are causing health problems. B.S.E. is one such disease that will be coming to light more and more over the next decade. Vegetarian animals being fed ground up animal carcasses is dreadful. What lengths will we not stoop to in order to make money. Animals have their own incarnations, they are not put on this earth for us to do just what we want to do with them. We are all beginning to pay the price of this callous treatment of our animals.

Most farmers care very much for their animals. Most people want to eat meat and farmers do their best to produce it for us. But they in turn are in the hands of the Ministry of Agriculture, who make most of the decisions today in modern farming, along with the government of the day. Most farmers don't want their animals driven hundreds of miles to abattoirs, it's very cruel to the animals and certainly very dangerous for us to eat traumatised animals. 2002 has seen the result of this folly. We have seen the slaughter of four million animals with foot and mouth, the result of modern farming methods gone mad. The disrespect for animals is amazing, and to show on every newsreel lorries tipping bodies into pits and then fires burning hundreds of bodies is nothing short of sick. We will all become very sick if we're not careful. Our crops are sprayed with so many chemicals, and then when the crops are harvested they use other chemicals to make the food last longer, and then colorants are used to make the food look better. Hedges, which housed the creatures which naturally did away with aphids that farmers now spray for, are constantly smashed to smithereens by machinery, instead of being trimmed neatly or layered like they used to be. Not only are we doing away with the natural habitat of many creatures, but also the countryside in some areas is beginning to look as vandalised as the inner cities.

And our drinking water goes through us six times. There are

chemicals which can't be removed from the water. It's already been proved that hormones going into the water from the birth pill and H.R.T. cannot be removed, and has been proved by some scientists who analysed thousands of dead fish. I believe it is making men more effeminate, and I take it one step further. I believe that with men becoming more effeminate, women are becoming more masculine. For the simple reason that if men don't want to do a lot of the things they used to do, women have to do them. Women have become more aggressive, a male trait. Working and doing DIY has had an effect on women. We are much hairier than we used to be, another male trait.

The Open University course had taught me such a lot about what life had been like years ago in Britain, from the turn of the century up till the reforms of the forties. I learnt about Social Darwinism, which drew on Darwin's ideas of natural selection, emphasising the contribution of the fittest and the strongest to the survival of the human species. People were locked away in asylums and institutions for a variety of reasons. You didn't just have to be mentally ill. If you were the victim of poverty, if you were ignorant, or what they classed as a mental defective, or even if you lacked moral values you could be put there. And you could be put there if you were just a slow learner. In fact any excuse to rid society of the week and feeble. It smacked a little of the Nazis selective breeding program that we were all horrified at, when we learned about it after the war. I learned all about asylums, institutions, and workhouses. On a positive note I learned about Beveridge's visions for a better fairer land, which included the setting up of the N.H.S. and the Welfare State, which was desperately needed. I must say that when I read about social Darwinism it made me feel sick to my stomach. All that information was very relevant to my story.

It started me thinking again about the possible causes of the breakdown of our society today. I'd thought a lot about governments and the powers that be over the last few years, and it made me wonder whether they really did have our best interests at heart. Many times I'd felt like an alien in my own country because I'd felt so pushed about by them and subsequently let down by them. Many is the time I'd felt like the unwanted, heterosexual, married, working, Christian woman. A lot of the values that most people held dear were simply swept away. The fabric of our society was gradually being eroded in the sixties and seventies, building up to a crescendo in the late eighties and nineties. I'd had cause to think about all this with everything that I'd personally experienced.

The attitude of the high street banks has gone from the sublime to the ridiculous. From money being pushed at everybody in the eighties, to not being able even to get a bank account for thousands who are on credit reference lists, where they will stay for up to six years. Even if you are late paying a bill you are logged on a register. Big brother is watching you.

Next, the seeming indifference of some doctors, who had made me feel at times as if I was a damn nuisance for bothering them, whilst they received large salaries in return, has added to my anger. When I was a child the doctor used to look at you, yes he actually took his eyes off the computer screen, then he'd pull your eyelids down to see if you were anaemic, look at your nails and ask you to poke your tongue out. Just by looking at a patient they could tell a lot about them, by their skin colour and their eyes. Now they practically ask you what you think is wrong with you. But in defence of doctors they hardly get a chance to know patients today as everyone is so mobile, statistics say that on average you move house every seven years. So there's not a lot of chance of having a family doctor today who knows several different generations of a family. People go to the doctor with the most trivial things wrong with them for which years ago they would have gone to the chemist, and then gone home and gone to bed. Having had a doctor live with us I saw the other side of the coin. I used to get wild myself at some of the call outs he used to get. But I think there is too much reliance on machinery and drugs and not enough self-help. We all need to take stock of our lifestyles and take care of the greatest machine of all, our bodies. I don't think I would be here today if it wasn't for the love and kindness and the treatment I'd received from alternative therapists and healers, and a certain surgeon.

Then there were all the hundreds of different rules and regulations for small businesses that in the end put a lot of them out of business. The upholstery law was only a minor one of those new rules. There was health and safety, employment law, business rates that crippled small businesses, and huge insurance premiums. It seemed as if every day something else was illegal. Big businesses were mopping up small businesses, and when there are no longer small family run businesses who have the community's best wishes at heart, the big boys who up until now have been undercutting and undercutting to get your business will then be able to charge just what they like, and prices will be able to go through the roof.

I resented the amount of crime I'd personally suffered, with no punishment for the criminals in any of the cases. The victim of crime is the person in this country who has to do the sentence.   It isn't kindness not to punish criminals, it isn't love to not punish the young who do wrong, it isn't love to let them do what they like in absolute ignorance of the fact that at the end of the day they, we, all have to answer for our lives. Far better to put them on the right track straightaway, that's love!

I'd felt the government was very lacking by not intervening when thousands of families were losing their homes in the recession, caused not by the people, but by the chancellor not keeping a tight enough grip on public spending, causing interest rates to rocket and businesses to go to the wall. I remember the chancellor telling us that unemployment was 'a price worth paying' in order to get the country back on its feet. What a cheek! It wasn't him who lost his job or his home. You cannot build a sustainable society on the boom and bust syndrome we seem to have suffered from since the war. In fact it seemed like a purposeful decision that the government had made, not to intervene with the building societies and stop the huge amount of repossessions. They also could have instructed the banks to stop pulling the rugs out from under so many people. I thought many times that it would have been better for the building societies to have brought in a new system where people paid a much lesser amount for maybe two years until they were back on their feet.

I became very suspicious about what was happening in my

country. Was it another way of institutionalising people? After all, most of them after having their homes repossessed would have to be housed by the council, and receive benefits. Was that another way of getting total control? What a frightening thought. And if more and more people go onto benefits you can then dictate practically everything they are able to do. And the chances of their children going on to further education gets slimmer. And the chances of them having good health is diminished through poor diet, as these are mostly the people who buy the cheap food in supermarkets which may be genetically modified. It cannot be nourishing food. They are the people whose kids are hyperactive because of their poor diets, the food with all the additives. The better off people are buying organic food, they are the ones who read all the labels on the tins before they buy.

The government seemed to dislike individualism and eccentricity. Suddenly we all had to fit a mould. We had to meet all the new criteria for loans, and of course most people didn't. Are we once again becoming institutionalised? Regulations appeared daily. More and more facts were compiled about us, surveys on everything came through the door, everything from what you earn what life insurance and pension provision you had to what cat food you bought, and where you went for your holiday. The potential for compiling information centrally on people has never been so great. Everything you buy in a supermarket has a bar code on it which goes into a central register so they even know if you have a budgerigar.

Workers have lacked security in the work place for years, what with six monthly and yearly contracts, with performance charts, along with part time jobs, and job sharing. This has added to the insecurity of the workers. How can they apply for mortgages and plan for a family? That's a joke! We certainly haven't admired and promoted marriage as the ideal way of living for some time. Married couples allowance was taken away, so as to not penalise those couples who were co-habiting. What rubbish! Why are we so afraid of saying anything that might upset someone. If people want to cohabit that's up to them but don't penalise those who are married and showing responsibility. We should offer many more advantages to married couples so as to make marriage more desirable, bring back married couples allowances and what about cheaper home loans as married people are a better bet? And the raising of children as a full time career, and making them into good citizens, is seen as something very unimportant. Well there's nothing in life that will ever be more rewarding than giving life to another human being, and raising him or her to the best of your ability. I like to think of women as human greenhouses, we should aim to produce the healthiest children possible, with eating good food and not smoking. To be a housewife has been regarded as lower than low ever since I can remember. It's thought much better that all women do work outside the home. But a lot of their outside work is more menial than housework and child rearing in my view. I worry about the lot of women in this country, they are supposed to be super human. They must be beautiful, clever, hold down a job, run a home, have babies, do DIY, drive, and be brilliant in bed. And on top of that not always expect marriage. It's total nonsense. Figures published on December 12th, 2001, state that women who work are more likely to get divorced in the first eleven years of marriage. I for one stand up for marriage, and for women being at home with their young children, at least during their children's formative years. Erikson's eight stages of man states that the first seven years of a child's life are the most important. This period is where bonding takes place and children learn trust and security. It's not a lot out of our lives to give up for a brilliant cause. Then mothers could go back to work if they want to. We do need women out there making their mark, because we've fought hard for the right to get out there. But not at the expense of your family. A women can have both because I have done it. Mothers at home could actually save money in several ways, because firstly it costs money to get to work, then they have the cost of buying fast food, and buying packets of nappies, and childcare is very expensive. All that must take most of what they earn anyway. If they were at home they could cook good food instead of buying fast food which is very expensive and unhealthy. They could even go back to washing nappies. Most women today have washing machines, and the cost of buying nappies is ridiculous. Add up the cost of those items, compare it with the wages of a working part time mum who has to pay childcare, and I think it works out cheaper to stay at home. We are creating more and more landfill sites and for what? Because parents won't wash

nappies and because the country isn't into re-cycling. Our landfill
sites are a bomb just waiting to go off. Think of all that methane.

A child's early years are such magic years to miss out on.
Children change daily, and what a shame to miss out on any of it.
I'd like housewifery to be regarded as a major occupation. I'd like
to see marriage contracts, so that if one party opts out, or where
there is real stress living together and divorce is necessary, then
the one that leaves causes as little disruption as possible to the
children.

We must stand up and take responsibility for our own actions. I
am quite sure that a lot of the problems that we face today with
uncontrollable youngsters are a direct result of the actions of
governments and institutions during the last two decades. The
dreadful greed of the banks and building societies, the insecure
workplace, the lack of moral guidance, the bad language
commonly used in films and on television is everywhere now.
Some of the language in American films is unacceptable and quite
vile. Have we become too soft as a nation? Why do we accept
bad language and bad behaviour? Why do we plumb the depths
instead of reaching for the heights, like we did when I was young.
Have we nannied a section of society to the point where they can't
take responsibility for themselves anymore? Have we gone too far
the other way? Have we institutionalised people again under
another guise? Do people have too many rights to benefits today,
with no thoughts of doing anything for themselves? If the benefits
dry up, which is possible, what are those dependant people going
to live on?

We expect childcare facilities as a matter of course, because we
either don't want to stay at home, or have been persuaded that it's
better to work than look after our children. We all exercise our
rights to do what we want. We have the rights of women to have
abortions on demand and the rights of women to have children
whilst not being married, or even living with anyone. But what
about the rights of the children to have two married parents as role
models? I'm not judging what's right or wrong. That's up to each
and every individual to do for themselves. Families are in danger
of becoming extinct, whilst at the same time the government is

cutting back on care for the elderly which will ultimately fall on the shoulders of the children, well daughters anyway! I think we should want to be responsible for looking after our parents and our children, and not expect the state to pay for everything, and what better way to do that than from the advantage point of marriage. The state should, however, still look after the general welfare of children, i.e. education and health, as well as still looking after the sick, the disabled and the elderly who have no family, which was what the welfare state was set up for originally. It was not set up to provide flats for unmarried mums and everything else they want. Neither was it set up as a hand out for those who choose not to work. But I certainly noticed when I had my flats, how everybody seemed to know their rights about benefits and their entitlements. I even felt the government was actively encouraging girls to have babies by giving them flats and benefits, and it was seen by some girls as an alternative to working. Was that another way of institutionalising them?

But what we do have as a result of everybody exercising their rights is a society spiralling out of control, with forty per cent of our children born out of wedlock. Our children pay a high price for our lifestyle. We have poverty on a scale not seen in this country for decades. We still have the illiterate, and on top of that we have half the nation speaking as if they are auditioning for 'EastEnders'. We have children from an early age out of control, who can't be punished at school or at home, and many are too young even to understand what they've done. Teenage crime is at record highs, and teenage pregnancy is rife. It saddens me beyond belief.

It is very worrying to hear that we have the highest figures in Europe for unmarried young mums. Girls from the age of thirteen are becoming mums. Goodness me, what have we sunk to? These are kids having kids, and if that isn't bad enough we are providing crèches in schools for them so that they can sit their exams, which in turn will enable them to get jobs, in order to keep their babies. I remember from my schooldays, it was bad enough having a period during an exam, I don't know how girls cope with the added pressure of having a baby in a crèche. What will happen to a lot of these girls is that they can look forward to very little. Well, not

296

strictly true. They can look forward to working full time, going home to an empty flat with a child to look after, and spending their young lives washing, ironing, and working to make ends meet. Ah, let me think. Where is the father of this child? Oh, he's off with his mates enjoying his adolescence. Are we all insane, or is anybody going to do anything about it? They have proved that the health of single mums is not as good as the health of married mums. We should help single mums all we can, as there will always be single mums, but no way should it be promoted as the ideal way to live. Some female pop singers and actresses could set a better example, as they are so hero-worshipped by young girls. Their lifestyles couldn't be more removed from the average young girl who watches and idolises them and if a pop star has a baby she has plenty of money for a nanny. If the young girl has a baby she is going to be quite hard up, and lonely.

Pray explain why Emily Pankhurst and the Suffragettes bothered to do what they did for us women if it wasn't to make women's lives better. Having a baby and not being married is not equality. This is men opting out of all responsibility. Wake up women, for goodness sake, before it's all too late. Throughout my life so far I have seen women dancing to the tune of men, and I am highly sick of it. We all know that in the past, men used to have all the say, and women dutifully followed. That was how it was, and women put up with it. But don't we have it again under a different heading? Aren't women again dancing to the tune of men? And this is worse. Men can have all the sex they want without having to marry you. You can have their kids and they don't feel they have to marry you, or support you financially. How nice for them not to have to wake up in the night to do the feeds. They can be out clubbing, making someone else pregnant. I can't believe girls think that's equality. I think it's the total opposite.

I can hear all the feminists screaming at me, but this is not true emancipation for women. It's true there are some women, who bring up children successfully without a man. I was one of them (but not through choice), who earned a lot of money, had a good job and a lovely home. But the vast majority of women have menial work, and therefore work harder than women have since Victorian times. And what happens to a single mum when she gets older? Well, she can sit at home and look after all her Grandchildren, because her daughters and daughters-in-laws will be out working. Oh, and she can also look after her ageing parents, because don't forget the government won't be supplying any facilities for them either. It's all up to you lady. But if she's in a good marriage she can share all that with her partner, if she's un-married the total burden will fall on her.

Women today have no idea what hardships our predecessors went through on our behalf. The suffragettes went to jail etc. on our behalf, and went on hunger strikes, and some died as a result of this. I often feel that if they could come back and see just how far the pendulum has swung the other way, with girls and young women throwing their lives on the scrap heap, they would wonder why they bothered. You don't have to go very far back in history to understand that women didn't have any real rights. Not only did they have no voting rights, they also were not allowed to own property in their own right. The average woman's lot was not a happy one. Their job was to continue the human race and not worry their little heads about anything else. What relevance has that on today's society you might ask. The answer is a hell of a lot. Girls today can choose a career, they can therefore choose whether they want a family or not. They have birth control at their fingertips. More girls learn to drive than not, so they can get about independently. Sounds good, doesn't it? If only! In reality girls are lagging behind her contemporaries in Europe.

Statistics show that we have the highest level of unmarried mums in Europe. This in cold reality is opportunities being taken away from our youngsters. These girls are not high-earners, with nannies living in nice areas with a BMW in the yard and a gorgeous man waiting to take them out. There are a few like that, and it is only a few. The majority are desperately hard up and desperately lonely, perhaps living on benefits. And it's no joke bringing up a child on your own. Some of them, because they are lonely, will have a relationship and end up having two children to bring up. Then perhaps they might be able to get some kind of work, but they won't be accountants, solicitors, doctors or the like. They do all the mundane work that no one else wants to do. Is this the equality that our predecessors fought so hard for, and more to the point do you think that a young man would settle for this if he was the one who had the babies? No, I think that if there was any danger of that he would be sterilised.

Now how do I see equality in the true sense of the word? Well I would like to see the end of the battle of the sexes once and for all. Let's celebrate the differences in the sexes for once and be real friends. We've talked about what women's lives used to be like. And we know the mess we are in now, with a lot of girls throwing themselves at every Tom Dick and Harry. Figures published recently said that two out of five babies in this country are born into poverty. What are we doing to our youngsters? We shouldn't even have poverty on such a scale in the twenty first century. Why can't we have true friendship between men and women?

This is how I see it. There has always been equality between men and women, if anything women have always been in the driving seat, but they haven't always realised it. I believe women are so desirable that the average man would do anything to get you. He'd do what he used to do, he'd marry you. And as neither can reproduce without the other, that makes us equal. I personally believe in marriage, and I think it is good for these reasons. Firstly children benefit from two parents. These are their role models. Secondly for financial reasons, why should a woman have to give birth, raise the children whilst financially supporting them. A man doesn't do both. Where you do get a man bringing up the kids he usually gives up his job and lives on the state. Thirdly I do not believe it is the job of the state to pay for absent Fathers. It takes two to make a baby, and I believe it takes two to raise them. Lastly, I believe that most of us want to be loved and cherished, and if everyone is so happy living on their own why are the local papers so full of lonely hearts?

CONCLUSION

What did I learn? Well I learnt so much about life, which I
couldn't possibly have learnt without experiencing the things
myself. Nothing replaces hands-on experience. Being a person
with ideals and morals, I discovered, was not admired, or even
wanted in modern day Britain. 'Live for the day' I was told
repeatedly. 'Live off the state' was another well known saying
and when I was going through my divorce they said 'Don't think
about the boys, they'll leave anyway when they're grown up, and
they won't thank you for all your sacrifices'. Fortunately none of
that was my philosophy. I do not live for the day. Most people
however do live for the day, with no thoughts or planning for their
futures. After all how often do you hear it said. 'We might all be
dead tomorrow'. These people are also the ones who, when you
have done well, say 'Oh you've always been lucky'. I reply quite
calmly 'Oh yes I have, and I've always found that the harder I
worked the luckier I got'.

We all have choices and chances, and I can hear some of you now
saying 'it's alright for her'. But was it? I came from a very
humble background, with the tin bath in front of the fire on
Sunday nights, so I didn't have the benefits that lots of my
contemporaries had. But I did have the advantage of a good
Christian family life, and the benefit of being told that it was very
much up to me to find my chances and go for them, which I did.

A lot of us decide to waste our choices or chances, which I think is a dreadful waste of a valuable life, and at the end of the day we all have to answer for our lives.

Before we come into this world we make a blueprint of our life, a life plan that is, about what we are going to do, and what we hope to achieve. When we die and go back over the other side they show us the blue print and see whether we followed it or not. Perhaps you decided to ignore your conscience and do something much more fun, for kicks. Well if you got it wrong this time you will have the opportunity to do it all over again in your next life, but you might have a long wait to come back, as so many want to come back and do it right. Perhaps you blame someone else for the problems in your life. Well most people have problems in their lives, whether it's the child who wasn't wanted or who was abused. Whether it's the person in the unhappy marriage, or the dead end job, whether it's the person with a terminal illness, or a chronic illness. Or the old person who's lonely and very isolated. But life is about taking responsibility for ourselves at the end of the day. I know from my own experiences that we can't be responsible for everything that happens to us. We can't be held responsible for our childhood, or the way other people choose to treat us but it's how we deal with situations that counts, and it really doesn't matter whether you win or lose, it really is how you play the game. You cannot rely on the government to make your life comfortable and give you what you want. We need to take back a lot of the responsibility for our own lives. The welfare state has become abused. Why not change your lifestyle now to one that maybe suits you better. What about bringing back communities and village life, people supporting one another. What about bringing back pleasantness and kindness, asking your neighbour if he or she needs anything. What about not smoking and not drinking too much, and generally looking after your own health. Thus easing up the pressure on the health service. What about being married, setting examples, and controlling your own children's behaviour. It's not up to schools to control our children. They are teachers, not policemen. And if we controlled our own children we wouldn't need to keep training more and more policemen and women.

What about not buying anything other than organic to eat?
Suppliers would then have to supply what you want to eat.
Politicians are generally very well motivated men and women, and
I believe that some of them do try to do the best they can for us,
but like everybody else with a job, they also want to keep their
jobs, therefore a lot of the decisions they make are made on the
basis of getting them votes, which keep them in office.

If I hadn't met all the homeless people sleeping rough in derelict
hotels in Hastings it would never have been brought to my
attention. How can we justify homelessness in the late twentieth
and early twenty-first century? Most of the homeless people fit
three categories: the mentally ill, including those turned out into
the community from mental hospitals; children who had to leave
children's homes at sixteen because that was the age we
considered our duty done; and thirdly, children who can't get on
with a step parent, so opt to leave, or sometimes mum or dad has
thrown them out. How can we give aid to other countries before
we give aid to our own people? I liken it to a mother feeding the
children of a neighbour whilst her own starve. Dr. Carey wrote an
article dated March 10th, 1999, entitled 'Britain has an allergy to
religion'. What has happened to Britain, to allow this to happen?
We mustn't stop teaching our children the basics of Christianity,
or whatever your religion is. Muslims, Hindus and other major
Religions wouldn't dream of not teaching their children their
religion. Religion is the foundation on which every society bases
itself. It's how we learn right from wrong. It's where we get our
values from. And at the end of the day it's a crime that people
grow up in ignorance, not knowing God. Not knowing that at the
end of the day, we will have to answer for everything that we have
done. What a thought!

THE END

STELLA STICKLAND

Stella is a woman unlike any other that you will meet. She is an enigma.

On the one hand she is sensitive and spiritual. As a child she could see auras. She felt rather like an outsider, seeing both the beauty in nature and the illogicality in human behaviour. She was sometimes regarded as a rebel.

She believes in God, and reincarnation, and regards the various religions as many paths to the same goal. She has an innate ability to guide others, and has become a skilled counsellor.

At the same time she is focused, practical and capable. When she was left to support herself and two small sons, what did she do? Despite having negligible capital and little experience she started a successful property development company, which converted large seaside houses into flats.

Stella is a very political person, with strong views on most subjects. She is also an inspiration to women, believing that – for them – nothing is impossible. Whilst not a feminist in the usual sense of the word, she does believe that women should have equal status and opportunities. She also advocates marriage, believing it to be the best way to bring up children